With many thanks for
such a marvellous visit
to the theatre

from
the Lacrosse Squad,
Wycombe Abbey School,
High Wycombe,
Buckinghamshire.

March 1984.

A Shell Guide

Buckinghamshire

A Shell Guide

Buckinghamshire

by Bruce Watkin

Faber and Faber   3 Queen Square   London

First published in 1981
by Faber and Faber Limited
3 Queen Square London WC1N 3AU
Printed in Great Britain by
Fakenham Press Limited
Fakenham, Norfolk
All rights reserved

Whiteleaf Cross

British Library Cataloguing in Publication Data

Watkin, Bruce
  Buckinghamshire: a Shell guide
  1. Buckinghamshire—Description and travel—
  Guide-books
  I. Title
  914.25'904857   DA670.B9

  ISBN 0–571–11784–8

Illustrations

Note: Captions to the photographs include place names in **bold type**. These refer to entries in the gazetteer, pages 35–189.

△ Gold Hill, **Chalfont St Peter**

Play places

Wooburn Green (*top*)
Stony Stratford (*bottom*) ▷

▽ **Haddenham**

The Landscape of Buckinghamshire

by John Nash (1936)

Buckinghamshire is a long and narrow county, and lying as it does across the natural grain of the land, is composed of bands of entirely different types of country.

It may be divided roughly into three parts, North Bucks., South Bucks., and the Chiltern Hills, which form a natural barrier between north and south, and have little in common with either.

These chalk hills cross the county diagonally at its narrowest point, from south-west to north-east, and are crowned with beech woods.

To the south the ground falls gradually to the Thames Valley, 20 miles (32 kilometres) away, in what appears at first sight to be a rather haphazard mass of hills and dales. It is in reality a plateau, deeply grooved by three small rivers, the Wye, the Misbourne, and the Chess, that rise a few miles from the chalk escarpment and make their way towards the Thames. The whole of this area is richly wooded, those on the southern slopes of the Chiltern Hills being mostly of beech, while further south, as the chalk dives further beneath the surface, we find mixed woods of oak and hazel, fir and beech.

During the past 30 years, London has reached out its tentacles into this part of the country and many of the villages and lanes have become ruthlessly suburbanized. Here also lie the two largest towns, Slough and High Wycombe, where prosperous industrial conditions have led to a sacrifice of the countryside. Down in the toe of the county, however, where Bucks., Berks., and Middlesex converge, there is a small stretch of county left over, as it were, from another century, where villages still lie surrounded by cherry-orchards and market-gardens, or meadows with little streams beside them bordered with willow trees.

The southern boundary of the county is formed by the River Thames, which produces another type of scenery, beautiful if sophisticated, and gay with the peculiar architecture and holiday life of the river-side.

The northern face of the Chiltern Hills is very different from the southern, the beech-woods end at the brow of the hills and the ground falls away abruptly to the great Aylesbury Plain, which stretches out up to the northern boundaries of the county. Near the foot of these slopes there runs from west to east an ancient track. It is called the Icknield Way, and during its course divides into two parts, the Upper and the Lower. Most of it is now a made-up road, but a good portion of the Upper Way remains as the old grass track. Long before the Roman occupation its purpose was probably the transport of goods from the mining parts of the west to the agricultural district of East Anglia. The old traders avoided the woods and swamps of the plain and followed the edge of the chalk escarpment; possibly also such a route afforded a safer outlook for bands of robbers or hostile tribes. Even where the deep-rutted grassy track gives way to the metal road, its characteristics can be felt—the wide grass margins, the curves following the lie of the land, and the presence in the hedgerow of two significantly-named plants, the travellers' joy and the wayfaring tree. The Icknield Way enters the county near Bledlow, where the original track runs under and round Bledlow Hill. At the first crossroads out of Bledlow towards Bledlow Ridge the junction of the old track and the modern road leading to Saunderton is very obvious. It can be picked up again south of Princes Risborough on the Wycombe Road, curving away towards Whiteleaf Cross, below which it emerges on to the road again at Whiteleaf Village, and after another short piece of grassy track beyond the Missenden Road is swallowed up in the main highway from Princes Risborough to Wendover. Between Little Kimble and Wendover even on the modern road, the characteristics above mentioned are very marked, and again between Marsworth and Ivinghoe Beacon, after which near Edlesborough it leaves the county. The steep slopes above the track are dotted with bushes of juniper and yew and in some places box. The grass is fragrant with the scent of thyme and bright with cowslips, sun-roses, and bell-flowers in their respective seasons.

The fields of the plain are cultivated up to the edge of each hill spur, until the earth loses all colour, as it is merged into powdered white chalk, while the crops become thinner and more dwarfed.

The sight of these white-edged fields against the downland is one of the chief characteristics of the Chiltern landscape.

The so-called Aylesbury Plain of North Bucks. consists of rich, undulating pasture lands, broken by ranges of low hills, and watered by innumerable streams, some of which turn back southwards and join the Thames outside the county. The rest flow northwards into the Ouse or Ousel. The most interesting and largest of these is the Thame, which rises in Hertfordshire and flows across our county parallel to the Chiltern Hills, and is responsible for a beautiful stretch of country before it reaches the town bearing its name and passes into Oxfordshire, and so to the Thames.

There are few woods in the north to attract the visitor, although near Brill there may still be found fragments of the great oak forests of Bernewood. Only the names of the villages are left to remind us of these preserves where the kings of England hunted the wild boar and deer: 'Boarstall', 'Oakley', 'Ashenden', 'Wotton', and 'Grendon Underwood'.

Near Aylesbury are the sites of three depopulated villages, Quarrenden, Fleet Marsdon and Creslow.

Quarrenden was one of the political centres of Elizabethan days, and a great tournament was held every year in the Queen's honour. Of the manor house nothing remains, and only the shell of a church shows where the village stood.

At Fleet Marston a small Decorated Church stands alone in a clump of trees in the middle of a field, and at Creslow, the beautiful 14th-century manor house is now in use as a farm, while the remains of the Norman church are converted into a barn.

The battles of the Civil War must have been fought uncomfortably near these villages, and it is said that several disastrous floods added to the work of destruction. There is a feeling of desolation and loneliness about this locality, which all but the most insensitive motorist must feel.

A little further north, at Hillesden, the most beautiful church in the county stands alone, surrounded by great meadows. This was another place to suffer from the effects of war. Hillesden House was utterly destroyed, and the handful of cottages that now form the village, is far from any road.

North of Buckingham, in the valley of the Ouse, the country becomes more comfortable again, the fields have more homely proportions, and the villages are cosy and populous. The 'sinuous' Ouse gives us some lovely 'typically English' scenery as it passes through Tyringham Park and again as it loops around through Cowper's country. Before leaving Buckinghamshire at the north corner of the county it is again responsible for some perfect river scenery. Everything is there, the cows knee-deep in lush grass, the church tower half hidden by trees on one bank, and the manor house standing upon a green rise on the other. Quiet backwaters where water-lilies lie between rows of yellow irises, and dragon-flies dart between them.

North of Olney there is a distinct feeling of the Midlands. The houses are built of grey stone, and there is an impression that the warm villages are being left behind and a sterner life is at hand.

Buckinghamshire remains an agricultural county, and with few exceptions, the industries that are practised have developed from the natural conditions of the land.

The origin of the furniture factories at Wycombe and Princes Risborough, and the dairy produce of Aylesbury and the Plain will be found respectively in the beech woods of the south, and the rich pasture lands of the north. Altogether, Buckinghamshire is not a remarkable county, but though it lacks the attraction of a sea-coast, the scenery of mountains and of waterfalls, or the glamour to be found in cathedrals and castles, it affords certain contrasts. In the north, you may see country as little changed during the last thousand years as any in England, and in the south, you may find all the advantages of a flourishing suburban life within 36 minutes of London.

But it is to the beech woods in mid-Bucks. that the county owes its reputation. Winter is by no means the least beautiful of the seasons in the woods. The sun turns the carpet of dead leaves to pale red and orange, over which the intricate shadows of tree trunks and branches curve and dip with every rise and fall of the ground. Or on a dull day after rain a blue mist hangs in the woods, changing the leaves to a dark red, through which the wet soil shows in black rifts. The smooth green pillars of the beech trees streaked in black stand in endless quiet arcades. In spring there is more movement; the trees wear sweeping dresses, trail flounces, carry parasols of shrill acid green. The play of light on these complicated lacy masses of foliage is bewildering. Full summer seems heavy and quiet between the brilliance of spring and autumn: then the range of colours in the foliage becomes extravagant, the woods are a conflagration of reds, browns and burning orange till the fire dies out and the skeletons of the winter trees emerge again.

For those who prefer homely landscape to rugged scenery, it would be hard to find a more congenial or varied piece of country than that which lies between the Thames and the Ouse in the County of Buckinghamshire, and its lack of spectacular features would only help to ensure for the motorist that quiet in which to enjoy 'a blest seclusion from a jarring world' (John Nash, 1936).

NOTE: *In 1966 Linslade was severed from Buckinghamshire and joined to Leighton Buzzard in Bedfordshire. In 1974 the southern tip of the county from Slough to Wraysbury, including Eton, was transferred to Berkshire. These places are nonetheless described in this guide.*

Introduction

John Nash's introduction to his *Shell Guide to Buckinghamshire* (1936) is reprinted here before the Introduction to the history and buildings of the county by the present author. Although written 45 years ago his description of the physical appearance and feeling of the county is still a true indication of its character. Old towns have sprawled, new ones been built, suburbs have proliferated, villages become dormitories and cottage industries vanished, but the lie of the land is the same and the things that influenced the way the county developed still operate. The same beauties—so well seen by the painter's eye and so lucidly described—can still be discovered and enjoyed.

One devastating change to the landscape has taken place since John Nash wrote those words. 'Dutch' elm disease spread like wildfire during his last years and particularly affected the north of the County. 'Devastating' is used here literally, for in the area north-west of the Chilterns (over a third of the County) over half the trees were elms and soon few of these will be left. Isolated or in groups in hedgerows, elms were a major feature of the Vale of Aylesbury and their loss will take years to repair. Money for replacement by hardier trees has been made available by acutely conscious local authorities, but, almost alone, at Lenborough near Buckingham, has a private owner anticipated the loss and made a new landscape of small woods in place of hedgerow trees on his land.

Lime avenue, **Turville** Heath

Beeches, Gussett's Wood, **Hambleden**

Fingest (*top*)
Fawley Bottom

Chiltern landscapes

Harecramp Farm and **Ibstone**
West Wycombe

Boveney

The Thames, Mill End, **Hambleden**, (*top*)
◁ **Marlow** Bridge

The Chess, **Latimer**

Historical development

As Nash made clear, the land, that is the underlying rock and the natural vegetation, has had a major influence on the county's development and history. Very broadly, the Chiltern ridge divides the better drained but poorer land of the south-east from the wetter but richer land of the north-west. These factors favoured the economy of the north-west from the time of the forest clearance down to the 20th century when farming improvements (chiefly more fertilizers) and the spread of urbanization from London gave the south-east the advantage. Development and history have been relatively peaceful but, like most English counties, Buckinghamshire came into being as a military district and took its name from the old County Town of Buckingham in the north-west, which was the only town to have achieved borough status before the Domesday Survey of 1086. Buckingham was the military centre and made up the county by taking into association first the adjoining Hundreds—the older administrative districts—and then the full sixteen which made something akin to the long and shaggy county of today. Buckingham, however, declined soon after the Norman Conquest and its functions were slowly usurped by the more central Aylesbury, which is still the county town.

The erratic areas of the original Hundreds, based on land ownership and made increasingly irregular by dowry and inheritance, account for the curious shape of the county. A number of minor changes were made on the borders (of Oxfordshire in the 18th and 19th centuries, Bedfordshire in 1965 and Berkshire in 1974) but none of these made the boundaries tidier or more rational.

Buckinghamshire was isolated from London in the early years because much of the intervening plain of Middlesex was still uncultivated forest. This early isolation and

Old Great Central Line, at **Quainton**

◁   Near **Mentmore** (*top*)
    Pitstone (*centre*)
    Chilton Park Farm (*bottom*)

the absence of the national resources (coal, iron, water-power) that later gave other counties their opportunities, kept it dependent on agriculture and consequently its population remained small. Many towns and most villages also remained small and have kept the plan of the early settlement and many of their old buildings.

The Romans improved the primitive tracks of the Icknield Way and Akeman Street across the centre and north of the county, and paved the route of Watling Street (the present A5) but these improvements did not encourage much settlement. The canals and early railways favoured the north-east corner. It was only in the late 19th century, following the opening of railways through the Chilterns (the Great Western to Princes Risborough in 1862 and the Metropolitan to Chesham in 1890) many years after railway development in Kent and Surrey, that there was the sharp rise in trade and population that came much earlier to the other Home Counties.

In spite of the increasing popularity with Londoners of the south-east, the 'leafy Bucks' and 'Metroland' of early railway advertising, there are still no large towns in the county. By 1974 Slough (now taken away and given to Berkshire), which was largely a creation of the 1920s and 1930s and of the motor vehicle rather than the railway, was the only town to have reached a population of 100,000. High Wycombe had reached 61,000. It grew from the 19th century concentration into factories of the furniture industry, hitherto a rural craft based on and in the Chiltern backwoods. Now High Wycombe occupies 11 kilometres of the narrow valley of the little River Wye, and has added other light industries to furniture-making and the occasional old-established paper mill. Aylesbury, the only town of any size in the central vale owed its early prosper-ity to cattle, sheep and, later, the renowned Aylesbury ducks. This was a cottage industry making good use of the many streams and ponds in area. But it was messy and smelly; the finer citizens of 19th-century Aylesbury complained constantly about the back-yard rearing that made their town famous. With modern methods of production, like most cottage industries, it died. Aylesbury was ignored by the early railway builders and in spite of its central position, and some forced expansion after the war, had achieved a population of only 41,000 by 1974. Bletchley, with its once important railway junction and declining brickworks had reached 33,000 and, of the rest, only Chesham exceeded 20,000.

The fact that all these decently sized towns are in the commuting south meant that the north had a disproportionally small population. The new city of Milton Keynes sited on land made available near Bletchley and Wolverton is intended to encourage new industrial and business development in the north and to discourage further dormitory building in the over-crowded south. Widespread building has already begun, turning heavy fields into mud and some hollows into lakes. Some of the enveloped villages have been preserved and although as yet there is little unity there has been tree-planting on a lavish scale. It should be a pleasant enough city one day.

Whatever the fate of Milton Keynes and the effect of this bold conception on the county's ambitions and rate-returns it has slowed up the proliferation of shopping centres and hypermarkets elsewhere, to the advantage of small towns and villages in the country. Elsewhere, too, the landscape is unspoilt except for some of the chalk ridges of the Chilterns that were disfigured in the 1930s by thoughtlessly conspicuous housing.

The Ouse at **Tyringham** (*top*) and **Thornton** ▷

The buildings

The buildings of Buckinghamshire are, on the whole, modest, with a few splendours. They depend for their interest on variety and excellence of materials and the charm of their sites. The primitive isolation and poverty of the pre-Reformation years account for the comparative rarity of important medieval and earlier buildings, and for the ruined state of the survivals of those that did exist. There are no cathedrals, no abbeys, no castles, no royal palaces and few large churches. But there are castle sites at Buckingham, Castlethorpe and Whitchurch; the gatehouses of fortified manors at Boarstall and Long Crendon; monastic remains at Chetwode, Notley, Missenden and Burnham and large churches at Aylesbury, High Wycombe, Chesham and Amersham.

Architectural innovation has usually come in from bordering counties: for instance, the stone churches and villages near Northamptonshire and Oxfordshire and the little steepled churches near Hertfordshire. Surviving timber-framed and plaster buildings have not got much of the spirited decoration found elsewhere. But there is a great deal of local variety. The use of 'wichert'—a chalky marl mixed with straw in parts of the Vale of Aylesbury—produces simple engaging buildings with soft white rounded shapes; well seen in the low buildings and long curved walls of Haddenham and Cuddington. The flint and brick building in the Chilterns is as much part of their character as the beech woods and the bluebells. The flints are not napped (that is cut and squared) as they are in Suffolk and Sussex; here the traditional skill is in the selection of the naturally split flint and the ingenuity with which it is made to fit

in to the required panel or pattern. Sometimes flints are used with stone quoins and mouldings or with chalk or both, as at Fawley Church, but usually with brick: apricot, ochre, pale and dark red, often chequered, in rivalry to the dazzling flints with blue or brown burnished headers. Some Chiltern cottages even have bottle ends incorporated as well.

Long Crendon Manor

◁ **Tingewick** (*top*)
Monks Risborough

23

In old buildings (like Hambleden Manor) flint seems to have merged with brick into a warm tapestried whole. In new ones, especially gothicized 19th-century schools, flints sparkle and gleam in aggressive contrast to the more sober surround.

As for the splendour: the great mansion at Stowe with its temples, bridge and landscaped park, and the house, church and landscaping at West Wycombe Park are pre-eminent. In both places human genius was harnessed to the genius of the place and in both the result is triumphant.

The Rothschilds built a series of palaces: Waddesden, Mentmore, Aston Clinton, Halton and Ascott. Except for the last there was no attempt to relate the house to the landscape of the county. The Chateau of Waddesdon was designed by a French architect, Destailleur. Aloof and golden amidst statues and formal gardens it looks, from its hill, on to a prim low range of brick and timber farm buildings. The combination is like a little bit of Northern France set down in Buckinghamshire.

Victorian taste is so grandly represented by these palaces that it is surprising to find so little of the revolutionary spirit of the great 19th-century church builders. Pugin built a Catholic church at Marlow; Street did a fine restrained new church at Westcott (1867) and added a graceful bell-stage to the tower at Beachampton (1873), while George Gilbert Scott, born at Gawcott, left a wide but somewhat distinctive mark on his own county by his excessive restoration of over 20 churches. He worked on Aylesbury's parish church for over 20 years.

◁ Olney

Hanslope ▷

Building materials

Chalk, flint and brick at **Medmenham** Church

Capped wichert walls at **Chearsley** (*above*)
and **Haddenham** (*below*)

Brick and flint:

◁ Dropmore (*see* **Littleworth**)

Wheeler End, Common,
Lane End ▷

▽ **Turville** Rectory

The Meeting
◁ House,
Jordans

Particular
Baptist Chapel, ▷
Winslow, 1695

The 20th century has less to be proud of. There are two large buildings at Medmenham by Romaine Walker and Lutyens designed one large plain house at Taplow (1910) and added pretty water pavilions close to Soane's Tyringham House (1926). Of the 'Modern movement' of the 1930s there are houses by Connell and Ward at Amersham and one at Chalfont by Mendelsohn. Notable post-Second World War buildings include a number of attractive schools (chiefly by Pooley), the somewhat brutal tower block of county offices at Aylesbury (Pooley), the Egyptian rudeness of bridges on the M1 motorway (Owen Williams, 1959) and, later, county libraries (chiefly by Markcrow). It is surprising that with the enterprising example set by the public architects there is so little of note by private ones until very recently, when there is some good domestic work by local architects at Aylesbury and Bledlow.

Buckinghamshire has some grand monuments, well worth a pilgrimage, but it is, above all, a county of unexpected small pleasures. Of particular interest, all over the county, are the early dissenting chapels. The best known is the Quaker Meeting House at Jordans (1688). The fine Baptist chapel at Winslow (1695) deserves to be better known, as do many others throughout the county. Non-Conformity has been strong here since Wycliffe was rector of Ludgershall in the 14th century and the chapels are symbols of a strong dissenting and liberal tradition that produced such political rebels as John Hampden of Great Hampden, John Wilkes of Aylesbury and Edmund Burke of Beaconsfield. Its conservative politicians, the second Dashwood, Baronet of West Wycombe, the Grenvilles of Wotton Underwood and Disraeli of Bradenham were more radical when young. Disraeli claimed that there was 'something in the air of Bucks favourable to political knowledge and vigour'.

But dissent, like most building in the county, has now been tempered by the modesty and the courtesy that have deep roots in the lovable but homely landscape of this most English of English counties.

Stowe: Queens Temple, Gothic Temple, Cobham Pillar and Palladian Bridge

◁ Fountain of Venus at **Ascott** by Waldo Story

Fountain at **Waddesdon**. Triton and the Nereids by Giuiliano Mozani (d. 1735), originally in the Ducal Palace Garden at Colorno

Amersham Town Hall

Gazetteer

The number in brackets following the place name refers to the square on the map at the back of the book where the place is to be found.

Addington [8] A private, remote and upland-seeming place of two big houses and a church inside a large park approached through open meadows, cattle-grids and gently sloping clay fields. Addington Manor is an impressive neo-Georgian brick house of 1929 by M. Waterhouse and has free Ionic pilasters supporting a central pediment. The more modest Manor House to the north-west is a fragment of a Queen Anne house in brick with stone quoins, drastically reduced by the first Lord Addington (1805–89) and partly rebuilt in a classical style by Hardwick in 1858. There is a late 16th-century cruciform tithe barn near by and long stables dated 1642. Between the two houses is St Mary's church in stone rubble and lead and tile roofs, basically 14th century but so much improved (by G. E. Street, 1859) that little of the old is left but the embattled west tower and the arcades with plain pillars without capitals. Above the arcades circular clerestory windows are filled with some 50 panels of early 15th-century Flemish glass, set in pink borders and grisaille in 1859. There are a number of Busby memorials including one to the father of Dr Busby of Willen and another to Thomas, signed and dated by Rysbrack 1753.

Adstock [8] A small village surrounded with clay pastures and arable fields, formerly punctuated with hedgerow elms; it has a few old houses with timber frames and thatch but most are Victorian and modern brick—even 'Cotteswold', i.e. superior concrete blocks. The church of St Cecilia is befittingly small and simple with a battlemented west tower, and nave and chancel almost rebuilt in 1854 incorporating fragmentary Nor-

man north and south doors. Minton tiles, pitch-pine fittings and Powell glass of 1875 in west window accentuate its Victorian architecture.

Akeley [5] On the Northants. border; it has a stone church and mainly pink brick and cream-washed cottages. The church of St James is nicely sheltered in trees and stone walls on a bend in the main road. It is by S. Tarring (1854), dull outside in spite of a jaunty turret on its south tower and an east window by Mayer & Co. of Munich (1884). There is a little square of buildings to the south of the church which includes the cream-washed 'Bull and Bush' and a school of 1834. The Manor Farmhouse on the east of the village is in 16th-century coursed stone. The biggest house is Akeleywood, gabled and half-timbered, by Devey (1867), over a kilometre west towards Stowe.

Amersham [15] Really two places: the Old Town—a large, preserved village in the Misbourne valley bottom—and Amersham-on-the-Hill—a sprawling piece of Metroland separated from Old Town by flinty arable slopes and remnant beech woods 60 m higher to the north. The Old Town is on the medieval route to Aylesbury through the Wendover Gap in the Chilterns; the New grew up round the Metropolitan Railway which reached Little Chalfont (at its London end) in 1890 and was extended to Amersham and Aylesbury in 1892. The nicest approach is from Aylesbury, where the beauty of the long High Street lined with attractive buildings (without exception) and gently widening down to the Town Hall can be enjoyed in one progression. How-

ever, most visitors first see it from London End, where remaining beech trees and Green Belt fields soften the impact of the New Town houses spilling down the hill, the sausage works and petrol stations and then the large London Transport garage of 1935. On the south side of this is Bury Farm, the home of Mary Pennington and Guilelma Springett, wife of William Penn of Pennsylvania. Beyond is Broadway. Thirty years ago it was still narrowed at its London end by an island of old houses and there was a real market square between it and the Market Hall. This has now gone and a large hole is left on its north to give windy exposure to a memorial garden and a view of the church. The Market Hall, which blocks the view beyond, is a two-storey, red-brick and stone building with a white painted cupola and was built for the Drakes of Shardeloes. Its west end is badly disfigured with traffic signs. The September Fair granted by King John is still held in the street on each side. St Mary's church is externally Victorian, large and flinty with a varied silhouette made dramatic by a spired turret on its heavy tower. It is white-plastered inside with an engaging starred-blue ceiling to the chancel. The interest of the church is concentrated at this (the east) end where the east window has 17th-century glass from Lamer Manor (Herts.) inserted in 1760 and the principal monuments line the chancel and fill the Drake Chapel on its north side. In the chancel are the following monuments: one to the 14-year-old Henry Curwen (d. 1636), which has a sinuous figure framed in doors held by chubby-faced angels, by Edward Marshall; one to Sir William Drake (d. 1654), which has a shrouded bust flanked by winged hour-glasses, curiously pedimented, by Edward Marshall; one to George Bent (d. 1714) and his mother (d. 1730), which has cramped kneeling figures which seem cut off at the knees, by Edward Stanton; and one to Montague Drake (d. 1724) and wife, which has two portrait medallions framed with columns and pediment above a big grey sarcophagus, by Andrew Carpenter. The Drake chapel has those of M. G. Drake (d. 1728), which has a reclining figure in Roman dress by P. Scheemakers; Elizabeth Drake (d. 1757) and children, which has fat cherubs weeping by a sarcophagus with a framed relief of Elizabeth and six children above, by Henry Cheere; W. T. Drake, which has kneeling figure and urn by J. Bacon jun. dated 1802, and smaller sentimental memorials to other Drakes. The last notable monument is to T. T. Drake (d. 1852), which has a reclining figure reading the Bible, by Henry Weekes. Buildings near by in Church Street include flint stables and an old brick brewery which make a photogenic group. The Rectory is at the top of the hill beyond, a wide two-storeyed, yellow-brick house with a broken pediment, overlooking the Old Town from its small beech wood. Beyond Church Street and the Market Hall, High Street resumes its full width and then gradually tapers westward to enclose almost unbroken rows of handsome and apparently 18th-century, though often much older, two-storeyed red-brick and tiled buildings. The best of these are the Crown Hotel, with columned porch and courtyard; the King's Arms, with extravagant timber gables; no. 47, a 15th-century three-gabled house; Elmodesham House, in three storeys and 11 bays of purple and red brick; the Drake Almshouse of 1657, and Little Shardeloes, with its 17th-century brick gables. At the rear of the King's Arms is a red-brick, two-storeyed Baptist chapel of 1783 with arched windows and a glazed lantern. These are all south of the High Street. Starting from the west on the north side are the late 17th-century chequered brick Mill and the bay-windowed, gabled 17th-century The Gables. Shardeloes is outside the town further on the south side of the valley. Built in 1766 by Stiff Leadbetter but altered by Robert Adam, it is a large, almost square, house of stuccoed brick. The giant portico by Adam faces north across the valley. The interiors, part Adam and part James Wyatt, are now converted to flats and maisonettes; the grounds with lake by H. Repton make a pretty setting for the local cricket club. There is a pleasant walk back by the Platt to the old town centre, along the backs of High Street houses with their old cottagey gardens. Along Whielden Street, the road to Wycombe, are more modest houses and, buried in a modern hospital with an incongruous 11-storey block, is G. G. Scott's Tudor-style workhouse of 1838. Near by is a Friends Meeting House, dated 1685, of almost ostentatious lack of pretension. Of course, more than a century earlier, the town had been the scene of Protestant martyrdoms, commemorated by a 20th-century monument in a field towards the station. To the north, Amersham-on-the-Hill incorporates traces of former rusticity—e.g. in Beel House and Raans Farm, towards Little Chalfont, and in Flint Cottage, at Amersham Common—but is largely the creation of late railway days, the greatest growth being just before the Second World War, when many houses made determined efforts to look older than Old Town (see, for example, 'Timbers'). But one group of rebelliously modern houses was built above London End which started with A. Connell's three-legged plain concrete 'High and Over' of 1931 and ended with four smaller 'Sun Houses' of 1934 by Basil Ward. They are in the so-called International Style of that day and, though still strange, do not look as foreign as much of the sham Tudor. The best new buildings are the more modest brick and timber post-war schools by the County Architect.

Ascott [8] A Rothschild mansion and park on the edge of Wing. The mansion is a picturesque jumble of half-timbering of which the centre, dated 1606 on the front door, is the house of the Dormers. This was bought by Leopold de Rothschild in 1874 as a family hunting box, and here he built kennels which were the headquarters of the Rothschild staghounds. He then employed Devey to extend the house, which was further extended in 1938 in a similar style. The house, gardens and contents, which include well-known Dutch and English paintings, were presented to the National Trust in 1950. The gardens are by Sir Harry Veitch of Chelsea—one of his few remaining designs—and have formal parts for Victorian bedding-out and informal parts in the manner of William Robinson. They contain an elaborate fountain of Venus by the American sculptor Waldo Story (cf. Cliveden), two rock gardens and a huge topiary sundial. Some sense of unity is provided by the fine tree-planting and the views through this towards the Vales of Aylesbury.

Ashendon [10, 11] A small village on a high, rather bare and isolated hill with a grey stone church and reddish brick houses. The best views are outward—particularly into the deep valley between Ashendon and Waddesdon Manor, whose turrets peer above the trees on Lodge Hill to the north-west. St Mary's church is stone-walled and lead-roofed with a stumpy embattled west tower and an over-restored interior. The nave was Norman (see the blocked north doorway). The chancel is 19th century. It has a plain late 17th-century pulpit, a defaced, late

own work. The south doorway is Early English and there is a piscina in the chancel. The highly coloured east windows are in memory of Rear Admiral Sir James Clarke Ross (d. 1862), who discovered the Magnetic Pole in 1831. He lived at the only large house, 'The Abbey', an 11-bay, grey stone building, looking 18th century, on a site of a country seat of the Abbot of St Albans, whence the village gets half its name. It still has its medieval moat.

Aston Clinton [11] Filled with red-brown brick Victorian terraces and villas, infilled and cemented over with bungalows which spread thickly north, sparing the retiring village of Buckland but enclosing the medieval Green End, where a timber-framed pub and a few modest 17th- and 18th-century cottages survive. The vast expansion coincides with the establishment of one of the great Rothschild mansions, that of Sir Antony, who bought Aston Clinton Park in 1851 and extended the earlier house instead of, like his relations, building *de novo*. This house has now been demolished and a modern Youth Leaders' Centre has been built in its place by the County Architect (1964) in simple brick and tile. The attractive park is still there, providing green shade to the overbusy road. The church of St Michael and All Angels is on the edge of the park, of flint with some stone, mainly late 13th-century and early 14th-century with elaborately crocketed sedilia, piscina and Easter sepulchre in the chancel and a 14th-century painted figure on its south wall. The Rectory, in brick and stone, neo-Elizabethan, is by E. B. Lamb (1850). The schools (by Gotto of Tring) and the Anthony Hall were given by Sir Anthony de Rothschild. The Bell Inn, the only other attractive landmark on the main road, is mid 18th century with

13th-century, cross-legged knight, and fragments of 15th-century glass. Upper Pollicott Farm and Pollicott Farm to the south are of 16th- and 17th-century brickwork with giant chimneys.

Ashley Green [12] A main-road village on a chalk ridge north of Chesham carpeted with orchards and turkey farms; it has red-brick houses and bungalows and some older cottages between sycamore, oak and beech trees. It is a modern parish formed in 1875 when it was given the church of St John the Evangelist at its crossroads—a 'dashing little design' (John Betjeman)—in grey stone, with nave and chancel and bellcote over east end of nave, by G. E. Street. Grove Farm, nearly a mile south-east, has a former 15th-century flint-faced chapel (now converted to a cottage) and remains of a gate-house within a moat. On Whelpley Hill, a kilometre further east, is an Iron Age hill fort.

Askett [11] Wet pastures in the Vale of Aylesbury with no church, or obvious centre. Cottages of all types—brick and tile, occasional flint and stone, wichert and thatch—are set among willows, garden trees and odd patches of pine. The best-looking building is the Three Crowns Inn, of late 18th-century brick, with broad eaves, slate roof and flint and brick stable block.

Aston Abbotts [8] A well-treed village on a slight hill rising above the Vale of Aylesbury with views west to Weedon and to 'Fred's Folly', the County Buildings tower at Aylesbury, has a small village green and mostly small red-brown and brown brick cottages, though some timber-framed, round a triangular pattern of lanes. The small grey stone church of St James has an embattled tower with projecting staircase but was otherwise so restored and rebuilt by G. E. Street in 1865–6 as to look like his

Market Square, **Aylesbury**

Venetian windows and rich menus. Evelyn Waugh (1903–66) taught at a preparatory school and wrote much of *Decline and Fall* here in 1925–7.

Aston Sandford [11] Isolated by streams down a cul-de-sac, in flat clay fields; it has one large brick house, a church, little stone houses, stone walls, chestnuts. St Michael's church is suitably small (about 18 m by 5 m overall) of light grey limestone and red tiles, with a weatherboarded belfry over the west end. Its plain interior exhibits a small 13th-century, green and yellow Christ in stained glass at the east end. The Rev. Thomas Scott, friend of Cowper, author of *Force of Truth* and grandfather of Gilbert Scott, was buried here in 1821. Gilbert Scott seems to have had a hand in the red-brick 'Manor'.

Astwood [6] A flattish main-road village of brick, tile and thatched cottages and a neglected-looking church on the Beds. border in the north-east of the county. The

church of St Peter was damaged by a bomb in 1940 and seems not to have recovered from its surprise. The Perpendicular west tower cuts into the first bay of the nave while the other buttresses of the nave seem supported by ivy. The best thing inside is the Royal Arms of William IV but there is a portrait medallion to one of the Lowndes family of Astwood Bury (d. 1775). To the north are The Bury, made from 17th-century timber and brick cottages, with a moat, and Dove House, an octagonal brick 17th-century dovecot converted to a three-bedroomed house, both relics of the once-important house of Astwood Bury.

Aylesbury [11] A mixed-up town with a long history, a central position and administrative dominance in the county; it is still neither as attractive nor as impressive as one would expect. It was a small medieval town, then an 18th-century market area, now an administrative capital dominated by a grey concrete tower, 19th-

century workers' housing and large 20th-century suburbs for the new middle class. It had a minor royal palace and minted royal coins in late Saxon times but did not have the County assize courts until 1218 or become a parliamentary borough until 1554. It lost its Members of Parliament to a wider County constituency in 1885 and even its borough status from neglect, until re-incorporated in 1917, only to be submerged in the larger Aylesbury District in 1974. It has always been a node for roads—a branch of the Grand Union Canal reached it in 1814, a branch railway in 1839, and direct rail connection to London by Great Western in 1863 and by Metropolitan in 1893. Large-scale printing arrived in 1867 and milk processing in 1872. Growth of the population was, however, surprisingly slow: 3,200 in 1801, 6,000 in 1851, but only 9,000 in 1901. Increase slowed down in the later 19th century, when most towns were booming. When Pevsner wrote his volume on the buildings of Buckinghamshire

Aylesbury

in 1960 he could still say 'the impression is of a market town, prosperous in the 18th century'. The town was then clustered round the church on its little hill and few buildings separated the 18th-century market square on its south side from the pastures and duck ponds on which its former prosperity depended. In the 1960s the town was artificially and grossly expanded by agreement between County and London boroughs to take their 'overspill'. Commanding offices for the county were built south of the 18th-century market and the whole area from Walton Street to the station was cleared and rebuilt. The area of small houses and professional offices between the Market Square and the parish church was left, though there are more offices and fewer houses, but the former character, scale and humanity of the central alleys, dissenting chapels, inns and duck ponds has vanished. The new shopping area is no worse than many of the period, and is, in some ways, better, since it is closely co-ordinated with new bus station, car stack and approaches to railway station. Church Square has the heart of the medieval quarter and the buildings of greatest interest, the parish church and the County Museum. The church of St Mary is at the highest point in the town, in a wide graveyard surrounded by a precinct of dignified 17th- and 18th-century houses. It is of grey limestone with lead roofs, large and basically cruciform in plan though with chapels added at odd points and angles. It has a thick 13th-century central tower and 15th-century panelled battlements within which rise a small turret and a 17th-century (strictly a 19th-century facsimile) lead spire. The church was extensively restored by Sir George Gilbert Scott for 20 years or more from 1850 when much of the 15th-century and other detail was turned to what he thought the 'purer' style of the 13th-century Early English. Inside, the church seems both cold and towny, largely because of this. The chancel, for instance, has only one genuine 13th-century wall, the north, with its original shafted lancet windows; others on east and south are copies. Outside, the damage at the east end is more apparent for the former wide and welcome 15th-century five-light window was replaced by Scott's triplets. Of other openings, only the 15th-century west window and a three-light window in the south transept are original. The nave is wide, with six bays with quatrefoil piers, and has narrow aisles which widen into 14th-century chapels. A Lady Chapel was added to the south transept in the 14th century and clerestories added to nave and transepts in the 15th century. The west end of the nave and its aisles were transformed (1978), by the insertion of a raised stage and new galleries so as to increase the social uses of the church. It spoils the scale but reduces the chill of its size and its copious Victorian glass. The best thing is the splendid late 12th-century font which with its scalloped base and spirally fluted bowl and band of foliage, is the archetype of many found in the centre of the county. There are also a few misericords in the chancel stalls, two poppy-head bench ends, a rare 15th-century vestment press, sculptured figures by Farmer and Brindley (1870), and windows by Willement, Oliphant, Gibbs, O'Connor and Burlison and Grylls, none outstanding but forming quite a museum of Victorian glass. Two interesting monuments are hidden in the north transept behind the organ: the damaged alabaster late 14th-century figure of a knight, found in the Greyfriars area, and the large alabaster monument of Lady Lee (d. 1584). She was the wife of Sir Henry Lee of Quarrendon (d. 1610), and this monument, with kneeling figures of mother and daughter, was brought here from the vanished church at Quarrendon. It is continuously decked with a fresh red flower. There are minor wall monuments in the body of the church including

one of 1703 by Edward Stanton and another of 1749 with a tall white obelisk attributed to Scheemakers. Behind trees on the east side of St Mary's Square, as the precinct is called, is the buff-stuccoed Prebendal House which was the home from 1749 to 1764 of the radical M.P. John Wilkes, who married a local heiress. It has an elaborate, rusticated, red and grey brick gate to Parson's Fee, the little curved street that dives down to the south-west. Adjoining this is the 17th- and 18th-century Prebendal Farm (now St Osyth's) and an even earlier timber-framed barn now made into a dwelling. On the north side of the Square is the three-storey red and grey brick frontage of the Derby Arms, an 18th-century screen of a smaller, older building, while, from the south-east corner, towards the present town centre, runs Church Street, the happiest-looking street in the town. At the church end of the County Museum, which occupies two buildings, are the old Grammar School of 1719 and the early 18th-century Ceeley House which has a contemporary staircase and a later doorway with arched fanlight and Corinthian portico, brought here from the Eythrope mansion demolished in 1805. The Museum is the head-quarters of the long-established Bucks. Archaeological Society and, apart from many other local collections, houses the County Council's displays illustrating rural life in the county. There are two 15th-century houses opposite the Museum: no. 10, refronted in dark brick with lighter dressings in the 18th century: and no. 8, which was refronted in stucco in 1840 when its three gables were given moulded barge-boards. It is a short distance to the tiny Temple Square (named after the Temples of Stowe), which is little more than the junction of the old central streets, Church Street, Castle Street (the old road to Oxford), Rickford's Hill, which runs south, and Temple Street, which continues on towards the

Market Place. There are more historic dwellings round the Square and down Rickford's Hill, though most have been altered. The best-looking is no. 1 Church Street, which has a red and grey brick front dated 1739 and pedimented door to a 16th-century body. Slightly north of this is Kingsbury, normally reached from St Mary's Square by the still-cobbled Pebble Lane. It is a triangular space with a few old pubs facing prominent shelters and lavatories but it was the earliest market place of the town and probably the site of the royal palace. At its south end it opens up across a nasty road junction into the 18th-century Market Place, the visual centre of Aylesbury. This is now an empty cobbled space surrounded with tarmac roads, for the cattle market has been moved south and the produce market translated to small regimented stalls in the new shopping centre on the west. On its north side, approached by one of the few remaining alleys, is the King's Head Hotel, which has a 15th-century hall with a big mullioned window filled with contemporary glass showing Royal Arms of Henry VI and Margaret of Anjou. Within the square are heroic statues of Hampden (by Fehr, 1912) and Lord Chesham (by Tweed, 1910) and a 20-metre-high pointed gothic clock tower (by D. Brandon, 1876). On the east side are a few unpleasantly rebuilt shops and offices and the handsome 18th-century brick Bedford House retained by Barclays Bank. The centrepiece of the south side is the tall three-storeyed County Hall built by Thomas Harris from 1723 to 1740. It is in brick, above stone facing up to the ground floor arches, not externally distinguished though approved by Vanbrugh. It contains, on the first floor, one perfect room, the Main Court, which has a raised judge's seat with royal crested pediment, panelled walls and box pews. It was almost destroyed by fire in 1970 but carefully restored by the County

Architect, down to details of the little recess for the judge's chamber-pot behind his judicial seat. On its right, at the corner of Walton Street, is the long, low, early 19th-century, stuccoed front of the older Bell Hotel and then, across the street, the stern concrete walls of the new County offices framing the tunnel which swallows up the bus station. From its two- and three-storeyed podium rise the grey, heavily modelled, 11 storeys of the County Offices by County Architect F. B. Pooley (1966), usually known as 'Fred's Folly', in commending whose design the Concrete Society said that its 'powerful impression' was 'appropriate to its role as the headquarters of the county'. It is difficult to see how an architect's department which designed the lovable County Library at Burnham could produce this unfriendly landmark. For a more humane view of architecture look at the same department's Police Headquarters and the Gollins, Melvin and Ward-designed insurance offices, both just off Walton Street.

Barton Hartshorn [7] A tiny village in flattish hunting country in the corner of the county. St James's church is a small, creamy grey stone building with a little belfry, largely rebuilt in 1841 and altered later with cast-iron Royal Arms of Victoria. The Manor House to its east has a north-east wing dated 1635 and considerable additions in a similar Tudor style made in 1903 and 1908 by Sir Robert Lorimer. These wrap, in an L shape, round an old walnut tree. To the west, and abutting on the road, is the gabled and mullioned 17th-century Old Manor Cottage.

Beachampton [5] A somewhat isolated village in N. Bucks., straggling down a slope to the Ouse; it has a church, two good farmhouses, some cottages and dying elms. The church of St Mary is in a yellowish limestone rubble

century stone-built and gabled manor house, Beachampton Hall. Other parts of the old house were cannibalized to make the present stone farm buildings. To the south is The Grange, a timber-framed and rough gabled farmhouse on a stone base, and opposite is Elmer House, the former grammar school of William Elmer of 1652, attended by Browne Willis, the Bucks. antiquarian.

Beaconsfield [15] The name means 'field of the beeches' and the place is still surrounded with beech woods on gentle chalk hills. The old town, in spite of its prominent Victorianized church, is the best 17th- and 18th-century 'village' in the county, with its four 'Ends' —London, Windsor, Wycombe and Aylesbury—filled with interesting and attractive small houses with timber frames or of brick and tile, though many have been improved to, and a bit beyond, the limit of good taste. The new town is a Metroland suburb round the Western Railway station (the railway reached here in 1862) to the north. The intervening space between the two was filled slowly with larger houses. The church of St Mary and All Saints is at the crossroads of the ancient Ends. It is in Victorian flint with Bath stone dressings and was greatly over-restored in 1869. Some Perpendicular features remain in the lower part of the west tower, in the chequered flint buttresses and in the western end of the arcades, but the heavy pinnacles, and spired stair-turret, which are such features, were added at the Victorian restoration. Inside, between chancel and south chapel, is a screen with flat ogee arches and in the chancel is a tomb recess sheltering an altar-tomb. The grave of Edmund Burke (d. 1797), who lived at Gregories, is marked by a discreet brass tablet in the floor. In the churchyard is a tall stone obelisk over a tomb chest designed by William Stanton, which marks the

Beaconsfield
Old Rectory (*above*)
London End (*below*)

with lead and tiled roofs and, though fundamentally an early 14th-century building, with Y tracery in the windows and quatrefoil piers to the three bay arcades, was largely rebuilt by G. E. Street in 1873. His addition to the 14th-century west tower, of a balustraded bell stage and tapering stone spire, is striking and attractive. Inside it is less memorable but for the memorial to Sir Simon Benet, a

benefactor of University College Oxford, who died in 1682. This standing monument, with bust, scrolls, inscription plate, pediments and columns, is supposed to have been put up by his old college in 1760, but the figures look 17th rather than 18th century. On the south bank of the Ouse, north of the church is Hall Farm. This is the remaining fragment, containing the banqueting hall, of the 17th-

grave of the poet and statesman Edmund Waller (d. 1687) of Hall Barn. The dramatic E-shaped Old Rectory, with upper storey of curved timbers projecting over the simpler brick walls of the ground floor, was built about 1500. In Aylesbury End to the north are the timber-framed Lloyd's Bank and the five-bay mid-18th-century Rectory, with its iron gates, and the mid-18th-century Wycombe House, with canted bay windows. Windsor End, with its avenue of pollarded elms, leads to Little Hall Barn, where, from 1809 on, William Hickey wrote the uproarious memoirs of his youth and hard times. Off this road, across the motorway, is Beaconsfield's grandest house, Hall Barn, home of Edmund Waller, who built this red and black house in 1660. It has three tall storeys with pilasters, hipped roof and a lantern. Remarkably like a contemporary doll's house it was called a 'town box' by John Evelyn. Originally square it was much altered, notably by Colen Campbell, who added a wing on the south, and by Devey, who added the giant porte-cochère. The grounds were beautifully landscaped with a lake, ornamental boathouse and garden temples, and much of this work survives. The main street is London End, which widens gently to the gates of Wilton Park and is architecturally the best of the 4 'Ends', lined on both sides with attractive houses, pubs and cottages. The best are Burke House on the south, which is plastered and has five canted 17th-century bay windows and 18th-century octagonal glazing bars, and Malt House on the north, which has a doorcase with Tuscan columns and broken pediment. Wilton Park is an early 18th-century white-rendered house in a large park but is now surrounded with temporary-looking buildings and a more incongruous tower block in red

Beaconsfield: ▷
Hall Barn Lodge, detail

Bledlow

brick with concrete bands, occupied by the Army's Education Service. In New Beaconsfield there is a church (St Michael) by Fellowes Prynne (1914), neo-Georgian Council offices, a library with low-pitched roof and timber slatting by County Architect (1956) and 'Bekonscot', in Warwick Road, north of the railway. This is a very large model village with a model railway in rock gardens, aesthetically distressing but of delightful naïveté and already a museum piece of the 1930s. Edmund Burke lived at Gregories, which he bought in 1768, and there entertained Crabbe, Sheridan, Garrick and Johnson, but his house was burnt down in 1813. G. K. Chesterton lived and wrote his Father Brown stories at Overroads in Grove Road from 1909 to 1935.

Bellingdon [12] (near Chesham) This ridge-top ribbon development runs from Chesham towards Cholesbury but ends, more or less, in an attractive group of buildings

clustered round Bellingdon Farm, a timber-framed and red-brick 17th-century house with 17th- and 18th-century farm buildings and cottages. D. H. Lawrence lived in one of the cottages from 1914 to 1915.

Biddlesden [4] An estate hamlet of stone buildings hidden in a wooded limestone valley on the Northants. border. Its centre is Biddlesden Park, a large house on the site of a Cistercian Abbey, whose church acted as the parish church long after the latter's dissolution. The old church was swept away in the early 18th century to make way for the sober, almost dull, stone house of nine bays which now faces a pleasant lake surrounded by trees. The long brick stables on the south-east side incorporate in their two southern bays the plain church room provided by the builders of the new house. The south side of this, the present tiny parish church of St Margaret, has a central entrance with pediment and, inter-

nally, contemporary fittings and a west gallery supported on Doric columns. North of the house are impressive, arcaded stone barns.

Bierton [11] A long large village on the main road north-east of Aylesbury follows a small ridge of cornbrash above the clay vale; it now seems a noisy suburb of the county town. The church of St James is mainly early 14th century, of grey stone with a square tower and little lead spire over the crossing. Tall arcades and crossing arches on shafted quatrefoil piers with moulded capitals give the interior a graceful look and a feeling of overall design rare in parish churches. Clerestory windows were added in the 15th century when steeper 14th-century roofs were replaced. The font is plain Norman with a cable moulding; the monument to Samuel Bosse (d. 1616) is full of small kneeling figures of his large family. There is a picturesque group of minor buildings north-east of the church which includes

44

no. 105 Main Road, an early 17th-century timber-framed building with brick infill—its front to the churchyard was refaced in the 18th century with red and blue bricks—but the village street is spoilt by through traffic.

Bishopstone [11] Scattered cottages in brick, tile and thatch with some wichert between oak, dying elm, hornbeam and willow in a flat stretch of Aylesbury Vale.

Bledlow [11] An H-shaped village on a spur of the Chilterns. Smoke from Chinnor (Oxon.) cement works mars its views somewhat. The cross-bar and main street of the village has the flint and grey stone church and the red-brick manor house and is a 'bridge' across the head of a little wooded ravine called the Lyde, which is cut by clear springs and floored with watercress. Holy Trinity church is overall grey with west tower and shallow eaves. The nave, aisles and chancel are of 12th-century origin but the chancel and south-east nave windows were enlarged in early 14th century and have distinguished tracery. Nave arcades have firm circular piers with stiff leaf capitals and pointed arches. The font is a cup-shaped Norman one of Aylesbury type, with scalloped base and fluted bowl. The reredos, now in the south aisle, is an 18th-century work by J. Gwynne. There are many 17th-century texts on walls; fragments of 13th- and 14th-century wall-paintings, including St Christopher on the north wall and Adam and Eve on the south and an early 16th-century brass. Across the lane and facing the head of the Lyde is the early 18th-century pale red-brick Manor House of the Carringtons, with a large weather-boarded barn at its rear. Adjoining the Lyde is a group of low brown brick houses with sharp roof lines of 1977 by Aldington and Craig, deservedly 'commended' by the R.I.B.A. To the west along the street are timber-framed and brick-filled cottages, and at its east end is a large stone-built house designed as a workhouse school for girls. Bledlow Cross, a prominent chalk cutting on Wain Hill about 23 m in length, is probably pre-Conquest —perhaps much earlier—but little is known of its origin.

Bledlow Ridge [14] Has small houses and bungalows of the 1920s and 1950s in red-brick or white rendering, softened by garden trees dotted along a high chalk ridge. The ridge has some views outward and from here Bradenham looks like a toy garden. St Paul's—a flint-bodied, small, bare church of 1868—has a bellcote at the west end and a big window (mid 1960s) by John Piper.

Bletchley [8] A Victorian railway town made from local (Oxford clay) bricks. The old village is to the west of the once-important railway junction, with lines to Oxford and Cambridge, and the newer terraces and shops are towards Fenny Stratford which it has now absorbed. It is the largest town and a 'cornerstone' of the Milton Keynes New Town. St Mary's church and the few old cottages on Church Green are surprisingly attractive. The rest is, not surprisingly, one of the least attractive places in the county in spite of efforts by the New Town Corporation to give it a new face. St Mary's, of limestone rubble with lead roofs, has a prominent early 15th-century west tower and some residual late Norman work, e.g. in the rebuilt south door, but it is most interesting for its restoration by the antiquarian Browne Willis, who repaired the church, post 1700, as a memorial to his parents, and for its later restoration by William White in 1868. Willis not only repaired the neglected building but added pinnacles to the west tower and had cherubs painted on the chancel roof. White removed the pinnacles and cherubs and other improvements as unseemly and anachronistic. It has 13th-century piscina and sedilia, alabaster effigy of a Lord Grey de Wilton (d. 1442), alabaster slab to Thomas Sparke (d. 1616) and, on the chancel floor, two plain slabs which mark the graves of the parents of Browne Willis. The church itself is partly their memorial. Bletchley Park, near by, was the home of the war-winning code-breaker 'Enigma' and is now the centre of bleak suburbs with a modern grammar school of 1966 by the County Architect. The station, still the natural centre of the town, has a large Jacobean, red-brick front of 1881. Near by are large curtain-walled offices by the New Town architects. Those on the east block the old spine road of the town and screen the 'Brunel' shopping centre. The east end of this old road is planted with plane trees and a glass-fibre canopy to provide a cockney-type street market. A more central and imposing shopping area for the whole New Town has been provided half-way between here and Wolverton.

Boarstall [10] Once deep inside Bernewood Forest, all that is left of the fortified medieval house, property for some centuries of the Aubreys and Aubrey-Fletchers, is the three-storey gate-house called Boarstall Tower, on a lawn within the remains of a moat. The house was given a fortification licence in 1312 and its gate-house is of that time, though much altered in the 17th century. It is rectangular in plan with four hexagonal turrets, of which the larger pair flank the outer gate to a stone bridge over the moat. The house was occupied during the Civil War by each side in turn and when finally surrendered to Parliament in 1646 was despoiled. The gate-house was converted to a substantial dwelling, which it still is, and was given by the Aubrey-Fletchers to the National Trust in 1943. The two-storey, dark brick stables with mul-

Bradenham Manor

lioned windows, outside the moated site, are now a separate farmhouse. The church of St James, of nave and chancel, is small and dull, built for Sir John Aubrey in 1818. It is enlivened inside by wall slabs, some in Coade stone with oddly worded inscriptions, to a 'Mrs May Aubrey, Spinster' and to Sir John Aubrey 'whose union with two women of such rare excellence he regarded as the choicest blessing of Providence'. In the wood to the north is a duck decoy which has a collection of European wild-fowl and provides demonstrations for visitors.

Botolph Claydon *see* Claydon, Botolph

Bourne End [14] A mixed bag of Thames-side bungalows, housing estates and industry left over from

days when the Bourne was a useful source of power. There is even a group of older and more attractive cottages at Well End, just enough to make a 'Conservation Area'. St Mark's is a dull church of red brick with nave and chancel in one, a bell-turret over the nave and exposed brick walls inside, by A. Blomfield (1889). The late 19th-century Abbots Brook Estate is early garden-village stuff with half-timbered houses laid out along a stream. The Thames is the best thing here, much used by small boats. The best local view is across it, to the unspoilt meadows on the Berks. side.

Boveney [17, 18] Select houses are isolated down a cattle-gridded lane from Eton Wick. Down a wooded footpath, with glimpses of oarsmen between willow and rushes, is the

disused church of St Mary Magdalen. It has chalk-rubble walls faced in flint with ashlar dressings enclosing a rectangle of nave and chancel with a weather-boarded bell-turret; fragments of an alabaster reredos. Boveney Court in the adjoining wood is an E-shaped house with a 15th-century timber frame filled with brick.

Bow Brickhill *see* Brickhill, Bow

Bradenham [14] A long triangular green slopes down from a beech-wooded Chiltern ridge. It is dominated by a flint church and a dark, red-brick manor house at the top and lined on its northern side by village houses. The Manor House was the last home of Isaac d'Israeli, who died in 1848 and is buried in the church, and the place is immortalized by his son Benjamin

△ Fibreglass cows, **Bradwell**

Disraeli in *Endymion*. The village was acquired by the National Trust in 1956. St Botolph's church is of flint and stone and so restored externally by G. E. Street in 1863 as to look Victorian. It has an embattled west tower, nave, chancel and north chapel of which the chancel and part nave were rebuilt by Street. The south door is early Norman and the rest later medieval and Street's neo-Decorated. There is a communion rail by Canon Staley of Ickford (of the 1920s); east window by Kempe (1887); a figured brass (of 1521); and, in the chapel, a monument to Charles West (d. 1684) with an altar-type base and inscription flanked by graceful columns supporting a pediment. The east window of the chapel has fragments of heraldic glass including a crest of Thomas, Lord Windsor, early owner of the manor, which is interesting as an early example of enamelled glass. The adjoining Manor House faces the Green through ornamental gate piers and iron railings. It was originally built in Tudor times by the 2nd Baron Windsor and rebuilt, about 1670, with nine bays in a classical style. A later addition to the east has upset the symmetry and made the fenestration look a little mean. The village houses are

pleasant but not notable. The White House, now greenish colour-washed on 18th-century brick, has castellations and pointed windows. The Rectory on the Wycombe Road is 18th-century flint and brick and has two large chimney breasts as its central feature. The little Nonconformist chapel north of the church is now a Youth Hostel. A steep lane through the beech woods beyond leads to a large Air Force camp scattered in the hill-top woods.

Bradwell [5] Brick and stone cottages with tiles and some thatch, isolated by a few fields from giant estates of the Milton Keynes New Town. St Lawrence's church is at the south end, next to the earthworks of an early motte and bailey castle; it is of grey stone and approached through heavy cast-iron gateposts. The latter were cast at the Deanshanger foundry a few kilometres away (in Northants.). This foundry's work is a feature of the area. The church has a small west tower, nave, south aisle, chancel and north porch; was restored in 1768 and is of little interest inside. There are east and west windows by Clayton and Bell and a chancel window by Powell but these are not their best work. The main railway

line to Glasgow hums alongside and cuts off from the village the few remains of a Benedictine Priory founded in 1155. Abbey Farm is a 17th-century house of coursed stone taken from its ruins and is now the archeological and preservation centre of the New Town. In its grounds is the little stone chapel of St Mary, which was reconstructed in the 18th century with a painted plaster ceiling and has been recently restored.

Bradwell, New [5] A railway workers' village built in 1854–61 on the east side of the London and North Western Railway's works at Wolverton. It originally consisted of 187 small, red-brick, two-storey terrace houses for workers and 17 three-storey 'pavilion' houses for the foremen. Much was demolished in 1974 and replaced by tidy, but boring, unbroken terraces but the south side of the High Street and part of Spencer Street were then more happily restored. The church of St James, built for the estate by G. E. Street (1858–60), is of stone with the stump of a north-west tower and Art Nouveau-ish glass in its north window. The Norman chancel arch from the ruined church at Stantonbury has been built into its west wall. The old

Little Brickhill

tower mill south of the deep cutting of the former branch railway to Newport Pagnell was restored in 1976.

Brickhill, Bow [5] Brown brick cottages and an ironstone church on a steep, sandy, pine-clad slope rising above the oak-fringed clay plain. The church of All Saints is by itself against the pine trees of the hill crest and has views down the long village street and over the Bletchley end of the Milton Keynes New Town. It is built of large blocks of local ironstone, partly plastered, mainly in Perpendicular style, with embattled west tower. The chancel was rebuilt in the extensive restoration by the antiquarian Browne Willis in 1757, and is in mixed brick and stone; whitewashed inside and enlivened only by the 15th-century timber pulpit. Adjoining woodlands belong to the Bedford Estate of Woburn which spills over the Beds. border.

Brickhill, Great [8] A spread-out village of brown stone church, brown stone walls and small houses, in the sandy hills on the Beds. border, with pine woods to

east and views west over the softer clay landscape of the Ousel valley. The church of St Mary is in clunch and rusty ironstone of attractive texture in Early English and Decorated styles, and has a 13th-century central tower and turret dividing the four-bay nave and 15th-century south aisle from the chancel and side chapel. It was restored by Browne Willis, the Bucks. antiquary, in the 18th century, and the roofs were heightened in 1867. There are some 18th-century tablets to members of the Barton family. There are some 18th-century houses around the church and further south, the Duncombe Arms, a pleasant pub on the main street with a long view to the west. A further kilometre south-east is Stockgrove, a large country house built in 1929 by W. Curtis Green in sprawling two-storeyed brick and pantile, heavy neo-Georgian, like a superior R.A.F. Mess in a formal layout of stables, steps and pools. Its rolling wooded sandy park is a popular 'Country Park' managed jointly by Beds. and Bucks.

Brickhill, Little [8] Straddles a sharp rise on the busy Watling Street in coniferous, lower Green-

sand hills. From 1433 to 1638 Buckinghamshire assizes were held here because this was the first place accessible (partly because on sand, not clay) to judges coming from London on their 'Norfolk' circuit. The little church of St Mary stands on a bank above the road. It is chiefly Perpendicular in style and in local warm ironstone, with an embattled west tower, four-bay nave, south aisle and chapel, chancel and south porch. The south chapel has piscina, aumbrey and a squint.

Brill [10] A small, decayed, 17th-to-18th-century town on a prominent, much-quarried hill top 200 m high, best-known for its prominent mill on a common facing west over the mid-Oxon. plain. Streets of seemly red-brick and tiled houses coil round the hill-top connecting the common to the pretty triangular Square and then the wedge-shaped Green with its stumpy church hidden in yews. It was a royal centre for hunting in Bernewood Forest which stretched north and over adjoining county borders. The church of All Saints has fragments of its early 12th-century rebuilding in nave and

Brill

chancel but was largely rebuilt by Oldrid Scott, who added the south aisle and raised the nave roof, thereby making the squat early 15th-century west tower and spirelet seem meaner. Inside it is attractively untidy but has few things of note: the early 17th-century roof to the chancel has a truss with radiating balusters; the font cover (*c.* 1920) is by Canon Staley of Ickford. There were

14th-century paintings on the chancel arch, protected by white-wash at the Reformation but faded since their exposure in 1867. The royal house, enjoyed by hunting-kings from Edward the Confessor to Edward II, was on the hill top close by and had its own chapel. The bank and ditch near the church are probably its last relics but have been confused by later earthworks built during the Civil

War. Also on the Green is Brill House, in red and grey brick with pilastered and pedimented door-case, and a Methodist church of 1841. Brill Manor House is a 16th-century building at the western tapered end of the Green. It is of brick and old tile, altered in later centuries. The windmill on the windy common is a post-mill dated 1668, with black weather-boarding and white sails on timber supports hidden (in the 1950s) by a round brick base to protect the timber. The Common is pock-marked by grass-grown clay-workings. From the 13th to the 19th century, bricks, tiles and pots were made. There were seven potteries still left in the mid 19th century, making mostly coarse garden stuff. The Common provides glorious long views, a good picnic spot and, thanks to the pock-marks, great fun for small children. If peace and more extensive views are wanted these can best be had from Muswell Hill, to the north. The hill is of some geological interest and has, on its east side, a chalybeate spring which was harnessed to the short-lived spa at Dorton. On the north side was the terminus of the Wotton tramway, an unsuccessful extension of the Metropolitan Railway made for the Duke of Buckingham across his estates from Quainton Road.

Broughton [5] Small church and brown brick cottages in flat clay country on the edge of Milton Keynes New Town, just bypassed by the Woburn–Newport Pagnell road. St Lawrence's is a simple grey stone church with lead roofs, embattled west tower, nave and chancel, well-known for its 14th- and 15th-century wall-paintings touched up by Professor Tristram. On the north wall are a pietà with backgammon players in the foreground and a Doom with hellish flames and a trumpeting archangel. On the south are two versions of the story of St George, one with a two-headed dragon and the other with St Helena and St Eloi. There is a stained-glass window by Gibbs (1864) on the south and other windows by Clayton and Bell. Manor Farm, a little south-east, is a picturesque muddle of tiled roofs, timber frames and brick walls. Cottages in the village show interesting varieties of Victorian patterned brickwork.

Buckingham Gaol

Buckingham [4, 7] A small, quiet, ancient country town of stone and brick buildings with red-tiled roofs, in a tight loop of the Great Ouse, here rather small. Its early history is misty but it was probably made county town in the late 9th century. In the 10th century Edward the Elder built forts here to keep the Danes at bay. It is put firmly first in the County inventory of Domesday, though it never seems to have had full control of justice in the county. In view of its position at the furthest end from London it is easy to see why. After the Norman Con-

quest the Giffards built a castle on the promontory above the Ouse but this was rarely occupied and by Leland's time little of it was visible. But the family gave their badge, depicting a golden-chained swan, to the town and the town gave this to the county. By Henry VIII's time the assizes were moved to Aylesbury, a much more central place in the county, but Buckingham was incorporated in 1554 and then neither gained nor suffered much from later events, even in the Civil War, until the early 18th century. Its fortunes were reviving when Browne Willis was M.P. (1705–8) and the summer assizes were brought back in 1708, but there was a serious fire in 1725 which destroyed over one-third of the 387 houses. Patronage of the Temple family of Stowe assisted its restoration and the 1st Viscount Cobham even gave the town a gaol to help it retain the assizes when people were complaining that it had not even got one. Meanwhile, the parish church, at the south end of the promontory, below the old castle, was decaying. The 50m spire collapsed in 1693, the tower in 1776, and in 1777 a new church was started, largely at the expense of the Temples, for it was the focus of their view from Stowe, on the more imposing site of the Giffards' castle. SS. Peter and Paul's (1777–81) is a large towny church with a six-bay nave and aisles, battlemented west tower and a spire nearly 50 m high, which makes it a dominating feature of distant views of the town though less so inside the town. The interior was originally in a debased classic style but was altered to a late Geometric gothic by George Gilbert Scott (born at nearby Gawcott) in 1862, when it was given timber vaults and alternating piers of black granite and yellowy stone. The chancel was added in 1882 at the expense of the last Duke of Buckingham and Chandos of Stowe, and a west window by the Buckingham Needle and Thread Society in 1890, a reminder of the importance of the local cottage lace industry. The Market Place is dominated by the Town Hall. This was a late 17th-century building with open arcaded market floor but was faced in red brick at the end of the 18th century when the market arcades were filled in, and a clock-turret added supporting the graceful chained swan. The elevation to Market Hill is somewhat assymetrical as part of the north bay was cut off to widen Castle Street. The large early Victorian White Hart Hotel has a big Tuscan porch over the pavement but the rest of

Buckingham:
Town Hall (*above*)
Trolley House, Castle Street (*below*)

Market Hill and its continuation into High Street is patchy and less impressive. To the west is the old stone Chantry Chapel, lately the Latin School, restored by Scott in 1875 and now owned by the National Trust. This has a Norman south door. At the junction of the Brackley road is the old Gaol, built in 1748 in the shape of a mock castle and given a new south front and small lodge by G. G. Scott in 1835. Scott also built a workhouse (he was a workhouse specialist as a young man) in his early classical style. West Street has the most imposing and attractive house in the town: Castle House, now offices, of eight bays with two storeys of red-brick stone dressed. The street front has a central section of four bays and appears to

have two front doors. This hides the remnants of the older house where Queen Catherine of Aragon stayed in 1514. A fireplace is dated 1619 and the north wall 1623. Castle Street was largely rebuilt after the 1725 fire. It contains one important building, Trolley House, which is in brick and in stucco dressed up like stone. Past the church and on down Church Street are the sites of the older church and the 16th- and 17th-century Vicarage and the Prebendal House (now called the Manor House). Beyond, in Hunter Street, new uses are being made of old stone buildings—notably of the handsome Yeomanry House—by the infant University College of Buckingham. The latter was opened in 1976 as a novel, independent, university with two-year courses instead of the conventional three. The college was attracted here, with other modern 'industries', by the Buckingham Development Company, an institution funded by District and County Councils to champion expansion of the town from its 5,000 in 1975 to a future 15,000. New housing is being concentrated to the north-east towards Maids Moreton. Near the church, St Rumbold's Street and Well Street are memorials to the legendary baby St Rumbold who expired after delivering a long sermon when only a few days old, perhaps in the year A.D. 621. His body is said to have been brought to Buckingham in A.D. 626 and, with the sacred well, was the centre of a miracle-working cult until the Reformation. To the north-west is the 3 km avenue of beech and elm leading to Stowe. This and the less complete avenue on Moreton Road are special features of the town's outskirts.

Buckland [11] A village of grey church and white and red houses and bungalows, hidden in trees at the foot of the Chilterns near Tring and screened from the main Aylesbury Road by the spread of Aston Clinton. The church of All Saints,

Burnham Beeches

near the south end of a long narrow lane which is the village spine, is a small flint building of chancel, nave, north aisle and embattled west tower. It was externally Victorianized and its tower rebuilt in 1894. It is whitewashed within and has a late 13th-century arcade with circular piers and alternate octagonal and circular capitals. The font is of the Aylesbury type (though 13th rather than 12th century), with the base scalloped and the cup decorated with a foliage band. The timber-framed and brick-filled Church Farmhouse nearby is the best of many old houses and cottages. Similar smaller houses up Pegg Lane have

been over-restored and altered. A brick Methodist church of 1831 is galleried.

Bulstrode Park [15] (near Gerrards Cross) A large house by B. Ferrey in a handsome park by Repton to the west of Gerrards Cross. The Park is named after a family who were its early owners. The original house was extravagantly rebuilt by Judge Jeffreys, who lived here from 1676 till his death in 1689, and was again rebuilt by its next owner, William Bentinck, Earl of Portland. It became a centre for intellectuals and statesmen, particularly in the time of the 2nd Duchess of Portland, when it

Burnham Beeches

housed the Portland Vase, now in the British Museum. Nash and Wyatt both designed additions and new buildings and Repton worked on the park in 1802. Gothic Tower, Swiss Cottage, 'The Dovecote' and a garden entrance are all relics of their improvements, but the new house by Ferrey (1862) is a rather gloomy, brick and stone, many-gabled building. There is an Iron Age fort, 9 hectares in extent within double ramparts, on the little hill in the south-east corner of the park. Much of the estate on the east side towards Gerrards Cross was sold off in 1932 and is now almost indistinguishable from other suburbs of that dormitory town.

Burnham [14, 15] Islanded in characterless suburbs of Slough are a compact medieval village and a once isolated medieval abbey. The spine of the old village is the High Street, which, with its one-way traffic, now leads from the Burnham Beeches end to an attractive green. The old church is in Church Street, a pleasant cul-de-sac, off its south end. St Peter's church is large, of flint and clunch with lead and tiled roofs; it has a four-bay nave, aisles, a north transept and a south transeptal tower. The nave is 12th to 14th century, the aisles and chancel and tower base mainly 13th, and the tower top and spire were rebuilt in 1892. The church

has been much extended in its time and has little consistency. The main interest is in the monuments: the chancel has a bust of John Wright, vicar (d. 1594); black and white marble figures of George Evelyn of Huntercombe (d. 1594) and wife; and a coffin, cushion and skull commemorating Bridget Friend (d. 1721). In the south aisle is a seated figure holding a portrait medallion of Justice Willes, designed by Bacon, while in the nave are brass effigies of Edmund Eyre (d. 1563) and wife and brasses to other members of this family which are re-used 15th-century Flemish engravings. On the south arcade piers are traces of anti-Papal slogans. The High Street has a number of pleasant but not outstanding houses of 16th and 17th centuries. In Burnham Park is the timber-framed and timber-lined County Library by the County Architect (1973), which, for visual warmth, inside and out, fully deserves its R.I.B.A. 'commendation'. The remains of the once-important Abbey are in fields of vegetables to the south, close to the motorway and its link road. It was founded in 1266 as a house for Augustinian canonesses but suppressed at the Reformation and converted into a private house. Long decay followed and many buildings remained only as farm storage until the site was restored by nuns of the Precious Blood for use as a convent. The east range of claustral buildings, including the chapter house, remains, with 16th-century additions and alterations and fragmented parts of other ranges but little sign of the large, aisle-less church. Huntercombe Manor, a short way north but still south of the present Bath Road (the older road went through Burnham village on its winding westward journey), was the home of a branch of the Evelyn family. It looks largely 19th century but contains a 14th-century hall with archbraced roof and a 14th-century kitchen wing. George Evelyn, the diarist's cousin, made extensive

55

alterations in the 17th century and left some plastered ceilings painted by Verrio with clouds and cupids. The House of Prayer, a convent in Britwell Road, has a chapel of 1935 by Ninian Comper. 2 km north in fields and woods, but still in the parish, is Dorneywood, a large house of the early 1920s in mixed Tudor and Georgian styles with some internal decoration by Rex Whistler. It was given to the nation by Lord Courtauld Thomson in 1942 as a minor 'Chequers' for use by the Foreign Secretary. (For 'Nashdom' see Hitcham.)

Burnham Beeches [15] The name given to 80 hectares of ancient woodland commons between Burnham and Beaconsfield, bought by the City of London in 1880 and maintained by them as an open space with controlled roads and rides and good, but short walks in most directions. It stretched west to Taplow and Wooburn in the 18th century. Dropmore was only reclaimed from its wild state in 1792 while it included Black Park and Stoke Common on the east and the Middx. border. Large areas are full of beech trees of an average age of more than 300 years, with huge spreading branches, relics of much earlier pollarding. The poet Gray stayed with his uncle at Burnham Grove and wrote to Walpole in 1737 of the 'most venerable beeches . . . dreaming out their old stories to the winds'. Other notable visitors included Sheridan, on honeymoon in 1773, Mendelssohn, and Jenny Lind, the last two being commemorated by landmarks in the woods.

Cadmore End [14] Part of the parish of Fingest, on a road which follows a chalk ridge between Marlow and Stokenchurch and provides a pleasant alternative to either the A40 or the motorway; it is a long drawn-out village of little red-brick houses peeping from the edge of ragged commons between beech, oak and birch trees. It is cut off from the north by the motorway

(M40), noisily close. St Mary-le-Moor, the parish church, is fronted with an incongruous group of pine trees, bungalows and casually parked cars, a small, flint-faced and red tiled building in an Early English style by Rhode Hawkins (1851). The interior is darkened by Hardman glass of 1855 in bright blues, red, gold and green, which makes it hard to see the little naïve pictures of Stations of the Cross which line the walls.

Calvert [7] (near Charndon) Large London Brick Company works with tall smelly chimneys, almost disused (former Great Central) railway and huge worked-out pits of Oxford clay with belemnite fossils spattered like machine-gun bullets. The pits are being filled, but oh so slowly, with rubbish from north London boroughs. The area has relics, e.g. notices in English and Polish, of the wartime occupation of this area by refugee Polish government and troops.

Calverton [5] An area of soft undulations between the Milton Keynes New Town and the Northants. border which may end up as a refuge from the former. It embraces the tiny village of Calverton—with its grey stone church, manor farmhouse and large former rectory, among meadows and trees—and a more open ribbon of mixed grey stone and red-brick cottages which form first Lower Weald and then Upper Weald on the wiggly lane to the south. The church of All Saints is the focal point of Calverton village and is of grey stone and tiles surrounded by trees; it was rebuilt on its medieval foundations with a neo-Norman west tower by H. Hakewill (1808–24). A south aisle was added and other parts 'beautified' by the rector, the Hon. Charles Perceval, from 1820 to 1858. The stained glass by O'Connor dates from the end of his term. The church was again restored in 1870 by the local architect Swinfen Harris. He added polychrome

decoration to chancel arch and stone pulpit and designed the mosaic-work reredos. Outside is an elaborate cross of 1873. Church and churchyard are an epitome of mid-Victorian Gothic Revival. The Manor Farmhouse is a rambling stone building on a slope above the road. It was built by the de Veres in the late 15th century, and extended in the 16th and 17th. In a pleasantly treed park on the site of a small Roman camp is Calverton Place, built of yellow brick with a red parapet as the Rectory in the early 19th century. Lower Weald consists of a few more farmhouses and cottages. Middle and Upper Weald have more modern, largely red-brick cottages.

Castlethorpe [5] Separated from Northants. by the little River Tove and by the electrified railway to Scotland; it seems to have settled down to sleep after the closure of its own little railway station which used to give it 'an air of Wolverton'. The church is inside the earthworks of an early medieval motte and bailey castle and the village is wrapped round the south-west edges of this site. The church of SS. Simon and Jude is of grey stone with lead and slate roofs with a short fat nave which was probably Norman, for a single circular pier of late 12th-century design with upright feathery leaves separates it from the north aisle, which, like the chancel, was itself rebuilt in the 14th century. The south aisle was added in the 15th century and the low embattled west tower was rebuilt in a Georgian style following the collapse of its predecessor early in the 18th century. The only notable monument is to Sir Thomas Tyrrell (d. 1672), which is of alabaster and shows a tired Sir Thomas resting his head on the knee of a worried Lady Tyrrell, an engaging and unusual portrayal for its time. The motte to the west of the church still rises to 12 m above the adjoining ground and the outer ditches of the castle are up to 20 m

Calverton

wide. Castle House, formerly Castle Yard, is a 17th-century stone farmhouse west of the church, built from materials of the former castle. The main part of the village is in a kidney-shaped pattern of twin North and South Streets closely lined with stone and colour-washed cottages.

Chackmore [4] East of the grand avenue from Buckingham to Stowe, within the parish of Radclive-cum-Chackmore, a few stone cottages, barns and walls cluster west and south of the pleasant Queen's Head.

Chalfont Common [15] (near Chalfont St Giles) Fills the north part of the parish of Chalfont St Peter with overspill from better-known Chalfonts. Here in 1895 was

established a large colony for epileptics, the first of its kind in the country, with brick and half-timbered gabled houses by Maurice Adams. Later community buildings in concrete blocks are screened by trees and adjoining 20th-century bungalows. Outside is an obelisk of flint rubble built in 1785, a cross between a beacon and an outsize milestone. At Newland Park to the north is a County College in a large early 19th-century white house with Doric portico. Near by will be a museum of old buildings.

Chalfont St Giles [15] Has a picturesque core of red-brick and timber houses round a tiny village green with a modest flint church but is surrounded, save on the east, where Misbourne meadows sur-

vive, by extensive modern bungalow and neo-Georgian cottage suburbs. The place is best known for its short association with Milton. St Giles's church is approached from the Green by a timber-framed lychgate under a timber-framed house. It has a Perpendicular embattled west tower but the exterior was otherwise restored in Victorian Decorated, by G. E. Street in 1863. The chancel is largely 13th century and has a double piscina. The nave and aisles are mixed 13th century and Perpendicular, the south arcade and the chancel arch being rebuilt in the early 15th century. There are wall-paintings, an architectural design of early 15th century on the chancel arch, and 14th-century scenes from the life of the Virgin and of Christ, together with a few

Chenies

scenes from the Old Testament in the south aisle. There are a number of 15th- and 16th-century brasses in chancel and south aisle, and a hanging monument with scrolly pediment and frame of black pilasters to Sir George Fleetwood (d. 1620). Sir Philip de la Vache, a friend of the Black Prince, is also buried in the church. The Vache is a brick Elizabethan re-building of a house said to date from 1277, now Coal Board Offices, north-east of the Misbourne. It was the home of the Fleetwoods, one of whom married the daughter of Cromwell. Their grandson signed the death warrant of Charles I and subsequently forfeited the property. In its Park is a late 18th-century monument, a pedestalled globe over an arch, in flint and brick, to Captain Cook. South-west of the church a timber-framed cottage is now a Milton museum. It was built by the Fleetwood family and was found by Thomas Ellwood, tutor to the Penningtons of Chalfont St Peter, as a refuge for Milton and his

family from the plague. Milton stayed here from 1665 to 1666 while finishing *Paradise Lost* (supposed to have been inspired by the Penningtons) and starting *Paradise Regained*. Other similar timber-framed cottages have been spoilt by the insertion of ill-considered shop fronts. The best remaining old house is the Rectory north-west of the church. This is a red and grey brick, early 18th-century, building with hipped roof and doorcase that has carved brackets and columns. East of the Misbourne and screened by trees from the eastern suburbs of St Giles is the best-looking house of the early modern movement in England. This is Shrub's Wood, built in 1935 by Mendelsohn and Chermayeff in one long east to west range of white plastered, reinforced concrete, but less aggressive and better sited than most contemporaries. At Dibden Hill, south of the old village, are some houses and bungalows which remain from a colony founded by the French socialist P. H. J. Baume in 1846.

Chalfont St Peter [15] A large suburban complex round a small medieval village; like Chalfont St Giles, but it is more modest, less self-conscious and also more disturbed by the main road to Amersham. There is a new shopping centre in brownish brick and tile, a Georgian rather than medieval church and just one picturesque house, the 17th-century Greyhound Inn on the Misbourne. St Peter's church was rebuilt as an early Georgian brick box with a west tower with stone dressings after the collapse of the medieval church, but this box was 'gothicized' in 1857 by Street, who inserted Decorated windows in the nave and altered the chancel. Inside interest is limited to the early 15th-century brasses to Whappelodes which have figures nearly a metre long, and outside interest to the late 18th-century iron railings and gates. The Grange convent school, up the hill west of the church, is on the site of the home of the Penningtons, a centre of Quakerism in the 17th century. Isaac Pennington's stepdaughter married William Penn of Pennsylvania and his tutor Ellwood found Milton the cottage at St Giles. He was gaoled four times at Aylesbury for his beliefs and the family was forced to leave St Peter's in 1665. His house was the temporary home of Judge Jeffreys during his rebuilding of Bulstrode. In Oval Way, at the south suburban end, is the unfinished church of All Saints, mainly a large north aisle in gothic style, by Temple Moore (1912). Chalfont House, east of the London Road, was once the principal mansion of St Peter's. It was built in the mid 18th century for General Charles Churchill, nephew of Marlborough and brother-in-law of Horace Walpole, by Walpole's friend John Chute, in a Strawberry Hill manner which was spoilt by Salvin's additions of 1836. The first Lombardy poplars in the country were introduced here, and there are remains of an Italian garden by Lutyens.

Chalvey [18] A suburban area on the west side of Slough, now in Berks., divided by a large road linking the Bath Road to the motorway junction. It has a church (St Peter), by G. E. Street (1861), with nave, chancel, north aisle and bellcote, faced with flint and brick bands. It is light inside, and has crude foliage capitals to its arcades and a curiously foiled circular east window.

Charndon [7] Houses scattered along a lane winding over a hill west of Calvert brickworks, in the parish of Twyford.

Chartridge [12] A seemingly endless ribbon of houses and bungalows stretching along one of the finger-like chalk ridges west of Chesham. Wide roads, tarred footpaths and lamp-posts frame some still attractive cottages but the extent of this development is itself unpleasant and only mitigated by glimpses to the north and south of

the green valleys below. The best building is Limetrees Farm, a late 17th-century house of dull red brick with bright red-brick dressings and an old tiled roof. Great Hundridge Manor is more isolated on the next finger-ridge to the south. It is a large house dated 1696 and has a flint rubble plinth and red and grey brick upper storeys roof. Behind it is a rare survival—a 13th-century domestic chapel in flint, with perpendicular east window and lancets.

Chearsley [11] A smiling village of colour-washed, mostly white, timber-framed or brown brick cottages with occasional stone or wichert walls along winding lanes. It slopes from the fragmented greens on the main road to a small stone church almost in the willow-framed Thame meadows, with hardly a jarring note in spite of infilling with new houses and strange plants between old cottages, and odd tanks occupied by traditional-looking Aylesbury ducks. St Nicholas's church is of light grey local limestone with tiled roofs and has an embattled west tower and a generally Perpendicular look. It was originally a chapel of Long Crendon, and is still simple, with no aisles, a low spreading roof and sloping plastered walls. There are light oak box pews, copied from those at Haddenham by Ivor Newton between 1935 and 1970, and a timber west gallery of 1762. The most prominent features of the interior are the Royal Arms: of George II on the north wall in a 2 m square surround looking like a brown carpet; and of George III on the west gallery. There is a simplified Aylesbury-type font with fluted bowl. East of the church is a 15th- and 16th-century H-shaped stone house behind a high surrounding wall of wichert.

Cheddington [8, 9] A village with a square pattern of streets, overlooked by an isolated chalk hill to the west and a long railway

embankment to the east. There are orchards on the heavier land, which is threaded through by the Grand Union Canal. The village rose to momentary fame at the time of the Great Train Robbery of 1963, which took place on the railway embankment at the junction with the main line of the former branch to Aylesbury. St Giles's church is on a slope north of the village, surrounded by orchards and chickens, and, more immediately, by yews and other churchyard trees. It is of a dark grey stone and has Norman origins, as can be seen from the Norman fragments in the south porch, but is now mainly Perpendicular with the usual west tower. It has a carved Jacobean pulpit with tester and a glass mosaic reredos by Powell and Sons of 1870. The Manor House on the west side of the village is in brown and red brick between timber frames. The once impressive lynchets on the slopes of the isolated hill are now being overgrown with scrub. The other notable earthwork, the railway embankment, is well-maintained. It is 8 km long, over 10 m high, and is made of chalk taken from the deep cutting at Pitstone (1834–8). Cheddington station is part ochre-coloured boards and part later (London and North Western Railway) cast-iron and brick.

Chenies [15] On a little hill above the Chess on the Herts. border, a model village of picturesque Victorian cottages, flint church and dark brick manor house round a fragmented Green, but unified and attractive, thanks to the benevolent landlordism of the Russells for over 400 years. The village was acquired by John Russell, the 1st Earl of Bedford (1486–1555) on his marriage to Anne Sapcote, and was the main seat of the Russells, later Dukes of Bedford, until their transference to Woburn Abbey (Beds.) in the 18th century. It was sold to pay duties after the death of the 12th Duke, in 1954. Manor House and church are screened by a grass-lined lime-tree walk from village houses near by. St Michael's church was entirely rebuilt in the 15th century, in flint rubble with stone dressings, with a west tower, nave, chancel and south aisle. The Russells' mortuary chapel, the glory of the church, was added as a long north aisle in 1556. The church was heavily restored in 1861 and later, and the nave was given a hammer-beam roof which has accentuated its Victorian atmosphere. Medieval relics include the Norman cup-shaped font and brasses of Lady Cheyne (d. 1484) and of her second husband. The Cheynes were landlords before the Russells and added their name to the original village name of Isenhampstead. The mortuary chapel is now separated from the church by locked plate-glass and ironwork, and inside this show-case the bright Victorian chequered marble floor reflects the grandest collection of family monuments anywhere outside Westminster. Monuments line all sides and range from that to the 1st Earl (d. 1555) through that to the 1st Duke (d. 1700), whose exuberant monument by Francis Bird fills the whole west end of the chapel with its figures, columns and baldachino; the 2nd Duke, designed by Chambers with white alabaster youth, maiden, clouds and cherubs; to that to Lord Arthur Russell (d. 1892), which is by A. Gilbert and has near Art Nouveau figures representing his virtues. The chapel also contains monuments to the 4th Earl, great drainer of the Fens, and to Lord John, 1st Earl and Prime Minister (1878), as well as memorial windows by Kempe (1895–7). The Manor House of the Russells is a thin L-shaped dark red-brick building with steep gables and ornamented brick chimneys. It is built a little east of the older manor house of the Cheynes whose stone crypt can still be seen. The present

Chequers Court

north block is mid 15th century and the south block was added by the 1st Earl in the early 16th century. By the mid 18th century the Russells were letting the House to tenant farmers, though they took an abiding interest in the affairs of the village. Chenies Place on the Chess was built for the widow of the 10th Duke in 1897 by Charles Kempe, the glass painter. It has red-brick Dutch gables and a garden designed by Lutyens. There is a Baptist chapel of 1778 built by a former Bedford Estate steward and at Dell Farm (towards Chesham) a modest Roman farmhouse was discovered in 1834.

Chequers Court [11] A large 16th-century brick house in a long dry combe in the Chilterns beechwoods above Ellesborough. The property descended in a tortuous family line to Lord Lee of Fareham, of the Lee family of Quarrendon and Hartwell. He employed Sir Reginald Blomfield to make considerable alterations to the house in 1912 and gave it to the nation in 1917, as a country retreat for its Prime Ministers. A public footpath which ran close to, and gave a good view of, the house has recently been diverted for security reasons. The north range of the house encloses on its first floor the Great Parlour, which has pilastered panelling, and the Long Gallery, which has Cromwell family portraits, but the rest of the formerly principal rooms in this range were converted to smaller rooms by Blomfield. The second floor still contains the 'Prison Room' where Lady Jane Grey was confined for two years. Blomfield remodelled the south range to make principal rooms but kept the original brickwork. Access to both house and grounds is now strictly limited.

Chesham [12] A prettily sited, historic, town at the source of the River Chess, which splits into separate channels to water the lower part of the town, and to run between old brick houses. It has a long connection with manufacture which was originally based on mills at Waterside. There were settlements here in Roman times and a Saxon township in the 7th century, but the town was ecclesiastically dependent on Amersham until 1454 when riots in Chesham led to its independence. It is still of disparate parts: part villagey, with old cottages and one grand house beside the church; part industrial; part 19th- and 20th-century shopping centre; part ribbons of houses and bungalows along chalk ridges; and part more solid Victorian and Edwardian housing, towards Chesham Bois and Amersham. St Mary's church is large and cruciform, on a bank above the river in the grounds of Chesham Park. It is in flint with a puddingstone base and has a central tower with slender octagonal spire. Parts are Norman, as can be seen in the north transept, but externally the appearance is Victorian, thanks to vigorous restoration at the expense of the Duke of Bedford by Gilbert Scott in 1869. However, the chancel and south transept are mainly Decorated and the rest, including the two-storeyed south porch, Perpendicular. On the south wall is a large but faint medieval painting of St Christopher. The east wall of the nave has scenes of the last days of Jesus by John Ward (1970). The mortuary chapel of the Cavendish family of Latimer has a sarcophagus of Sir John Cavendish (d. 1617), the younger son of the 1st Earl of Devonshire. In the chancel are a bust of Richard Wood (d. 1623), preaching, a memorial by N. Skottowe (d. 1800) by John Bacon jun., and stones to members of the Lowndes family of The Bury near by. This is a tall brick house with quoins and parapet built in 1712 for William Lowndes, Secretary of the Treasury, and has decorated rooms and staircase but has been a good deal altered. It has two little lodges to Church Street which face an attractive assortment of Georgian cottages. There is also a late Georgian red-brick vicarage. Waterside is downstream to the south-east and starts badly with a mixture of ugly factories, railed off river and parking lots, but improves to end in picturesque mills and watercress beds. It has its own flint and Bath stone, Christ Church by R. Brandon (1864) with mixed lancets and quatrefoils. The town centre once had a central market hall like Amersham but of the 18th century. It was swept away for road improvement in the 1960s, which reduced bottlenecks but exposed northern Chesham. The centre has little interest today but Arthur Liberty (see The Lee) had a draper's shop next to the George in the High Street, before moving to success in London's Regent Street. Lace and bodging of chair legs were ancient industries of the town; woodware and leather goods are still made. On the Amersham Road, Mineral Cottage marks the site of a chalybeate spring, source for a short-lived 19th-century spa, while around and outside the town some good farmhouses survive, such as Vale Farm to the north, Blackwell Grange Farm to the south-east and Great Hundridge Manor to the west. Pleasant walks abound.

Chesham Bois [12] On the high wooded chalk ridge between Chesham and Amersham; it is full of Victorian, Edwardian and later houses which followed the extension of the Metropolitan Line into the area. St Leonard's church, approached up a suburban drive, was largely rebuilt on medieval foundations in 1884, when the present tower was added at its south-west angle. It has a 17th-century pulpit and 16th-century brasses of Cheynes.

Chetwode [7] A remote pastoral parish in the north-west of the county; it was an Augustinian Priory founded in 1245, with no

Chetwode

village. Now there is a nice group of yellowish-grey church, farm buildings and Priory House, joined by stone walls and wide, tidy, grass verges. The Priory was dissolved because of its poverty in 1460 but the remaining parishioners obtained leave to abandon their former small church of St Martin, which was half a kilometre to the east, and to convert the chancel of the Priory church into the parish church of St Mary and Nicholas, and to add a low pyramid-capped north-west tower to it. The present nave and chancel are consequently undivided and retain at the east end a group of five stepped lancets with shafts and foliated capitals which so delighted Gilbert Scott when, as a boy, he came over from Gawcott and looked through the keyhole. There are also groups of three stepped lancets to north and south and these have late 13th–early 14th-century figures, including St John the Baptist in a brilliant yellow robe on blue background, within almond-shaped panels—the best early glass of the county. The east windows were glazed in imitative style by William Holland in 1842. Biblical verses (1696), a slab to Sir John Giffard of Twyford (d. 1350) with inscription in Norman French, and a tablet with two little mourning girls of 1668. The Manor House of mixed Jacobean and later brickwork is now isolated about 1 km east. It stands near the site of the older parish church.

Chicheley [5] A large, early 18th-century mansion in red brick, glowing down its avenue of limes to the nearby grey church, east of the Newport–Bedford road, and a pub and a few thatched cottages on the main road, in pastoral country. St Lawrence's church, on the approach to the great house, is of stone with tile roofs and largely Early English in style with a central Perpendicular tower. The chancel was rebuilt in 1708, in a classical style. It is screened from the cross-ing by Tuscan columns and wrought-iron gates and has a plaster ceiling decorated with a central flowered wreath. The approach under the crossing has a lower plaster ceiling with a bell-ringers' gallery and a carved oak rood loft above which were inserted by N. Comper in 1907. The nave has box pews thoughtfully raised at the west end. There are monuments to Anthony Cave (d. 1576), with a naked cadaver and caryatids supporting a pediment, and to Sir Anthony Chester (d. 1635) and wife, with kneeling figures. Chicheley Hall was built for Sir John Chester in 1719 by Francis Smith of Warwick. It has the giant pilasters (Corinthian to the south and Doric elsewhere) and prominent attic storey above the main cornice which are typical of many big houses of its time, but is unusual in that the central three bays are swept upwards, cornice and attic storey as well, to give the illusion that these bays project considerably to the south. The interior is elaborately decorated up to the attic storey. The entrance hall, in a slightly more Greek manner, is by Henry Flitcroft. A long two-storeyed stable block and a balancing office range were completed in 1725. The Hall was the home of the Chesters for two centuries and is now in the hands of the Beattys who have made it appropriately ship-shape and opened it to the public.

Chilton [10] A small village on the long southern slope of a limestone ridge which gives views over lush clay valleys; it is a place of pictorial charm with a castle-like church, a large early 18th-century, mainly brick, house and many smaller stone houses. St Mary's church is not large in spite of its towering impression above the adjoining lane. It has a cruciform plan with a low north tower, with higher stair-turret balancing a south transept. The chancel is lopsided as the 15th-century nave was rebuilt over the site of an older nave and south

Chetwode

aisle. The porch is of two storeys and has a tunnel vault with transverse ribs. Inside are a timber screen between chancel and south chapel, stalls made of part earlier screen and part older stalls, an 18th-century organ from Chilton House and Royal Arms restored in the east window is filled with heavy Victorian glass but there is an engaging view, through the clear glass of the south chapel, of the adjoining Chilton House. This chapel has three good monuments of 1608, 1631 and 1755. That of 1608 is to Sir John Croke, and has recumbent alabaster effigies, that of 1631 has a kneeling figure of Elizabeth Tyrrell, née Croke. The Croke family were owners of Chilton House but the present house was built for Chief Justice Carter (d. 1755) whose monument, a composition of columns, pediments and cherubs in marble, is on the north wall of the church. Chilton House is screened by big trees and high grey stone walls. It was built about 1740 with three storeys of rose-coloured and stone-dressed brick above a rusticated stone basement. It was said to have been based on a reduced model of Buckingham House, London, but shares little with the latter but giant pilasters. The House faces east across rolling fields to Upper Winchendon, incorporates diagonal Tudor chimneys of an earlier house, and has fine wrought ironwork to its entrance court. Townhill Farmhouse in stone with brick pilasters is early 18th century and there are earlier brick and timber cottages.

Cholesbury [11] Old cottages and modern bungalows are scattered along a high wooded common on a chalk ridge. The northern boundary of the parish is also the county boundary with Herts., and follows the line of the early Saxon earthwork of Grim's Ditch. The church, near the central crossroads, is hidden inside an overgrown 6-hectare Iron Age hill camp which also encloses some small fields and

Chicheley

two ancient ponds which mark the site of the early village. St Lawrence's, formerly a chapel of Drayton Beauchamp (over 5 km away), is small and flinty and was almost rebuilt in 1873. Towards Hawridge is a tower mill converted from an earlier smock mill in 1884. In its turn it has been made into a dwelling but its sails in red and white were restored in 1977.

Cippenham [18] This suburb of Slough, now in New Berkshire, has one pleasant old building, the timber-framed and brick Cippenham Place, and an early single-storey Bucks. county school (1952), neatly set in an old orchard.

Claydon, Botolph [8] A line of scattered cottages with no church. Botolph House, a five-bay, early 18th-century, brick house, is a dower house of the Verneys of Middle Clayton. A prominent tree in the village street is surrounded by a timber bench and conical thatched roof.

Claydon, East [8] A group of black-and-white cottages around crossroads, and a grey church and white house looking south-east from a gentle ridge over clay fields fringed with dead and dying elms. St Mary's church has an embattled west tower, 13th-century south chapel, 14th-century chancel and

64

15th-century nave, but all so restored and rebuilt by Scott in 1871 that little feeling or interest are left. The Decorated chancel arch rests on corbels carved with grotesque animals and there is a wall monument to Abells. The Abells lived in the nearby colour-washed White House which became the dower house of the Verneys. Here Edmund Verney lived with his wife Mary Abell after their marriage in 1662, a date cut in rather Victorian-looking figures on the porch. The house is screened by mixed brick and stone 18th-century walls and has formal gardens of clipped box and yew hedges. The 17th-century Verney Farm at the west end of the village was the former manor house. Botolph Claydon down the lane to the south is within this parish.

Claydon, Middle [8]

Has no village, just the grand Claydon House and the modest church in a land-scaped park with a few small houses and cottages on its edge. The House, home of the Verneys for four centuries, is of two parts. The north is most of the 17th-century Manor House, the south some of the over-ambitious rebuilding plan by the 2nd Earl Verney which ended in bankruptcy. A considerable reduction of the building followed, in the late 18th century. The Manor was purchased in mid 15th century, after some favours by Edward IV, by the Verneys (a Bucks. family from Fleet Marston), who let it to Giffards until Sir Edmund Verney took up residence in 1620. He married Margaret Denton of Hillesden and was killed, as the king's standard bearer, at Edgehill in 1642. He was succeeded by Sir Ralph, a prudent Parliamentarian who died in 1696 and was succeeded by his son John, the 1st Baron Verney and Viscount Fermanagh. It was the 2nd Earl Verney (1712–91) who, succeeding in 1752, determined to make Claydon a political and cultural centre rivalling that of Temples

Chilton

and Grenvilles at Stowe. He started by rebuilding the large brick stable-block and then went on to extend the house, first by the south wing, which still exists, and then by a domed rotunda and a north wing to match the other, only enclosing a great ballroom. His building was now 75 m long. The architect was Sir Thomas Robinson and his south wing was extravagantly decorated, woodwork being largely by a Mr Lightfoot and plasterwork by James Rose, who also worked for the Adam brothers. In 1784 the Earl was declared bankrupt and creditors moved in to strip mantel-pieces, doors and other movables. The whole of the domed section and the newest wing was pulled down. Luckily, the south wing escaped almost intact and this contains three fine principal rooms: the double-cubed Hall with its ceiling decorated with trophies and gar-lands and walls with niches and rococo heads and birds 'such as the world never saw' (as Lightfoot

himself said), as well as the more subdued but still heavily decorated Saloon and Library. A delicately decorated staircase leads up, under a heavily coffered oval dome, to two of the most extravagantly deco-rated rooms of all, the Gothic and Chinese. The Gothic has sunk panels in the ceiling and 'gothic' detail around all openings and fireplaces, while the Chinese has a large alcove carved with unique rococo chinoiserie, including a pagoda and figures. The Earl was succeeded by his niece and the property descended through her half-sister to Sir Harry Calvert who gave his name to the Calvert brick-works but adopted the name Ver-ney. He married as his second wife Parthenope, sister of Florence Nightingale. Florence settled here in her later years and many of her possessions can still be seen. The House and part of the garden were given to the National Trust by the family, who continue to live in it, and it contains the best collection of

portraits in the county, including Van Dyck paintings of Charles I, Sir Edmund Verney and Dame Verney, as well as one of the pirate Sir Francis Verney (d. 1615) attributed to Mytens. The church of All Saints is on a knoll by the house and shares its pleasant view over the park's lake to the steeple of Steeple Claydon church and the more distant chimneys of the Calvert brickworks. It is joined to the house by garden walls and is of stone rubble with stone dressings and lead roofs, with embattled tower, nave and chancel. The nave is mainly 13th century, but much restored, particularly by G. G. Scott. The chancel was rebuilt and the tower built by the Giffards in 1519. The pulpit is of the early 17th century with arched panels but the chief interest of the interior is in its Giffard and Verney monuments. There are brasses of 1523, 1526 and 1542, the last to Roger Giffard who rebuilt the chancel which has nearly full-size figures. In the chancel is the altar tomb of Margaret Giffard (d. 1539), with an alabaster effigy, and a wall monument to two Verneys of Jacobean times, with kneeling figures facing across a desk. There is a large monument in dark and light marbles erected by Edward Marshall in 1653 to Sir Edmund Verney, who died at Edgehill (1642), and his wife and son and daughter-in-law. This has busts in niches on each side of the inscription and was originally intended to be one of twin tombs of Sir Edmund and Lady Verney which would have faced each other across the small nave. There are many later monuments including a bronze portrait bust to Sir Harry Verney (d. 1894).

Claydon, Steeple [7] The largest of the Claydon villages and like them is closely associated with the Verney family. It is in rolling, clayey landscape and built round a

Claydon House:
North Hall, detail (*top*)
Chinese Room, detail (*bottom*)
The Chinese Room ▷

square pattern of lanes with a radial lane at each corner. Three of these serve the medieval 'ends'— Church End, North End and West End—while the fourth leads south to the extensive Calvert brickworks whose chimneys are such a landmark. The church of St Michael stands on a little hill at the east end of the village next to entrenchments called The Camp from which Cromwell's force set out in March 1644 to overwhelm Hillesden House. It is of stone and largely medieval but looks entirely Victorian thanks to the zealous restoration, alteration and enlargement of the Scotts (G. G. and J. O.), who gave it little originality or charm in return. The major alterations were made in 1842 when the transepts were rebuilt in brick, but retaining 15th-century stone windows, and in 1862 when the heavy broach spire was added to the tower as a memorial to General (Sir Harry) Calvert, who adopted the name Verney on inheriting the Verney estates. The interior is wide and bleak but contains an early 16th-century pulpit and another memorial to Sir Harry Verney (d. 1894) and Lady Verney (d. 1857) which has two medallion portraits in a timber frame. The village hall and library incorporate an early village school founded by Sir Thomas Chaloner in 1656 and extended later. It is of brick with a little 17th-century bell-turret and contains a collection of books to which Florence Nightingale contributed—her cheque is framed inside. A number of timber-framed and brick-filled cottages, many colour-washed and some thatched, are scattered around the 'ends'. The old square of fields between them has been filled by mid-20th-century houses for workers at the Calvert brickworks. (*See also* Calvert and Middle Claydon.)

Clifton Reynes [5] Stone church and small stone and brick houses with old orchard trees, on a little lane winding down to a bluff overlooking the Ouse meadows and the town of Olney. There is no large house in the village but the church is rewarding for its fittings. St Mary's church is predominantly Perpendicular necklaced with late 14th-century battlements: plain Norman west tower, heightened in the 14th century. The nave is taller than long and has narrow arcades. The north aisle was rebuilt in 1901 when the interior was given a 'church-warden-gothic' feel, subsequently undone by scraping of the chancel and the Reynes Chapel. There are carved piscina and sedilia and a 14th-century octagonal figure-decorated font, but the main interest is in the effigies in the Reynes Chapel. Here are two knights and their ladies carved from black oak about 1300. One pair is on a late 13th-century tomb chest decorated with shields in quatrefoils and the other has been moved into a white stone recess of contemporary date. There is a later 14th-century tomb with recumbent stone figures and little mourners in ogee arches below, and brasses to Sir John Reynes (d. 1428) and to a man and woman in shrouds of about 1500. There are also a number of wall monuments. That to Alexander Small (d. 1752) has a bust by Scheemakers and an obelisk, and was cut by J. Andrews, the mason of Olney who was a friend of the poet Cowper. Fragments of 15th-century and some early 19th-century glass brighten the interior but most glass is clear. The medieval Hall of the Reynes was on the little hill north of the church.

Cliveden [14] A great mansion in a beautifully landscaped park on a chalk cliff (hence the name) above the Thames. The house is let to Stanford University (U.S.A.) as a European centre but the grounds are open to the public. The house is in the northern half of the park and its history is confusing as two earlier houses were destroyed by fire but left some mark on the construction of those following. The first house was built on the flattened hill top for the 2nd Duke of Buckingham (1628–87), by the Dutch architect W. Winde in 1677–9. It had nine south-facing bays and three tall storeys. Here the Duke brought Lady Shrewsbury after killing her husband in a duel. He made a great terrace in front of the house and the parterre, which was levelled by piling up earth to form the terrace. Evelyn described the building as 'of extraordinary expense', but admired the wide views, since limited by the growth of beech and other trees around the house. Lord Orkney, the first Field Marshal in British history, bought the estate in 1696, employed Thomas Archer to add colonnades and wings to the house in about 1706, and used Henry Wise on the garden. Frederick, Prince of Wales, father of George III, leased the house from 1739 till his death from a blow by a cricket ball in 1751 and here was first played Arne's 'Rule Britannia' at a masque held in the Rustic Theatre. In 1795 this house was destroyed and a new house to a classical design by William Burn (on the lines of Winde's and retaining Archer's colonnades) was not built till 1829 and this was destroyed by another fire in 1849. The new owner, the Duke of Sutherland, employed Sir Charles Barry to build a new mansion. Barry's is not so different from Winde's but is cement rendered, has long wings, more pilasters and a more vertical but crowded emphasis. Henry Clutton built an eccentric, and incongruous but jolly, clock tower on the north-west wing in 1870 for the Duke of Westminster and in 1893 it was bought by the American, W. W. Astor. He employed Pearson to restore the interior and bought the great stone balustrade of the Villa Borghese to rebuild it at the base of the great terrace. In the 1930s it was the centre of the 'Cliveden set', a term coined by

Claude Cockburn to describe the Astor family and their friends who thought peace could be kept with Hitler. The Astors gave part of the Park along Taplow Road for a Canadian War Hospital and the house and remaining park to the National Trust in 1942. The main public entrance is from the Taplow Road on the east, but cars have to be left at the top of the grand, yew-framed avenue north of the house. Viewing of the house is limited but the gardens and park are as interesting and, to most people, more enjoyable. At the head of the avenue near the car-park are the great fountain by W. W. Story (of the U.S.A.), with happy French-type nudes in a giant cockle shell; to the east is a lovely water garden and to the west the formal Long Garden of box hedges and topiary. Up the avenue, past the giant terrace and round to the south of the house are the giant terrace and formal gardens of the parterre, with a view of the long Taplow reach of the Thames framed in trees. On the chalk slope to the Thames west of the parterre is Astor's chapel (and burial place) converted from a little garden temple by Leoni (1735), while to the east and south are less formal areas of woodland, including a wide area of rhododendrons.

Cold Brayfield [2]

A tiny village of house, farm and church down a lane on the Beds. border; it faces Newton Blossomville across the Ouse. St Mary's church is of limestone rubble with much shelly oolite which gives it a dull, brownish look from a distance but has an interesting texture when seen closer. The nave, chancel and low west tower are mainly 13th century and the late 13th-century porch is its best feature. It is of little interest inside. Brayfield House, nearer the river, is a wide, two-storeyed stone building, mainly early 19th century, with an iron verandah to its river side. The few cottages around are mainly Victorian estate buildings.

Coleshill [15]

Has a straggle of Georgian and Victorian villas on a pleasant Green Belt ridge with beech and mixed woodlands and lots of ponies. All Saints, in brick and flint with some stone, is an undistinguished church by G. E. Street (1861). Bottle Cottages, dated 1809, have bottle ends as decoration to their first floor, a not uncommon decorative feature of Bucks. cottages in chalk and flint areas. Coleshill House is a tidy, cream-stuccoed Georgian building, now flats, and Stocks Place is near the site of the vanished Manor House where Edmund Waller was born in 1606. The parish was once in Herts. and became a refuge for Bucks. dissenters.

Colnbrook [18]

A long narrow street of pubs and houses of all ages on the former Bath Road, for which it was an important staging-post. It is now bypassed by the unattractive inter-war road fringed with dumps and small factories. The part of the village beyond the Colne is in the old County of Middlesex, now Surrey. Henry VIII and Catherine of Aragon stayed here, as did the future Queen Elizabeth I. The Ostrich Inn, with over-sailing upper floors and half-timbered gables, was notorious for a murderous landlord. See the model in the bar, which distracts customers from the noise of aircraft at nearby London Airport. St Thomas's church is a small, flint church in Early English style, by Benjamin Ferrey (1852) with a west gable corbelling a little stone spire. Inside is a screen by B. Champneys (1886) and glass by Kempe (1884).

Crafton [8]

(near Mentmore) A hamlet of Mentmore; it has the stud farm of brick and barge-boarded gables, built for the Roseberys of Mentmore in the late 19th century, a few older red-brown brick cottages and a timber-framed farmhouse up a narrowing lane to the north-west.

Creslow [8]

No village or church, but a large, old stone manor house, the centre of a pastoral farm with huge fields on a low limestone hill. A former possession of Knights Templars, it had a rectory till this was suppressed by Queen Elizabeth I. The Manor House is a remarkable survival of an early 14th-century dwelling, one of the most complete of its date in England and probably the oldest inhabited house in the county. Its pastures have long been famous, for they supplied royal tables in Tudor times, while a more recent owner, John Westcar, as can be seen from his monument at Whitchurch, was an agricultural pioneer and the first to send cattle to Smithfield on the new Grand Union Canal in 1801. The oldest parts of the house are the great hall, which forms the much altered north end of the house; the central solar wing, which has a star-vaulted crypt under its eastern half; and a tower at the south-west end with a higher stair-turret. There is a walled garden with 17th-century gate piers and a detached chapel which goes back to the 12th century—its north doorway re-uses a Norman arch—but was desecrated in the Civil War. The medieval feeling of the whole complex is diminished by the handsome upkeep of the place, its carefully controlled approach road and the radio station on the hill top which has wide views.

Cublington [8]

Has a stone church and brick cottages in heavy clay fields on a slight ridge, isolated enough to preserve old gated roads. St Nicholas's is a small, mainly Perpendicular church with a squat west tower. It has a simple west gallery and a chancel arch on corbels with carved monkey and man; early 18th-century Royal arms and Victorian oil lamps converted to electricity. Over-restoration as late as 1927 removed much character. 18th-century brick stable block and grain store of the former Manor House are nearby. The Beacon is a

mound about 6 m high, all that is left of Norman castle. There is a little spinney planted to commemorate the success of the inhabitants and the County Council in preventing the establishment of the Third London Airport here on the site of the disused wartime airfield, of which some concrete buildings still remain (cf. Stewkley and Wing).

Cuddington [11] Has an involved pattern of narrow lanes, little greens, grey stone or white wichert walls and rendered or pink brick cottages, on a rolling ridge-top with views over the Thame valley and Lower Winchendon. The church of St Nicholas is in a stone-walled graveyard hemmed with pollarded elms and is of light grey, local limestone and dark red tiles. The tall

Cliveden: the gardens

embattled west tower is a landmark. The church has a complicated history of antiquarian rather than aesthetic interest, but like so many Bucks. churches has a Victorian feel inside and out, this time due to Street's restoration of 1857. Street designed the glass in the blue, red and green east window executed by Powell. The east window of the south aisle has two small 14th-century angels. The font is a tapering 12th-century tub with blank arches. Across the road is the ungainly, tall, early 17th-century, stone Tyringham House. This was the home of the Tyringhams which was later inherited by the Bernards of Lower Winchendon to whom much of the village now belongs. Many buildings with stone base and timber and plaster, or brick, upper storeys survive—the village hall near the church is a caricature of them—and the whole village north of the Aylesbury Road seems full of picturesque cottages as good as those in the better-known villages of Haddenham and Long Crendon. The best group is centred on the whitewashed plaster and timber-framed 'Three Cottages' at Lower Green (east of the church) but the connecting lanes are attractively lined with waving wichert walls topped with thatch and tile. Gibraltar, a hamlet on the Aylesbury Road towards Westlington, is still in this parish and has a nice old pub, the Bottle and Glass.

Dagnall [12] A brown-brick, somewhat suburban village overshadowed by the Whipsnade Downs.

Datchet [18] A large Edwardian-looking riverside place which incorporates an older village round a little Green, now cut off from the river by the Victorian Railway Line to Windsor. St Mary's church, a

Dinton:
church path (*top*)
tympanum

Dinton Castle

little east of the green, is by R. Brandon (1860), on the site of a medieval church. It has a curiously set, ornate, octagonal tower with a spire. The interior is dark but enlivened by the red and purple O'Connor windows of the 1860s. Three of them are memorials to the Prince Consort. The east window shows Christ in Majesty between SS. Peter and John. There are three 17th-century wall-tablets with busts (of the Wheeler family), probably by a pupil of Le Seuer, and a plainer tablet to Christopher Barker (d. 1599), who did much to improve English printing in the 16th century, as his inscription tells us. A brass with kneeling figures of R. Henbery (d. 1593) and wife with books is in the chancel. A short High Street leads from the Green across the bumpy and disruptive railway crossing to the river by way of some Georgian red-brick houses and a few early-Victorian yellow ones. The best are Datchet Lodge and Old Bridge House facing the river. The motorway divides the town from Ditton Park, a romantic, moated, mock-castle (by W. Atkinson, 1817). Parts of a 14th-century tower and other old bits are built into it. Atkinson added a gothic chapel. All are now incorporated in a Defence establishment.

Denham [15] Part of Greater London, with two large modern suburbs: one of small houses on the old Oxford Road; the other of larger ones between film studios and golf course. The old village is the most attractive near London and a good advertisement for its owners (and perhaps for planning control). It stretches from the handsome Denham Place across a humped-back bridge over the River Misbourne and ends near the church and the lime avenues leading to Denham Court. Lined with dark red and brown brick varigabled houses and cottages with giant wisterias as porches, it looks like, and has often been, a film-set. St Mary's church is of flint and ashlar, in a churchyard with good trees at a sharp angle to the Street. It has an embattled west tower, Perpendicular above a Norman base and Perpendicular arcades and clerestory. It is dark and Victorian inside. There is an octagonal Purbeck bowl font (13th century), a damaged Doom painting (of same date) and some late brasses, including one to the last Abbess of Syon. Also a tomb chest with stone effigies (Sir Edmund Peckham, d. 1564) and a bust on a plinth between looped curtains (Sir Roger Hill, d. 1729) by Thomas Bull. Denham Place, hidden from Village Road behind high walls and elaborate stables, is the principal house. Built for Sir Roger Hill in 1688–1701, it is a conservative H house with heavy dormers, chimney stacks and an elaborate door. Many of its ceilings are delicately plastered with rustic and sporting scenes, and a chapel contains fittings brought from elsewhere, such as the old house at Bulstrode. The stables and garden landscape with lake are late 18th

Dorney

century, the latter by L. Brown. The garden frontage to the Watford Road has fine late 17th-century wrought-iron gates and screens. Denham Court at the east end is also hidden, but this time by its avenue of limes. It is a large house, now mainly in 18th-century yellow brick. Charles II is supposed to have hidden here after the Battle of Worcester and John Dryden, staying later, called its garden 'one of the most delicious in England'. Between this and the Place there are many good minor houses such as Hill House, with alternate stepped and Dutch gables; Wisteria Cottage, overloaded with flowering creepers; Wrango, and the former Charity School; but hardly a house is without interest or charm, or both. Across the railway and the fields is the Savoy, which encloses, in a somewhat drab exterior, the late 14th-century great hall of the original timber house and a 15th-century solar. Additions are of all ages, among them mural paintings dated 1606. It was the inter-war home of Sir Oswald Mosley, whose wife was buried (till 1970) under a garden monument by Lutyens. The Rank Laboratories and film studios have a long white concrete building by Gropius and Fry of 1936, a little recognized monument to the 'modern movement'.

Dinton [11] A small place of limestone walls, brick and timber-framed, red-tiled cottages, stone church and hall, wrapped in chest-nuts along a sheltered fold in the limestone ridge flanking the Vale of Aylesbury. The church of SS. Peter and Paul is in a stone-walled graveyard with views. It is of a coursed shaly rubble with stone dressings but has been much cemented over. The sturdy embattled tower is Perpendicular but the body is mainly 13th century, though much restored, and the chancel extended, by G. E. Street in 1868. He also removed the internal plastering and left the interior with a Victorian air. The glory of the church is the south door, replaced after the 13th-century building of the aisle. This has zigzag and billet mouldings and, in the tympanum, characterful sculptured scenes of

Garrard monument, **Dorney**

two wyverns eating fruit from trees and, rather squashed in a panel below, a St Michael attempting to push a cross down the throat of a large dragon. Inside are a Jacobean pulpit, Decorated; font with carving and two dates; a carved and inlaid altar table dated 1606 and communion rails of about 1770. Brasses include one of Simon Mayne (d. 1617), father of the regicide. The stained-glass windows in the chancel and south aisle are by O'Connor. The Maynes lived at Dinton Hall, a long brick and stone house with many gables and chimneys. A long row runs south along the centre roof-ridge. The house seems to have had 14th-century origins but looks much later, particularly of the 16th century. The gate piers are of the 17th century and there is a circular dovecote. Simon Mayne the regicide (1612–61) was imprisoned in the Tower after the Restoration and died there, but his body was brought back to Dinton. His secretary, John Biggs, then became a recluse and retired to a tiny thatched cottage called 'Hermit's Cave'. He is commemorated in the local public house called 'The Dinton Hermit' and in a satyrical journal issued in the Vale under the same name. The regicide's grandson sold the Hall and manorial lands to the Van Hattams, who built, in 1769, the eyecatcher on the Thame–Aylesbury Road known as Dinton Castle—a hexagonal building with turrets in a ruinous condition but set against a little pine-clad hill and an attractive feature. Glebe House, Dinton, is supposed to be the highest building in wichert in Bucks. Waldridge House, on the east side of village, is a modernized 16th- to 17th-century building with timber frame and herringbone brick infilling, large central chimney and diamond-shaped shafts. Westlington village is joined to Dinton by the stone walls round the grounds of Dinton Hall.

Dorney [17] Preserved in its trees and Thames-side meadows by past landlords, the Palmers and Eton College, and now by Green Belt controls. It has a flint and brick church, a rambling brick and timber manor house in a park, cottages and some 20th-century half-timbered houses at a distance from these. The textures of old mixed clunch and flint walls of the body of the church (St James) and the early brickwork of its additions are interesting and attractive. The brickwork is of various dates, the

Dorton

former early Tudor, the Gerrard Chapel early 17th century and the porch of 1661. Inside, 17th- and 18th-century fittings include a three-sided balustered, timber gallery round the west end (1634), the pulpit, the large Palmer pew and other smaller box pews. The font is a decorated Norman tub. In the chapel is the large monument to Sir William Garrard (d. 1612): the alabaster figures of the knight and his wife kneel, with 15 children kneeling below. Dorney Court wraps round the north side of the church. It has a long history but, due to antiquarians' improvements, has lost much of its aesthetic interest and now looks a large, dull, dark version of 'stock-broker's Tudor'. It is nevertheless a big and

remarkably complete large house of about 1500 with a well-documented history, which has been in the hands of Lyttons, then Garrards (or Gerrards, wealthy London grocers), and then Palmers, who inherited it from Garrards and have been here uninterrupted since 1629. The earliest part is the Great Hall, with a fine open roof of thin arched braces, screens, dais and panelling (from Faversham Abbey), a solar (now Library), and the projecting Parlour. The original entrance was also on the north but was moved to the centre of the east front when this was 'restored' to something like its early appearance by the removal of a dignified 18th-century classical façade and the addition of more cross gables. The west end, built round a small courtyard, seems to have been a rebuilding of part of an earlier house. A gabled gate-house north of the house and ranges of outbuildings were demolished in the 19th century. The Hermitage, a flint and brown stone building with some bottle decoration, on the village road, was a former lodge of the Court. The Pineapple Inn commemorates the offer of the first pineapple grown in England to King Charles II at Dorney.

Dorton [10] Largely consisting of a big house and its park hiding a little church and estate cottages in clayey pastures, at the damp eastern foot of Brill Hill. St John's church, next to a wooded stream behind the big house, is of stone rubble with a weather-boarded bell-turret over the west end supported internally by timber pillars. Largely Decorated in style, it was over-restored as late as 1904 and is now the chapel for the school in the adjoining house. Dorton House is large, Jacobean H-shaped and red brick, with many gables; it is now used by Ashfold Preparatory School, whose playing fields make good use of the open meadow east of the house, but whose extra classrooms and other temporary-looking buildings have cluttered up the west and south. It was the home of Dormers from 1541 to 1773 and then that of Aubrey baronets of Boarstall. Inside the house the main staircase starts with an arched screen supported on tapering Ionic columns and has decorated plasterwork ceilings dated 1626; the Hall has an ornate screen and elaborate fireplace. From the back of the house and church is an attractive walk up the little valley to Brill. Here Spa Farm commemorates the short-lived and unlucky spa dependent on a spring under Brill Hill which produced exceptionally unpleasant sulphurous-chalybeate waters. Henry Hakewill built a classical pump-room for the Spa Company which was formed in 1830, but the Company collapsed in 1839 when Queen Victoria went, not to Dorton as had been expected, but to Leamington. All that now remains is a green and slimy pool in Spa Wood.

Downley [14] Once an independent village, approached by a precipitous hill from the Wycombe Road, with a few old cottages and Donkey pub on the edge of a rough common, it is now the north-west bastion of overgrown estates from High Wycombe with blocks of flats and an ecumenical church.

Drayton Beauchamp [11] On a long lane down a shallower slope of the Chilterns with scattered cottages linked by chestnut, ash, elm and fields to its church at the top end. St Mary's church is isolated on a hilly spur up a gated road across meadows and is seen against a background of beech woods. It is part chequered or rubbly flint, with stone dressings, and part ashlar, with bands of ironstone. The whole church, from embattled and chequered west tower to chancel windows, is consistently Perpendicular in style though the body is 13th and 14th century. The east window has a group of ten late 15th-century stained-glass figures of apostles (SS. Luke and Barnabas were omitted) which have been restored with modern glass. The chancel also has two brasses, with figures nearly full-size, to Cheynes of 1368 and 1375. The first was armour-bearer to Edward III and his family held the Manor down till 1732. The dominating monument on the north wall is to Viscount Newhaven (d. 1728) and his second wife (d. 1732) by William Woodman. The Viscount's semi-reclining figure is in robes and ruffles on a grey sarcophagus between Corinthian columns and pediment. His wife's figure rests on the verge of the sarcophagus and is dressed in fur mantle with a white marble coronet at her feet. She was added later and upsets the balance of a monument already too large for its setting. The font is an arcaded Norman tub. Richard Hooker (1553–1600) was rector here for a short time and herded real sheep near his rectory. The present Rectory is a pleasant yellow early 19th-century rebuilding of his house. The Beauchamps, after whom the village is named, were manor-holders in the 13th century.

Drayton Parslow [8] A village flowing in a stream of holly, stone church, elm, oak and brick houses dividing and re-uniting down the clay slopes towards Bletchley, but still remote. Holy Trinity church has a 12th-century origin but looks mainly Decorated outside with a plain west tower and south porch and Victorian inside thanks to restoration and reseating in 1863. Above the altar is an early 15th-century panel of Nottingham alabaster carved with the Crucifixion. The font is a crocketed octagonal, 15th-century bowl and there are fragments of medieval glass. The best house in the village is near the church at the top of the hill. It is of the 16th century, dark grey and red brick, partly rebuilt in 1754 when the garden side was given a chequered brick skin and pointed windows in an early example of domestic gothic. Lower parts of the village are in red brick and have a towny look.

Dropmore [14] The 240-hectare wooded estate created out of scrubland by Lord Grenville at the end of the 18th century. Dropmore House is a long, white, simple building started about 1792 for William Wyndham, cousin of the younger Pitt and later Lord Grenville and leader of the 'Ministry of All Talents' on Pitt's death in 1806. The house is notable for its gentle bow windows and extensive trellis work which joins it to an elaborate but delightful aviary of red metal trellis and green Chinese pottery panels, capped with a hexagonal lantern.

Lord Grenville undertook extensive planting of conifers, rhododendrons and azaleas until his death here in 1834, and brought here the 'alcove' from the pre-19th-century London Bridge to decorate a lake and created, by the removal of a little hill, a splendid view to the south over miles of apparently endless woodland. The north-east lodge to his Park, facing Littleworth Common, is a 19th-century caricature of flamboyant Tudor timber buildings, using bench and bed ends in its panelling.

Dunsmore [11] A modern settlement in Chiltern beech woods, with a red-and-white pub, The Fox, and red or white gentrified cottages in the woods around. Beyond these are good hill and woodland walks in all directions.

Dunton [8] A remote hamlet of church, rectory, manor farm and a few cottages, far from any town or large village. The southern approach is still by a gated road. St Martin's church is a small building of grey stone with red-brick dressings, with a Perpendicular west tower and a Norman body, much altered. The blocked north doorway still shows a zigzag arch and little figured panels left and right of its lintel. The interior furnishing is late Georgian and there are arched windows in the south wall to keep it company. Oak beams disappear into whitewashed ceiling, the west gallery is in timber and decorated with texts and there are high box pews. Brasses with small figures on the nave floor are of 1420. The rectory is early 18th century.

East Claydon *see* Claydon, East

Edgcott [7] A little village with a nice grouping of church and two old farmhouses on a steep slope overlooking the wide, low fields which run away towards Brill. It is now squeezed by the growing brickworks at Calvert on one side and the open prison at Grendon on

Newhaven monument, detail, **Drayton Beauchamp**

the other. The church of St Michael is small and has an embattled west tower, nave and chancel, in grey stone and of the 14th and 15th centuries, though of little interest inside. It has been scraped and given green glass, a colour best left to nature. Parts of benches are of the 16th century. On its west is the 17th-century timber-framed Rectory Farm and on its south is the 18th-century, chequered brickwork on large stone base, Manor Farm.

Edlesborough [9] A spread-out village. Churchtown is the medieval settlement round a little circular chalk hill, itself a low stepping promontory from the Chilterns. On this the church stands like a lighthouse on a rock in the Vale, with a few old houses at the foot. The larger part of the village is spread over a square pattern of lanes on heavier land interlaced with orchards and poplars. St Mary's is a beautiful church with the best fittings in the county, but, to the shame of a large and prosperous-looking village, is now disused. It is built of Totternhoe stone, a hard chalk which weathers badly but gives sharp white sculpted interiors. The west tower is unusual in being more Decorated than Perpendicular, and taller

West gallery, **Dunton**

The following text appears in the photograph (wall panels):

ll things losse for
ke of Christ Jesus
judg them as dung
Christ.Phil.III.8
Pastor. 1609

I am not ashamed of the gos
pel of Christ:for it is the power
of God unto salvation to every
one that beleveth. Rom.I.16
Sam: Clutterbuck.Pastor:1622

I am determined not to
know any thing among
you, save Jesus Christ,and
him crucified.1.Cor.II.2
Thomas Willis. Rector.1664

thias Mayo.*Rector*.1776

Samuel Masters. 1695.
James Moody.   1717.

John Ollyffe.
D. Preedy.

(21 m) and more massive than usual. It bore a spire till 1828 when it was struck by lightning. The body of the church is embattled all round, has a clerestoried nave of four bays—the oldest part left—and a chancel with five-light, geometrically patterned, window which seems to overflow the east end. The church is exceptionally rich in woodwork: the open timber roofs of the nave and chancel; the Perpendicular chancel screen of tall three-light divisions; the carved stalls with misericords and the slender wine-glass-shaped pulpit. The last has a superb canopy of panelled sounding board crowned with four tiers of minute pinnacles and finials. The font is a simple Perpendicular octagon. There is Victorian stained glass, including an early work by Clayton and Bell (north aisle) and a south chancel window by Kempe (1901). The nave was decorated in red lines in 1867. There is an almost full-size brass effigy of John de Swynstede (d. 1395), a rare brass of 1412 in the shape of a rose, and a 16th-century brass of John Rufford (d. 1540), which re-uses a brass of an early 15th-century lady. The pattern of old lanes to the east has been crudely infilled by modern housing of saw-tooth-roof and plastic-

weatherboarding varieties which is not up to the usual Bucks. standard. There is, however, one magnificent barn, 60 m long, at Church Farm, not far east of Churchtown and near by a medieval moat. Manor Farm to the south-east has another medieval moat. Further south-east on the Beds. border is a sail-less tower windmill. The area is open to south-west and north-east and not short of renewable wind.

Ellesborough [11] Not unnaturally confused by 'foreigners' with Edlesborough, for it has a similar name and another church on a little hill projecting from the Chilterns into the Vale. This one is a sheltered tiny village on the Upper Icknield Way with an isolated church and some thatched cottages on a grassy spur but is more closely backed by beech woods which rise to Cymbeline's Mount and the Chequers Court estate. The church of SS. Peter and Paul has a tall embattled south-west tower with higher stair-turret and is of flint, in mixed Decorated and Perpendicular styles, though it looks, outside, a hard Victorian from the drastic restorations of 1854 and 1871. Inside, the nave is a chalky white from the use of Totternhoe stone, as at Edlesborough. It has four tall bays to its south aisle and is mainly late 14th century. The most handsome fitting is the alabaster monument to Bridget Croke (d. 1638), which has an effigy of the lady reclining, uncomfortably, on her side under a black-columned and coffered arch. She was the heiress and last of the Hawtreys of Chequers Court and there is a brass to one of her ancestors, Thomas Hawtrey (d. 1544). Cymbeline's Mount on the hills above is a popular viewpoint which has a 7-metre-high mound and two small baileys near by. Iron Age and Roman finds near by led to the tradition that Caractacus was born here, but no connection is known with Cymbeline.

◁ **Edlesborough**

Emberton [5] Traffic to Olney passed right through, making an acute bend at the village clock tower, until a recent bypass was made. The church of All Saints is at the south-west corner of the village on a slight rise above the centre. It has a substantial Perpendicular embattled west tower with higher stair-turret. The rest is largely Decorated with generous flowing tracery in windows, particularly the five-light east window. There are five-bay arcades to the nave with quatrefoil piers and the clerestory has quatrefoil windows, but their interior is a little lifeless owing to an over-restoration in 1859. The font is octagonal Perpendicular and there are remains of the timber chancel screen (now on the north side of the chancel), piscina and sedilia with ogee arches, a brass of 1410 to a former rector and a sickly war memorial by Farmer and Brindley (1919), which has an alabaster angel on a rosso pedestal. Outside, at the central crossroads in the little square, is a creamy ashlar clock tower with pinnacles and large lancets which was built as a memorial to a rector's wife in 1846. It is ill-proportioned but in a lovely stone, cleaned and restored in 1972, which makes it an attractive eye-catcher in the village centre. Up the

stone walled lane past the church is the 18th-century Church Farmhouse and there are a number of other pleasant minor stone buildings in the village. In the Ouse valley, where Olney's steeple is a prominent landmark, is one of those contradictions in terms, a 'Country Park'. This one has 70 hectares of camping and boating and, with an adjoining wet nature reserve, was created from disused and flooded gravel pits.

Eton [18] A tightly packed little town, islanded between wide playing fields, willow-fringed commons and the Thames. Eton College, the best known public school in the world, dominates the one end of the main street; the Bell Tower of Windsor Castle, across the hidden Thames, overlooks the other. The town was transferred, with Slough and some villages in S. Bucks., to the Royal County of Berkshire in 1974. This entry is therefore shortened. The College was founded by Henry VI in 1440, together with King's College, Cambridge, to which its scholars were intended to proceed. The seventy scholars on the Foundation are known as King's Scholars (or Collegers) and live in the old College buildings. The other pupils,

numbering nearly 1,200, are called Oppidans and live in masters' houses spread around the school, mainly on the west side. The focal point of the College is the 'Burning Bush', an ornamental iron lamp-standard of 1864 at the junction of Common Lane with Slough Road; the medieval college is to its east, the expansions of the 19th and 20th centuries to its west. Henry intended his foundation to be the grandest in the country with a chapel larger than most cathedrals. Work was started on the chapel in 1441, the Hall, Buttery, Lower School and Headmaster's and Provost's Lodgings soon after. Work on the chapel was redone in 1449 and 1459, but in 1461 Henry was deposed by Edward IV, who attempted to suppress the College, and, while this was resisted, ambitious plans were retailored to reduced expectations, and the nave of the chapel, which had been intended to stretch right across the Slough Road, was abandoned for a modest antechapel. The latter later served as parish church in place of the decaying medieval church in the adjoining graveyard. The present chapel is 60 m long, in a late Perpendicular style and, with its great stone buttresses capped with delicate finials, its tall windows and

brick tower which rises above all these was added by Provost Lupton in 1520. The Upper School, attributed to Wren, was added on the roadside of the School Yard, arcaded over the modest entrance to the College in 1691. The Library and a south arcade to the cloister were added in 1729. The Library is the most beautiful room in the College but is rarely open to the public—and a second storey was added to the cloisters (now called Green Court) in 1766. The statue of Henry in the centre of the School Yard is by Francis Bird (1718). West of Slough Road buildings are usually disappointing and dull but the Memorial Buildings housing the school's hall and new library (by L. K. Hall, 1908) are triumphantly florid, while Woodyer's New Schools (1863) in a neo-Tudor style and the Lower Chapel by A. Blomfield (1891) in a neo-Perpendicular, are up to the standard of most of the older College buildings. A number of the old boarding houses are of historical interest and some are externally attractive, such as the group near Gulliver's and Old Christopher's around Barnes Pool (at the top of the High Street), and two of the oldest, Godolphin (1722) and Angelo's (1790 in Common Lane). Apart from them there are in the High Street numerous good minor buildings. In the middle is the sad-looking 'new' parish church of St John's, set back in a narrow yard, by B. Ferrey (1854).

Eton Wick [18] Mainly a large inter-war housing estate and a small Victorian church, isolated by flat commons and an elevated road, now in Berks. St John the Baptist's is a simple, red-and-blue-brick, rectangle with a little central bell-turret to its tiled roof, and an exposed brick interior by A.

its little lantern-topped staircase towers, is externally more impressive than the sister chapel at King's, Cambridge, though internally not of such fine quality. The most important item inside is the series of wall-paintings, in a monochromatic, Flemish-style, of the Miracles of the Virgin by two English painters, Gilbert and Baker (1479–87). These were whitewashed in 1560 and not restored until 1923 and 1975. The great east window is filled with stained glass (Crucifixion and Last Supper) by Evie Hone (1952), and eight of the north and south windows have more abstract glass by John Piper. The vaulted roof is a false fan-vault inserted by Sir William Holford using suspended concrete panels in 1959. There is a genuine 16th-century fan-vault in the Lupton Chapel on the north side which was used as a model.

There is a 'museum' of 16th-century to 19th-century brasses in the antechapel, cut off from the nave by Street's screen of 1882. The chapel is wholly of stone with lead roofs; the hall is largely of stone but has patches of brick where work was interrupted after the deposition of Henry VI. Most of the other school buildings are in an attractive mellow pink-red brick, and many show the earliest brickwork found in its old county of Bucks. The cloister was originally intended to be built north of the chapel, but here is the present School Yard, with the first school room (1443) on its north side. Smaller cloisters were built north of the Hall away from the road with a range of lodgings and school buildings around them whose elaborate drainage and garderobe towers give this part of the college its interesting silhouette. The great

Blomfield (1869). A window by F. Spence is based on Holman Hunt's *'Light of the World'*.

Eythrope [11] A large Rothschild park between Waddesdon and the River Thame. It is now largely farmland with good tree belts. It once had an important house which was the home of Dynham, Dormer and Stanhope families, but the chapel built for Sir Roger Dynham in about 1490 was pulled down by one of the Stanhopes in 1738, to build a little stone bridge across the Thame, while the large house was pulled down by another Stanhope, the 6th Earl of Chesterfield, in 1812, in what seems to have been a fit of pique concerned with local political rivalry. The estate was acquired with Waddesdon by the Rothschilds, and here, near the head of the 'lake'—a flooded arm of the Thame—a brick and stone 'Pavillion' was built for Alice, the unmarried elder sister of Baron Ferdinand de Rothschild of Waddesdon (by Devey, 1883). It was much enlarged in the 1950s. The estate has a number of fancy rustic Victorian lodges decorated with the five arrows, badge of the Rothschilds.

Farnham Common [15] The northern end of Farnham Royal; it has a large post-Second World War housing estate and a little church, of St John the Evangelist, designed by C. F. Whitcomb (1908). At Egypt, across the Beaconsfield Road and close to Burnham Beeches, is a solitary example, by V. Harding (1936), of the so-called International Style of those days. It is an L-shaped reinforced concrete house with spiral iron staircases inside and out.

Farnham Royal [15] A long, thin, suburb of Slough stretched north along the road to Burnham Beeches and Beaconsfield and relieved at intervals by commons and beech woods. The main church, near the Slough end, is St Mary's, big and

flint-faced, largely by E. Nesfield, who, in 1869, added an aisled nave and a west tower (with a pyramidal roof and an eccentrically placed clock) to the medieval, largely 12th-century, chancel of the former church. Inside are a brass to E. Mascoll, who was Wolsey's clerk of works for Christ Church at Oxford, and a window by Kempe (1900). Nesfield also built the large house in Farnham Park, with its heavy gables and tile hanging which has been much altered since.

Fawley [14] This parish is the south-west corner of the county, sharing woods and Henley Regatta with Oxon. The village is along a north to south ridge above the Thames and is approached by steep beech-wooded slopes which makes it seem isolated. Beech slopes, hazel and thorn hedges and some unhappy pine-trees grade into mixed oak woods as the ridge runs north, while beech and holly and yew threaten to overwhelm the little meadows in the adjoining bottoms. The church is near the centre of the village and cottages and farms stretch along the ridge for a kilometre in each direction. St Mary's church is almost hidden in the yew and other trees of its graveyard. It is of flint with stone dressings and has a tower of the late 13th century, with corbels below the 16th-century top. The chancel was rebuilt, with a round-headed chancel arch, in 1748, and the north transept was added and the whole church restored in 1883. Except for the chancel the church preserves the late Victorian atmosphere of its restoration. It does, however, have a 17th-century carved pulpit and a lectern, brought from the Chandos chapel at Canons, and in the chancel are other carvings and panelling from Canons. This was installed when the Freemans of Fawley Court rebuilt the ruinous chancel in 1748. The chancel was re-ordered in 1965. In a transept is a large monument, to Justice Sir James

Eton School Yard

Fawley church and Freeman mausoleum

Whitelock (d. 1632), with recumbent figures of him and his wife (née Bulstrode), under a black marble canopy with figures of Justice and Mercy. Some glass of about 1635 with Arms of Bulstrodes and Whitelocks originally in Fawley Court or its dower house was placed in the church in 1973. There is also a small window of 1978 by Piper and Reyntiens. The churchyard has two mausolea. One, for the Freemans, is an ashlar octagon crowned with rusticated dome of 1750. It was designed by Freeman himself (and the drawings for it are preserved in the Gloucester Record Office). The other mausoleum, for the Mackenzie family, is in granite. In the village street the earlier rectory was converted to stables and a new rectory (now Fawley House) was built in 1740. Roundhouse Farm at the north end of the village is an 18th-century cottage attached to a cylindrical wing with a conical roof. There is an early 'modern' house with reinforced concrete and steel frame by C. Nicholson (1937)

and a more modest house by L. Brett (1959) at Fawley Bottom, but most modern houses here are unhappy strangers screened by keen gardening. Fawley Court, the great house of the parish, is 2 km south-east in Thames meadows and woods. Now a Roman Catholic school for Polish children, it was built for the Freemans in 1684 (on the site of the Whitelocks' mansion which was destroyed in 1642) in a Wren style with bright red brick with stone quoins, of two storeys with hipped slate roof. The central section is joined to two projecting pavilions by curved single-storey links. James Wyatt altered the exterior adding a large Ionic colonnade, which gives the house a mid-Victorian look, and gave the interior much Adam-style decoration. Luckily the saloon retains its splendid plasterwork with grapes, garlands and little animals, dated 1691. The house has several good fireplaces and an interesting collection of Polish armour and antiques. The interior was badly damaged by

fire in 1974 but has since been restored. The gardens were laid out by L. Brown in the late 18th century, but have been much altered by nature and by farming, and the trees are magnificent. Near the house is a clutter of temporary classrooms. A new, bronze-clad, tent-like church has been placed, more discreetly, in trees. The Henley reach of the Thames can be enjoyed from an adjoining footpath and there are other good walks in the area north and east of Fawley village.

Fenny Stratford [8] Once an independent market town on Watling Street; it still has a pleasing group of pub and old cottages near the Grand Union Canal, and a picturesque timber railway station on the Bedford Line, but it is now a run-down end of the younger Bletchley, and part of Milton Keynes New Town. St Martin's church is at the central crossroads. The north part was built as a complete church by Browne Willis, the antiquarian, as a memorial to his grandfather, who died on St Martin's Day. He built it with the help of an architect called Edward Wing of Aynho (whom he sacked), and John Simmonds, a Herts. joiner. It is of red brick with a west tower of 1726 and has rounded arches but gothic detail to windows and, inside, a wide ceiling panelled with the arms of the subscribers to the church. The early 18th-century galleries and pews have now gone and the south wall has been cut through for the large Victorian nave added by W. White in 1866. Browne Willis was buried here in 1760 and is commemorated by his original floor slab, reset in the east wall of his church. The Victorian nave is in wild patterns of red, black and white bricks. A south aisle was added to this in 1908 and plain vestry and kitchen in 1965. The 'Fenny Poppers'—little hand-guns which are fired in celebration of St Martin's Day (11 November)—are kept in the church but they are now fired not in the churchyard but in a local recreation ground each year. The former villagey, stage-coach, nature of Watling Street has vanished leaving the Swan Inn looking uncomfortable at the old cross-roads. Further north where the railway crosses Watling Street by the 'Denbigh Hall' bridge, was the temporary terminus, until 1838, of the London–Birmingham railway. From the adjoining pub, now gone, railway passengers from the south were taken by coach to Rugby where they rejoined the railway to Birmingham.

Filgrave [5] (near Tyringham) A hamlet near the Ouse. There is a disused graveyard with the site of a medieval church (St Mary's), already a ruin in 1637, now gone altogether.

Fingest [14] Has shrunk since the 18th century. It is in a deep, beech-fringed, dry valley in the heart of the Chilterns. Its massive church tower dominates the tiny body of

Fleet Marston

the church and tidy flint and pinkish brick houses, cottages and Chequers Inn. The tower of St Bartholomew's is early Norman, with walls over a metre thick, in plan nearly 9 m square, and nearly 20 m tall. It is of flint with stone quoins plastered over in light ochre. It has elaborate arched openings to its third (bell) stage and a later twin-gabled roof. The present nave is joined to the tower by a 12th-century arch, slightly narrower than the tower, which may itself have served as the original nave. There is no arch to the present chancel, which is divided from the nave by a late 19th-century pine screen. The chancel has original late 13th-century lancets on the north and 15th-century windows on the south. The atmosphere inside is much that of its over-restoration in 1866 but is lightened by the restoration of white plasterwork in the chancel and repainting of the rest in 1967. The font has an octagonal 14th-century bowl and there are Royal Arms of Queen Anne. North of the churchyard is the site of a palace of Bishops of Lincoln. To the south is the chequered brick pub and to the east some timber-framed cottages. In Chequers Lane is a vil-

lage pound, described as in 'good repair' in 1780.

Fleet Marston [11] Has no village but three farms, a few cottages and a small church, in flat, and once marshy, meadows on Akeman Street. The church of St Mary's is, not unnaturally, now redundant. It is a small stone building of the 12th and 13th centuries with a nave and chancel and a small west bell-turret, plastered inside, with a 15th-century queenpost-type roof to its nave and an east window by Burlison and Grylls (1868). It was over-restored by Gilbert Scott in 1868.

Ford [11] A hamlet in Dinton parish with a chapel and pub and some cottages in large flat fields with dying elms and willows and distant views of the Chilterns scarp.

Foscott (formerly Foxcote) [5] Secluded among trees and byroads, it has an indeterminate-looking village green with a sadly disused and overgrown church, an over-restored manor house and half-timbered farmhouses and cottages. St Leonard's church is a stone building of small nave and smaller chancel and south porch, but with no tower or turret, in a wildly over-grown churchyard. The south door is in simple, dignified Transitional style. Inside, the walls are plastered: the east wall of the nave is decorated with commandments and hatchments and the chancel with wallpaper-like flowers. The communion rail is 17th century. The Manor House, an early home of Grenvilles, has an Elizabethan centre which was rebuilt in 1639 with Tuscan pilasters and then partly restored in 1868. 1 km south-east in the Ouse valley a Roman villa was found in 1837. One of the two tesselated pavements unearthed is now in the Queen's Temple at Stowe. North of the village is an ugly brick pumping station built by the Bucks. Water Board in 1953 in connection with a 20-hectare reservoir. The latter was filled in 1956 and, formidably fenced, creates a useful wild-fowl refuge, well seen from the road between Maids Moreton and Leckhampstead.

Frieth [14] A place of brick and flint cottages and a Victorian church on a single street through high, wooded Chiltern country. The church of St John the Evangelist was built as a chapel of ease to Hambleden; it is a flint-faced and tile-roofed barn of nave and chancel by J. P. Harrison (1848) in a 14th-century Decorated style. This was enlarged by a south aisle with steep cross gables in 1872. There is an east window by Hardman (1849) to a design by Pugin and three windows by Kempe.

Fulmer [15] A well-kept village with brown brick church and brown brick cottages in a little wooded valley with large houses in small parks and well-hedged little fields full of ponies. Careful retention of brown brick for new buildings in the village centre and continuous whitening of the late 18th-century and early 19th-century mansions make the place seem somewhat artificial, as do the effect of Green Belt restrictions, which keep Wexham at bay to the south; but the brick church in the valley bottom seems homely and lovable. St James's is a complete rebuilding of the former medieval church, in a dark brick with tiled roofs, carried out for the then Lord of the Manor Sir Marmaduke Dayrell, Treasurer to James I and Charles I, in 1610. It has an embattled west tower and all openings are of brick. It was extensively restored from 1877 to 1884 by G. E. Street, who rebuilt most of the chancel and added the south aisle. The 17th-century interiors are largely yellow-washed and the chancel is in undressed brick, but the whole is well-kept and slightly lacking in the homely atmosphere of the outside. Its greatest attraction is the monument of its builder, Sir Marmaduke Dayrell (d. 1631). He and his wife have recumbent effigies, he in armour and she in a black dress, while their two sons and their families kneel below. The monument is set in a roundheaded and recessed canopy supported by black marble columns, whose architraves are decorated with small figures. Fulmer Hall is an 18th-century house on the site of the Dayrells' manor house.

Gawcott [7] Has a plain stone church and plain red-brick houses and a mildly industrial and unloved air to it. It was the birthplace of the architect Sir George Gilbert Scott (1811–78), son of the Rev. Thomas Scott, who was then vicar of Gawcott and is buried here.

Fenny Stratford station

Fingest ▷

Gayhurst church

Thomas Scott designed the church of Holy Trinity. It is in a simple Georgian classical style, of grey stone with slate roofs. The west tower has a parapet and ball finials while the east end has a polygonal apse. The benches, pulpit and organ are contemporary fittings but the ceilings were altered in 1895. Gilbert Scott did not learn to love gothic architecture here, or at nearby Buckingham, but was inspired by the isolated church at Hillesden 3 km to the south. Lenborough, a hamlet 2 km east, has the 17th-century Manor Farmhouse, later refronted with flint and stone quoins, which was the home from 15th to 18th centuries of the Ingoldsby family. The best-known, Sir Richard, was one of the regicides but was pardoned by Charles II and sat in four Parliaments before being buried at Hartwell. It belonged later to the historian Edward Gibbon.

Gayhurst [5] A splendid group of creamy stone buildings, Elizabethan mansion, 18th-century stables and classical church, round a lawn in a landscaped park sloping down to the Ouse opposite Tyringham. The Manor and the former Manor House, whose early 16th-century foundations are in the present cellars, were given to Sir Francis Drake on his return from his voyage round the world. He promptly sold them to a William Mulsoe who started building the present house in 1597. This was completed by his son-in-law, Sir Everard Digby, early in the next century. Sir Everard was hung following his complicity in the Guy Fawkes Plot of 1606, with other conspirators who had actually hidden in his house, but his son Sir Kenelm (born here, 1603) was restored to favour and became an early member of the Royal Society. Wrightes bought the house in 1704 and George Wrighte made considerable alterations to the north front and to the interior in the mid 18th century. Further alterations were made by William Burges in the 1860s for the Carringtons. The house is of three storeys with five gabled bays to the centre, and has projecting wings on each side. To the east is a further projecting bay with a round-headed porch on heavy square piers. The projecting wings have flat roofs as stark as any County School of the 1950s. The original plan has an H shape but space between the north wings was filled in the mid 18th century. Internal alterations made by Burges were light-hearted and included the addition of an oriel window to the kitchen, a caryatid supporting a corner of a staircase while crouching over a door, and a series of panels painted with English flowers to a south-east ground floor room. The stables are in two bold blocks at right angles to the house and have a 17th-century dovecote over an adjoining gateway. The grounds were laid out by L. Brown in about 1760 and then remodelled by H. Repton in about 1790. Old fishponds were smoothed between lawns to make 18th-century lakes and 'Digby's Walk' created, with a sunken track

◁ **Gayhurst:** Wrighte monument

and a Gothic-arched tunnel under the road to a wooded spring near the Ouse. The church of St Peter faces the stables across the main lawn. It is a small Wren-style building, a complete rebuilding of the earlier church, done for George Wrighte about 1728. After Willen, it is the most important classical church in the county. It has a west tower with an upper stage supported on thin pilasters at angles, carrying a recessed lead-covered cupola. The nave, chancel and tower have matching arched windows and arched doors centrally on north and south of the nave. The interior is in white plaster with giant pilasters supporting a baroque plaster ceiling decorated with fruit and flowers. Fittings of panelling, box pews, two-decker pulpit, reredos, iron communion rail and little font on polygonal pillar, are all contemporary. The Royal Arms came from the previous church and are Stuart, altered in the 18th century. South of the chancel arch, and planned to fit the decoration, is the grand monument of Sir Nathan Wrighte in the robes of Lord Keeper of the Privy Seal and of his son George. The dramatic figures of father and son framed in Corinthian columns and baldachino are attributed, though without proof, to Roubiliac. On the main road the little 18th-century lodge was converted to mock-Elizabethan in the late 19th century and later to make a small pub.

Gerrards Cross [15] Has a large triangular, birchy, common on the London–Oxford road with Victorian villas on the south and a large commuter suburb, round the old Great Central Railway Line, to the north. The principal church is on the south edge of the common in a strange, yet appropriate mixture of Venetian–Byzantine and Victorian gothic, and the place feels more like Surrey than Bucks., in spite of the dry chalk valleys and beech woods of the southern Chilterns that flow round it. St James's

church was designed by Sir William Tite and built in 1861 as a memorial to a General Reid, M.P. for Windsor. It is cruciform in plan, with an octagonal, Byzantine-looking, lead dome over the crossing, but with four Chinese-looking turrets around it and gothic detail below, while at the north-west it has a tall Italianate campanile. It is mainly of yellow brick but with some white and red. The interior is light and polished and the massive scaliogla pillars supporting the painted dome are impressive. North beyond traffic lights is the long, white, early 19th-century front of the much older Bull Hotel, a reminder of the place's importance in coaching days, and northeast of this are a few small Georgian cottages. To its west, on the edge of Bulstrode Park (q.v.), is an 8-hectare Iron Age fort.

Granborough (or **Grandborough**) [8] A little village, not at all grand, in muddy pastures south of Winslow. The church of St John the Baptist (originally dedicated to God and St Alban) is a stone building with embattled west tower, early 14th-century nave and a chancel higher than the nave, rebuilt in the late 14th century. The Perpendicular east window has stained glass of 1889, and the chancel walls are stencilled with figures of angels done by a Victorian vicar. A 15th-century alabaster panel of the crucifixion and a rare 15th-century chrysmatory (a pewter box with lidded cups for wine, oil and water) were found in 1880 during the zealous restoration by Gilbert Scott.

Great Brickhill see Brickhill, Great

Great Hampden see Hampden, Great

Great Horwood see Horwood, Great

Great Kimble see Kimble, Great

Great Linford see Linford, Great

Great Missenden see Missenden, Great

Great Woolstone see Woolstone, Great

Grendon Underwood [7] Formerly called Grendon under Bernwode—the forest that stretched north and west along the Oxon border. Until the recent establishment of an open prison in the grounds of Grendon Hall, it was a sleepy village along a winding willow-fringed lane with a church and varied old brick and timber-framed cottages and farmhouses backing on to heavy clay meadows. The church of St Leonard is in grey stone with 15th-century embattled tower, tall 13th-century nave and chancel, all over-restored in 1866 and 1902. Only the early 13th-century south door with its decayed mouldings combines character, beauty and a feeling of age. The nave has a carved pulpit dated 1620, set, in 1902, on a Bath stone base; the chancel has a semi-reclining effigy of John Piggott of Doddershall (d. 1751) on an altar tomb, signed by Scheemakers, and two facing wall monuments in coloured marble to Lord and Lady Saye and Sele (1781 and 1789). Grendon Hall on Spring Hill, with the extended development of neat prison staff houses, is now more of Edgcott than Grendon. The Hall itself is the solid, gabled, neo-Elizabethan, late 19th-century home of the Piggotts, designed by the two brothers for their own occupation. House and immediate grounds are being privately restored. Shakespeare Farm on the village street not far east of the church is of mixed 16th-century timber frame and 17th-century brick. It was once the New Inn and said by Aubrey to have inspired Shakespeare with the story of *A Midsummer Night's Dream*. As the village street was part of the old road between Stratford and London this is possible.

Grove [8] (near Horton) A tiny hamlet in the Ouzel valley; it has meadows with a tiny church adjoin-

Gerrards Cross: parish church

ing locks on the Grand Union Canal. St Michael's church is 14th century and of stone, but now disused. It makes a pleasant group with the lock-keeper's cottage and the humped-back bridge taking the approach road into the fields beyond.

Haddenham [11] A large semi-industrial village. This statement, while true, gives a totally misleading impression of the place, for the newer housing estates and the scattered engineering works enclose a large, long medieval village with one crooked street stretching 1½ km from Church End in the south to Town's End in the north, passing other 'ends' called Diggs, The Croft, Stockwell Furlong, Fort End

and Dollicot on the way. There is no centre to this strange village but the church and some of the larger houses cluster round a Green at Church End and make this the most natural focus of the place. From the Green north-west there are long narrow streets of white plastered cottages with tiles or thatch, and patched walls of wichert with stone or brick bases and thatched tops, and these are threaded through by a brook connecting old duck-rearing ponds. Another, more isolated, pond at Crabtree Road is so enclosed in thatched walls that villagers said they thatched the pond to keep the ducks dry. The village is a butt of local jokes and is said to have 'put up gates to keep out the plague'.

The Green is a broad area of rough grass dominated by the medieval church, with a large pond which reflects white-plastered houses. St Mary's is of plain local limestone with a 13th-century west tower decorated with blank arcading round its top, and inside is large, airy and plain plastered. The nave has 13th-century aisles and the 13th-century chancel has a mainly 15th-century north chapel. The church has three piscinas, brasses of 1428 and an early 16th-century palimpsest of an early 15th-century one, a rough Norman font with frieze of dragons above rough fluting, Royal Arms of Queen Elizabeth II (1953), some 15th-century stained glass with apostle figures, and a modern window by

Church Farm, **Haddenham**

the native artist R. O. Bell. Its woodwork includes three 16th-century screens, and parts of 16th-century pews. The pulpit and clergy stalls (1955) and an organ case (1969) are by Ivor Newton. The big tiled and slated roofs provide the chief catchment area for the adjoining duck pond. On the east is Church Farm, which has a 14th-century stone base and ground floor, and 15th- and 16th-century upper floors, the upper floor with projecting timber frame. Its foundations are said to be even earlier. Grenville Manor, a little further east, has a Victorian date-stone (1569) and a genuine core of 16th-century building, though woodwork is of various dates. Manor Farmhouse has a large 15th-century barn. Other good buildings are found the length of the medieval village core. The best groups are at Skittles Green, a little north, at the road junctions in Ford End and round the Green at

Town's End. In mid High Street is Dove House, with a big stone chimney and the knuckle-bone decorated Bone House of 1807, but there are few modern buildings of note. Even the County Architect's Library and Health Centre of 1971 and the Fire Station of 1976 seem to be trying too hard, with rendered brick and pitched tiled roofs, to be 'in keeping'.

Halton [11] A large Rothschild house and park on the lower beech-wooded slopes of the Chiltern scarp. Most is now covered by Defence establishments, though still attractive thanks to the retention of the old trees. The little church of St Michael's is not much older than the Rothschild house, for it was rebuilt by Henry Rhodes in 1813. It is in an Early English style, with grey-squared stones and flint decorated joints, with an embattled west tower and five-bay nave. It was remodelled in 1886–7

to suit the more luxurious current taste, and Rothschild money. The only medieval relic is a brass with kneeling figures of Henry Bradschawe, Chief Baron of the Exchequer (d. 1553) and wife and children. Pseudo-Jacobean cottages, near the canal bridge, have the Rothschild family crest (five arrows) and motto. Halton House, south-east of the church, was described by Eustace Balfour as a combination of French chateau and gambling house, and by the Department of the Environment's investigator as an enormous mansion 'in the French railway station-chateau taste of the mid 19th century'. It was built for Baron Alfred de Rothschild in 1884 by W. R. Rogers, with ghastly splendour inside, the fault more of the architect than patron (the former was given a free hand). It was occupied by the fighting services in the First World War and acquired by the Crown on the death of Baron Alfred in 1918. The present west wing was built for the R.A.F. as senior officers' quarters in 1937 on the site of a large domed Winter Garden which had been the apple of the Baron's eye, for he had everything from concerts to his own circus within it. On Boddington Hill in the woods, above the barracks and hospital buildings of the armed services, is a 7-hectare Iron Age hill fort.

Hambleden [14] A small village at the centre of a large parish in the gently falling chalk valley running south from Fingest to the Thames at Hambleden Mill End. The valley sides are edged with beech woods, protected by National Trust and local authorities. The meadowed valley bottom is broken by the closer pattern of village cottages, church and trees, and dominated by the square tower which rises above them all. The two larger houses—the present Manor House and Kenricks—a former manor house and the new rectory, are below the fringe of the wood on the

Hambleden Manor

east side. St Mary's church has a handsome tower, complicated plan and long history, but is more interesting than beautiful. In its earliest 11th-century form it was simple cruciform with central tower, but the north transept was extended with an ambitious east aisle in the early 13th century and the nave rebuilt. The central tower collapsed in 1703 and a new tower was built at the west end in 1721, and this was encased in flint and given four little turrets in 1883. There was a general restoration in 1859, when the 'sheepfold' for farm labourers was transformed into a south Lady chapel and near the end of the century the chancel arch was rebuilt and porch added. Externally it looks polished Victorian; inside is a plain narrow nave, and Victorian improvements at the east end. The chancel has carved heads to sedilia and there are monuments to Sir Cope d'Oyley (d. 1633) and wife ('To the world a Martha and to heav'n a Mary') and kneeling children in painted alabaster. In the south transept is the so-called Wolsey Altar, made from an early 15th-century carved oak screen with arms of Wolsey and Bishop Fox. Among the yew trees in the churchyard is the stone-domed, mid 18th-century mausoleum of the Kenrick family. Outside the lych-gate is a square of small reddish-brown or grey brick houses round a single yew tree, and near by the flint and red-brick early 17th-century, many-gabled Manor House, the present home of Viscounts Hambleden, and birthplace of the 7th Earl of Cardigan, Commander of the Light Brigade at Balaclava. (The 1st Viscount Hambleden, the great W. H. Smith (d. 1891) lived at Greenlands near Mill End.) South-east is Kenricks, of red and grey brick with giant pilasters, built in 1724 on the site of the earlier Manor House where St Thomas of Cantelupe, Bishop of Hereford and last English saint before the Reformation, was born. Mill End is the south 'end' of

Hambleden, on the River Thames. It has a photogenic group of timbered Mill and Mill House on the edge of a wide roaring weir, and is a busy and dangerous place at summer weekends, owing to the narrowness of the Henley Road between its old brick cottages.

Hampden, Great [11] A church and mansion, in the care of the Hampden family from the 11th century, in a high downland park, set with beeches, sycamore, elm avenues, yew, cedar and chestnut trees. It is surrounded by Chiltern beech woods and arable fields and good walking country, long protected by owners and planning authorities but without feeling artificial. The church of St Mary Magdalen is of flint with some stone, particularly as dressings, with a clerestoried 13th- and 14th-century nave, 14th-century chancel and a small embattled south-west tower. It has some early 16th-century benches with linenfold panelling but the chief interest inside is in the Hampden monuments: the brasses to John Hampden (d. 1496), with a figure in armour over a metre in length, and to Sir John Hampden (d. 1553) and his two wives; a tall wall-tablet to Elizabeth, wife of the great John Hampden (d. 1634) inscribed 'in perpetual memory of his conjugall love'; and a large hanging monument to John himself. He died after wounds at Chalgrove Field (Oxon.) in 1643 and was buried without monument. This monument, designed for his grandson by Henry Cheere in 1743, has two cherubs, one waving a funny hat on a stick and the other looking tired, sitting on a sarcophagus which is surmounted by a large oval medallion decorated with a family tree rising from a spirited bas-relief of the battle of Chalgrove. Confusing, but as pretty and gay as a Christmas card. There is also a monument to Thomas Kempthorne (d. 1759) and wife, Anne Hampden, which has marble portrait medal-

lions and a garlanded urn. The mansion is alongside though almost hidden by trees from the church. It was, for centuries, the headquarters of the extensive Hampden estates which Hampdens and their descendants, Earls of Buckinghamshire, held from the time of Edward the Confessor. It is now a girls' school and, considering its long history, a somewhat disappointing building. It embodies parts from the 14th to the 18th centuries but now looks, with low battlements and muddy rendering, the large gothic revival building which it predominantly is. A tower known as King John's in the centre of the 60-metre-long south front, which is otherwise mid 18th century, may be of the 14th century, while the Hall behind the tower has a genuine medieval roof, though this was brought from a former barn at Great Kimble. Over a kilometre south-east, on the axis of one of the great park avenues, is the Old Rectory, a 16th-century house refaced in 18th-century red brick and given a Doric porch. The Saxon earthwork of Grim's Ditch is well seen in the Park, most with its 2-metre-high bank and 11m ditch. Its line directly adjoins the drive to the House, though here the bank has been flattened.

Hampden, Little [11] Church, farmhouse and a few old cottages on a lane that climbs up to an overgrown common of beech and thorn high in the Chilterns; picturesque and popular walking country. The church is on a steep slope above the road, screened by a row of Scots pine with a backing of beech woods. It is of flint, patched with grey and yellow plaster and is very small (only 50 sittings). It has a nave, 13th-century chancel (rebuilt in 1859) and a 15th-century two-storeyed and timber-framed porch, which makes the whole look like a picturesque but primitive farmhouse. The interior has wall paintings discovered in 1907, which are mainly 13th century. There are

Saints Peter, Paul and Christopher, bishops and a Doom. In the chancel is a late 12th-century stone statuette of a bishop with crozier giving a benediction and under the 17th-century communion table is the original altar slab with consecration crosses. Opposite is the white plastered Manor Farm with weather-boarded barns. The lane past ends ½km north in a dusty car-park created in a little wooded clearing with a pub. From here there is a walk north to Wendover through mixed woods and then the purer beech-stands of the Chilterns scarp. To the south-west, across ridges and bottoms, another good walk is to Great Hampden.

Hanslope [5] The finest steeple in the county, a landmark from the M1 motorway and for miles around, calls attention to this interesting N. Bucks. village on its windy ridge in Midlandish arable fields, more akin to Northants. than Bucks. It has two parallel main streets and a number of stone buildings, but road widening and windy gaps have made it a place to linger less than it deserves. The church of St James the Great is of light grey limestone with lead roofs, and has a 12th-century nave (wide for its time), chancel with Norman chancel arch and wide 13th-century aisles. The chancel has blank arcades outside its south wall and a corbel table dotted with grotesque heads. The nave has 15th-century gargoyles and a bear (representing Nevilles) under its plainer parapet. The tall spire in crocketed Ketton stone was added to the five-stage west tower in 1409 and is grasped between four flying buttresses with crocketed pinnacles. It was struck by lightning and rebuilt a little shorter (its total height is now about 57 m) in 1804. There is a brass of Mary Hitcham (d. 1602) in an Elizabethan child's dress and, on the wall of the stair-turret, fragments of wall-painting where the Nevilles' bear with ragged staff appears again. Rectory Farm is in

17th-century stone with mullioned windows, and in both High Street and Gold Street are many more 17th- and 18th-century stone buildings, a number of thatched cottages, some plain almshouses of 1712, two early 19th-century chapels and, at the top, the late 18th-century Watts Arms with big blank arches like giant eyebrows. 2 km south, Hanslope Park, now a radio station, was landscaped by Repton at the end of the 18th century; trees hide its plain 18th-century house. At Tathall End, a separate hamlet 1 km east, is Tathall Farmhouse, stone-gabled and dated 1602 and 1625 with a square stone dovecote.

Hardmead [6] No village, only an isolated church and farmhouses and moats of once-important houses in the clayey upland of N. Bucks, towards the Beds. border. St Mary's church is small, of stone, with a clerestoried two-bay nave and a low embattled 13th-century west tower. The arcades and chancel are all Decorated, but the south arcade is early and the chancel late in that style. The font is elaborately patterned 15th century but much restored. There are some fragments of 14th-century stained glass in the chancel, a brass to Francis Catesby (d. 1556); a recumbent effigy and a background of books of Francis Catesby (d. 1636); a wall monument of Robert Shedden (d. 1849) by Gaffin brothers which has a relief of the ship in which he died searching for Sir John Franklin; and a late 18th-century organ. The Catesbys lived at a long vanished manor house near the Manor Farm. The family was nationally important until its implication in the 1606 Gunpowder Plot (*see* Gayhurst). The Manor Farmhouse is 1 km south-west of the church and is a 17th-century building of brick and timber-framing, much altered in the 18th and 19th centuries.

Hardwick [8] A village on a low hill; it has a square plan of streets with a central green. The church and manor farm are on the south side, the rectory to the west and the Bell Inn to the north. The church is of stone, the houses of mixed materials, many using stone in their base. Garden walls are commonly ornamented with fossils found in the Kimmeridge clay here. St Mary's church has a wide nave, apparently pre-Conquest, to judge from the double-splayed window above the north door. The embattled west tower of white limestone is mid 14th century. The church was restored and chancel rebuilt by G. E. Street in 1873. There is a monument of Sir Thomas Lee (d. 1616), with kneeling figures of himself, wife and 14 children. Outside in the churchyard is a monument to 247 men killed at the Battle of Holman's Bridge, near Aylesbury, in 1642. Their skeletons were found near the bridge and were re-interred here in 1818 by Lord Nugent, local historian of Weedon. Manor Farm is of early 17th-century brick and timber but the south front has a later moulded brick cornice and is faced entirely in headers, blue and red. The Rectory, which has a 16th-century core, was similarly refronted in the 18th century with blue and red headers.

Harleyford [4] (near Medmenham) A former manor and now a neglected, grand, mid 18th-century house in Thames-side lawns backed by beech woods. It is a squarish brick block of two storeys with a great bow of three bays to the Thames; a canted bay to the east and a pedimented projection to north; stone string courses at each floor level; a bracketed stone cornice; and a brick parapet decorated with stone balls and a hipped roof. In spite, or because, of all this it has a curious angularity and only seems happy against the simple long lawn and trees when seen from the west. It was built by Sir Robert

Taylor in 1755 for Sir William Clayton, M.P. for Blechingley, who made it his principal home. The drawing-room, behind the big bow to the Thames, has elaborate plasterwork panels decorated with tools of sports and arts. The landscape is attributed to L. Brown and is now maintained as a caravan park.

Hartwell [11] A Jacobean stone mansion in a landscaped park with its own early Gothic Revival church on the Portway. Meadows stretch north to the Thame. The manor was acquired by the Lee family through marriage with a branch of the Hampdens in 1570, and remained in the family for some centuries. The house and park were occupied by the court-in-exile of Louis XVIII from 1807 till 1814, and are now used as a girls' school. The Manor House is symmetrical, early 17th-century stone, square-looking and, in spite of large mullioned windows, solid. It is of two storeys with an attic hidden by a plain parapet, only relieved by stone vases on the slightly projecting wings. There is a central porch to the north which has ornate tapering pilasters decorated with fleur de lys, a visual pun on the family name. The original Jacobean house had long wings projecting to the south. The space between was filled and a new front added in the mid 18th-century. A new east front was also added with a central porch and canted bay windows. The grand staircase of the Jacobean house, decorated with figures on newel posts and smaller figures as balusters, is still there, but most of the interior was remodelled in the early 18th century and again later in the same century—lastly by Henry Keene, who built the church in the park. Many rooms have finely plastered ceilings and walls and good fireplaces, of the 18th century. The house is approached through an arch between noble mid 18th-century stables, and the surrounding park was redesigned by L.

Harleyford Manor

Haversham [5] Stone walls and stone cottages in elms and willows not far from Wolverton, whose visible overspill mars the western part of the parish. The church, manor farm and rectory, with the site of the old moated manor house, are tucked away in a little cul-de-sac towards the river. St Mary's church has an embattled west tower with late 12th-century base, 12th-century nave, chancel rebuilt in 13th century, and 15th-century aisles. It was severely restored in 1857 but some bench ends of 16th century and brasses of 1390, 1427 and 1605 remain. The best of the monuments is an early 15th-century tomb chest with a white alabaster recumbent old lady in a stone, crocketed and canopied recess. There is Powell glass in the chancel and north aisle. The Rectory is a chequered brick building of the early 18th century. South of Manor Farm is the moat of the former manor and a stone dovecote with a tiled cupola, dated 1665. At the north end of the village is Grange Farm, which has a late 14th-century hall and a doorway and window of the same century incorporated in later rebuildings and alterations.

Brown in the period when the formal gardens (seen in a series of paintings now in the Aylesbury Museum) were replaced by lawns, trees and a curved lake. The bridge over the last was formed from the central arch of a former Kew Bridge. The avenue across the park to the north is early 19th century, and the park wall to the road was rebuilt with giant local ammonites framed in flint and dated 1855. The Church of the Assumption stands on a little mound in the Park ringed with pine trees. It was built by Henry Keene in 1756 and is an important early Gothic Revival building but has been in a state of dangerous disrepair since John Nash wrote the first *Shell Guide to Buckinghamshire*, in 1938. It is at last being restored. It has an octagonal

body with a lacy fan-vault (collapsed but being replaced), apparently imitating the chapter house of York, with identical small square towers: that to east providing a diminutive chancel and that to west a porch and organ loft. The north and south bays of the octagon have rose windows; the others have tall windows under crocketed ogee arches. Details are incorrect, and all the prettier for that. On the lane to Lower Hartwell is what looks like a well-vandalized bus shelter. This is the remains of a stone pylon designed by Bonomi over the original spring which gave the place its name. Lower Hartwell and the nearby Upper Hartwell—both largely in the parish of Stone—are hamlets on lanes petering out in Thame meadows.

Hawridge [12] A scattered place on a high ridge. The parish church and only grand house are among chestnuts and conifers; smaller houses are spread out along the thorny common towards Cholesbury. St Mary's church is small, 13th-century in style, of cut flint with stone dressings and brick bands, completely rebuilt by William White (1856), who retained only the 13th-century font and some minor monuments from the old church. The adjoining manor farm, now called Hawridge Court, is a big black-and-white timber house in a moat with big black barns. Its site cuts across a prehistoric earthwork with a single rampart 5 m high and ditch 15 m wide.

Hazlemere [14] A parish formed in 1845 from scattered development along the Amersham Road from High Wycombe, on high ground surrounded by woods. It is now consolidated into a large northern suburb of Wycombe. Holy Trinity, its first church, is a small neo-Norman, white and yellow brick, building, with a nave of 1845 and a chancel and modernistic bell tower of 1958. In the churchyard are the graves of Philip Barnes (d. 1874), founder of the Royal Botanic Society, and Sir William Ramsay (d. 1916), discoverer of argon. Near the central crossroads is a County Library, by the County Architect (1977), with its friendly exposed timbering.

Hedgerley [15] A small village hidden in a fold of chalk hills and approached by twisting lanes through woods and small fields, a remarkable survival for a place so close to Slough, Gerrards Cross and Beaconsfield. A flinty Victorian church stands above the sinuous village street of old timber-framed or red-brick and tiled cottages. The church of St Mary's, in flint but with engaging patches of puddingstone rubble, is a complete rebuilding with Perpendicular-style west tower and Decorated nave and chancel by B. Ferrey (1852). Internally it is nothing special but has a few fittings from earlier churches, such as the octagonal font with Tudor rose, faces and flowers; a framed piece of red velvet said to have been given as altar cloth by Charles I; brasses of 1498 and 1540 (the latter a re-used brass of an abbot of Bury St Edmunds of 1312); a painting of 1662 showing the fate of those breaking the Ten Commandments; and a pulpit and reading desk made from 17th-century satinwood from a church in Antigua. In the village street are some 16th-century timber-framed cottages, now painted black-and-white and renamed 'Old Quaker's House', which face the early 19th-century

Hartwell church

Tudor-style brick Rectory. Up the hill is the late 17th-century 'Shell House', in soft red and blue chequered brick, while at the top the road unexpectedly widens to jump the M40 motorway.

Hedsor [14] A church and mansion hidden in a hill-top park above the twisting leafy Thames landscape of Hedsor Wharf with its few cottages in the valley below. St Nicholas's church has an attractive site with views over the Thames valley but little architectural interest. It is in flint with some

clunch with medieval nave and chancel and a bellcote. These were ruthlessly restored and a north aisle added by the 4th Lord Boston in 1862, leaving little but piers and arches, and then altered again in 1886. In the churchyard is a flat stone to R. Hyde (d. 1606), who 're-edifyed this churche' in 1575. The mid 19th-century Hedsor Priory near by contains fragments of the medieval manor house, but the main house was moved by the Bostons to a higher hill to the south, leaving the church as a park ornament on its own hill. The present

Hedsor House is a blancmange of Italianate and French chateau styles. Further north on Tower Hill is an 18th-century folly by an earlier Lord Boston, which has three flint towers and some walling designed to look like a ruined castle.

High Wycombe *see* Wycombe, High

Hillesden [7] An isolated hamlet at the top of a gentle hill with a broad view, and the finest Perpendicular church in the county. Little else beyond the vicarage, a large farm, cottages and traces of a former mansion. The church of All Saints has a remarkable pinnacled and embattled silhouette, only spoilt by the weaker and more conventional, but somewhat earlier west tower. The rest was rebuilt by monks of Notley Abbey on orders of the Bishop of Lincoln in 1493. Their work has lasted well and it is sad that their own abbey has disappeared. The work is 'an exquisite specimen of the latest phase of Gothic art' said Gilbert Scott, who lovingly restored the church in

16th-century glass, Life of St Nicholas ▷

◁ **Hillesden** church (*and below*)

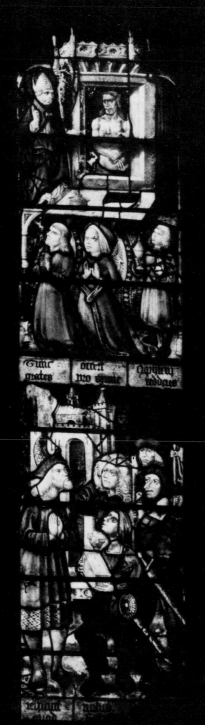

1875 and gave the north porch a vaulted ceiling and four pinnacles. He was the son of the rector of Gawcott and his visits as a boy inspired his love of gothic architecture. A drawing he made when only 15 hangs in the vestry. Exterior and interior are in finely cut limestone and there is embattlement all round and a prominent staircase tower, crowned by pinnacled ogee-shaped flying buttresses simply supporting a high pinnacle. The interior is light and harmonious. The nave has continuous clerestory windows and there are small transepts and a north chapel as long as the chancel. Arches and pier between the latter are especially graceful and there is a tall, coved, rood screen to the chancel and a panelled screen to the chapel. There is other good woodwork in the mid 17th-century family pew and the linen-fold panelled benches. Stained glass includes late 15th-century saints in the nine-light east window, 16th-century illustrations of the life of St Nicholas and in the south window of the transept, an acceptable pastiche of the 16th-century glass made by Burlison and Grylls in 1875. In the north chapel are two grand monuments, one to Thomas Denton (d. 1560) and his wife, which has alabaster figures on a chest and the other to Alexander Denton (d. 1574), with a narrow sarcophagus squeezed into what looks like a pedimented Renaissance fireplace but has another sarcophagus in place of its mantel-shelf. Other monuments are to Thomas Isham (d. 1676)—an oval cartouche framed in seaweed, into cherubs and skull—and to Sir Alexander Denton (d. 1740) and Lady Denton (d. 1733), with busts and obelisks on a white marble base, by Henry Cheere. Outside is a mutilated 14th-century cross. Beyond a blocked door in the red-brick churchyard wall is the site of Hillesden House, now remnants of three terraces and a pond. This was the home of the Dentons from 1547

to the mid 18th century. Sir Alexander Denton married a cousin of John Hampden and fortified the house for the King in the Civil War. He was, however, overwhelmed by Cromwell, the house was burnt down and Sir Alexander died in prison. The fighting is related in the Memoirs of the Verneys of Claydon. The house was rebuilt in 1648 and was later the home of Justice Denton, friend of the antiquarian Browne Willis, but this was completely destroyed in the mid 19th century and the church left with a lonelier silhouette. Now the approach road is again crowded with estate cottages of a prosperous farm, and pony jumps cover the site of the house.

Hitcham [14] A hamlet preserved by jealous landlords, and now by Green Belt controls, from the expansion of ever-popular Taplow and over-flowing Burnham, from which it is separated by a steep and well-treed valley. It consists of the church and Hitcham Farm, a Victorian mansion and the site of a former mansion where Queen Elizabeth I in 1602 and statesmen in the reign of Queen Anne were entertained. St Mary's church has an embattled Tudor brick west tower, 12th-century nave and 14th-century chancel and is in flint and stone. The chancel arch is large, round and simple. The Decorated east window is delicately shafted inside and has 14th-century glass with some large figures of angels on wheels and parts of four Evangelists in the tracery panels. There is more 14th-century glass in the north chancel window. The pulpit with carved panels and tester is 17th century. There are monuments to Roger Alford (d. 1580), with small kneeling figures; to Sir William Clarke (d. 1624), in white marble with recumbent effigy between framing curtains; and a First World War Memorial tablet by the architectural historian Banister Fletcher. Hitcham Farmhouse, an

early 17th-century building clad partly in brick nogging and partly in weather-boarding, stands between the church and the site of the Manor House, and with its barns makes a good pictorial group with the church. Nothing is left of the manor house where Sir William Clarke entertained Queen Elizabeth I and, later, Dr John Friend entertained Harley and Bolingbroke, except the extensive 17th-century brick garden walls, an iron gate and some good trees. The present Hitcham House is in a brick gothic style by T. R. Smith (1870).

Hoggeston [8] A small village in flattish clay fields with dying elms. It has a dull brown church, a red-brick Jacobean manor house, late 18th-century rectory and some thatched and whitewashed and red-brick and tiled cottages, and still shows signs of its once stockaded ring bank. The church of Holy Cross is of ironstone-patched creamy limestone, which sounds interesting but is drab, with a shingled broach spire over a north-west tower, nave with 13th- and 14th-century aisles, and a chancel rebuilt by William White in 1882. There is a stained-glass east window by N. Comper (1949), a recumbent 14th-century effigy (possibly of one of the de Berminghams who owned the manor from 13th to 16th centuries), holding a model chapel in his hands, the tomb chest of Elizabeth Mayne (d. 1599), and other Mayne monuments. The Manor House is Jacobean brick with blue diapering, some giant pilasters and a shaped gable obscured by a large chimney stack. Inside are a massive oak staircase and a panelled room. The Rectory, opposite the church, is a pedimented two-storey, red-brick house with arched door and windows to its tall ground floor, built in 1784.

Hogshaw [8] A pastoral, heavy clay parish with a tiny population in a few cottages and farmhouses. The site of the former church of St John the Baptist is south of Hogshaw Farm, which has old worked stones in some of its barns.

Holmer Green [14] A shapeless collection of red-brick houses and white bungalows in garden trees joined by way of Hazlemere to High Wycombe. The village green has a pond and pleasant flint-faced pub. Christina Rossetti lived with her uncle Polidori for many years in a Victorian house, now gone. Christ Church is a chapel of 1894.

Horsenden [11] A hamlet set in elm, beech, chestnut and sycamore down a dead end, isolated by old railway lines. Once on the old main route to Oxford, it has a few small houses and remnants of a moat which enclosed the manor house and church. St Michael's, of flint and stone, is only the 15th-century chancel of the medieval church plus the 2·5-metre-square west tower which was constructed from the stones of the decayed nave in 1765. The 16th-century chancel screen, carved with lions and roses, is now against the west wall. The chancel was lengthened by William White in 1869. The octagonal font is from the 1851 exhibition. There are a number of modest monuments to Grubbs, who held the manor from 1662 to 1841, including a diamond-shaped stone recording the death in 1666 of B. Grubb aged '143'. Horsenden House, a generous white-rendered, bow-windowed, house facing the church across lawns, was built in 1810 on the site of the previous Manor House owned by Sir John Denham, the Carolean poet who fortified it against Parliament in spite of being surrounded by Parliament-supporting families. He survived to sell it to the Grubbs after the Restoration. The grounds contain a large section of the former moat and an extensive fishpond. Near the church is a large, two-tiered, timber dovecote.

Horton [18] A scattered Middx. village in formerly flat, market-garden country now hollowed into large gravelly lakes and mounded to make giant reservoirs. The church of St Michael is central to Horton village but is alone and screened behind old brick walls. It is flint-faced, but has a Norman nave with an imposing Norman north door with chevrons and lozenge, four zigzags and knotted cable moulding inside a 16th-century porch, a transitional south aisle, rebuilt in 1876, and a stone chancel rebuilt in the same year. The Norman tub font has more cable moulding on the cup. There is a worn slab on the chancel floor marking the grave of Sara Milton (d. 1637), mother of the poet. John Milton lived here from 1632, when he left Cambridge, until 1640, at a house now vanished about ½km from the church and there wrote *L'Allegro*, *Il Penseroso* and *Lycidas*. There are some pleasant late Georgian houses near by.

Horwood, Great [8] A compact village on a little ridge in Whaddon hunting country; it is mainly of brick and tiled cottages though with occasional ones of plaster, or timber-framed and thatched. There is a particularly nice mixed group on the little rectangular Green, which is now a dusty car-park but was once the site of a weekly market, and another round the church, which is hidden behind the Crown Inn. A lot are of the late 18th century and were rebuilt after a fire of 1781. The village had another late misfortune when plague hit it as late as 1859. St James's church is of yellowy grey stone with lead and tiled roofs, and has a prominent embattled 15th-century west tower, but is otherwise mainly 14th century, though over-restored by Gilbert Scott in 1868. The nave arcades are tall Perpendicular and the south aisle has big Perpendicular windows. The chancel has piscina, sedilia and flowing tracery windows, the

four-light east window being especially good. There is a somewhat reduced 15th-century screen with traces of its original colouring and a brass of 1487. There is an early 19th-century Rectory; also, late 18th-century Crown Inn. The Congregational chapel of 1824 has a Doric pillared porch, original internal fittings and timber gallery. Manor Farm, towards Nash, is early 17th century, refaced with 18th-century panelled room and staircase with twisted balusters.

Horwood, Little [8] A village of winding roads in Whaddon hunting country. The church of St Nicholas stands high above the main road junction, with a 15th-century embattled west tower in large limestone blocks but the rest looking all of 1889, thanks to the overzealous restoration in that year by J. P. St Aubyn. Inside is an early 13th-century south arcade and Decorated chancel arch, early 16th-century painting of the Seven Deadly Sins and a 13th-century and fragmentary St Nicholas. The pulpit is Jacobean. There are pleasant 16th- and 17th-century cottages in timber-frame, brick and colour-washed plaster around, particularly on the triangular green on the road to Mursley. The only big houses are more remote and both of the early 20th century: Horwood House in a park, 1 km south-east, in light brick, symmetrical, neo-Elizabethan by Detmar Blow (1912), and Little Horwood Manor, to the north, built in 1938 in a pale imitation of Lutyens manner.

Hughenden [14] The manor house in a hilly landscaped park surrounded by beech woods in which Benjamin Disraeli, 1st Lord Beaconsfield, made his mid-19th-century mark. St Michael's church is at the side of the drive leading up to the manor. Of the medieval church only the 14th-century north chapel and its 16th-century arcading were kept in the rebuilding with

three-bay nave, north aisle and north-west embattled tower with pyramidal roof by A. W. Blomfield (1874–90). The 12th-century font and monuments in the north chapel were also kept, and these include a brass of 1483, the effigy of a 14th-century knight and three imitation 15th-century knights which were faked in the 16th century to give a spurious connection with the de Montforts to the local family of Wellesbourne—anyway worthy enough. In the chancel is the white marble memorial to Disraeli, Prime Minister 1868 and 1874–80, who died in 1881, erected by 'his grateful and affectionate Sovereign and friend Victoria R.I.', which has his portrait in relief by R. C. Belt. His body is in a vault under the north chapel. The chancel is separated from the nave by a low, open, wrought-iron screen and is deco-

rated with a painted roof by Heaton and Butler and stained glass by Willement. The present Manor House on a plateau above the church was the site of a plain brick farmhouse until 1738, when the former farming estate was converted into a gentleman's park. The original manor house was on another hill, and has vanished. Disraeli, who knew Hughenden from residence in his father's house at Bradenham, bought the estate in 1848 with help from the Bentinck family, and in 1862 had the plain house dramatically converted by E. B. Lamb into what Disraeli called 'Jacobean'. This meant the addition of angular brickwork, varied battlements and skewed pinnacles, plus the insertion of panelled ceilings even in the smallest spaces. Of the plain 18th-century interior only a fireplace

and a plaster ceiling in the Library were left. The house passed to the National Trust in 1946 and is a Disraeli museum. The Park is shared between the Trust and Wycombe Borough. There is a pleasant walk via Common Wood to Disraeli's boyhood home at Bradenham, 4 km away. To the south can be seen the red granite pillar 15 m high, erected as a memorial to Isaac d'Israeli by his grateful daughter-in-law in 1862.

Hulcott [11] Has a large rectangular green planted with lime trees and surrounded by a single lane along which are dotted manor house, church, farmhouse and cottages, nicely away from through traffic. All Saints Church is on the south side behind a 19th-century lychgate. It is a stone and tiled building, mainly 13th and 14th

104

century, with a nave, chancel and aisle and weatherboarded broach belfry, whose supporting timbers are exposed inside the church. The south aisle is wider than the nave and is of one Perpendicular bay running into an early 14th-century south transept. In the latter is a plain altar tomb, probably of Benedict Lee, Lord of the Manor (d. 1547). The Manor House is south of the church and contains a mid-17th-century staircase and stairwell painted with 17th-century representations of Hercules, Jupiter and Leda. West of the church is an overgrown moat and east is Church Farmhouse with an 18th-century brick front to its 17th-century timber frame.

Hyde Heath [12] (near Chesham) A common with small houses, probably an early squatting settlement, with larger 20th-century houses and bungalows in trees. There is a small 20th-century brick and tiled church on the common's edge. Off the lane to Little Missenden is 'Castle Tower', a grass-grown bank that marks the motte and bailey of a medieval castle.

Ibstone [14] A long village scattered around a rough common on a ridge. The lane along this connects the disparate elements of the village, the tree-shaded early 19th- and 20th-century villas at the south-east, the little side lane leading to the church and manor farm, then the long common and the increasingly close small cottages, mainly of the mid 20th century. The church of St Nicholas stands apart from all the rest on a flinty shelf at the head of the valley leading to Turville, surveying its beechwood-framed fields. It is small and simple, of nave and chancel of flint facing, roughly plastered over, and stone dressings. A small, weather-boarded bell-turret stands on the square shoulders of the prominent west wall. It has a Norman south door and a small Norman west window, a plain

three-light Early English east window to its 13th-century chancel and one more elaborate late Perpendicular south window. Inside is the exposed Perpendicular timber roof, a west gallery, a Perpendicular oak pulpit with arched panels and a simple Norman tub font. Manor Farm, a little below the church, is a 17th-century brick farmhouse with two original chimneys, much gentrified in the 20th century.

Ickford [10] A soft, homely village of thatched and timbered cottages, modern red-brown brick cottages, willows and dying elms in lush meadows near the Thame. St Nicholas's Church is large with plain Norman west tower capped with saddleback roof, late 12th-century nave and early 13th-century chancel and aisles. The pulpit with tester is 17th century and the communion rail 18th, and there is modern woodwork, including a canopy-shaped and tiered font cover by Canon Staley of Brill. The tomb chest of Thomas Tipping (d. 1595) has panels in low relief showing nine kneeling children, while strapwork round the inscription is decorated with little heads in Red Indian type headdress. Stained glass by N. Comper dated from 1919 to 1947. The Rectory has 16th-century, timber-framed and gabled wings, infilled in the 19th century. Seldon was a rector here on his way up to become Archbishop.

Ickford, Little [10] (near Ickford) A pretty smaller brother of Ickford to its west, full of timber-framed and brick cottages and willows and bridges. Two houses are exceptional, both timber-framed and colour-washed: the Manor Farm, 16th and 17th century, has arabesque wall-painting inside; and 'Close', 17th and 18th century.

Ilmer [11] Half-timbered cottages, Shell Demonstration farm with black barns and a few later red-brown brick houses hidden in

willows, poplars and sycamores in flat pastures behind the railway north of Princes Risborough. St Peter's church, a small grey stone building with red tiled roofs, has a simple 12th-century nave and 13th-century chancel, and a weatherboarded turret at the west end capped by a tall, shingled, late 19th-century flèche. Its whitewashed nave is separated from the richer chancel by a dark oak, medieval screen on a stone wall. The chancel is enriched with a stone reredos with inlaid cross in porphyry and marble dating from Street's restoration in 1860. In its north window are small carvings of the Trinity and St Christopher.

Iver [18] A large but compact village between the larger suburban settlements of Iver Heath to north and Richings Park to south, just kept separate by gravel pits and by meadows preserved by Green Belt restrictions. The small area around the church and near the bridge over the Colne, which is the boundary of Greater London, retains a historic, villagey feeling. St Peter's church, of mixed flint and pudding stone with stone dressings, has an embattled 13th-century west tower, a pre-Conquest nave extended by a north aisle of 12th and 14th centuries, and a south aisle of 13th and 15th, and chancel rebuilt in the 13th. Of pre-Conquest detail only a north window with roll moulding can be seen. 13th-century trefoiled-arched piscina and sedilia are exceptional; the font is a late Norman Purbeck marble tabletype; part of the 15th-century rood screen survives in the south aisle, and the pulpit is decorated with 17th-century cherubs and garlands. Monuments include brasses of 1508, 1604 and 1610; a complicated composition showing Lady Mary Salter (d. 1631) rising from a black coffin framed in cherubs, columns and pediments; another framed in columns and books for Henry Plant (d. 1784); and a marble bust of Edward Ward (d. 1838) by Chantrey. A wall slab in the chancel commemorates Elizabeth Kederminster (of Langley), granddaughter of the poet Waller (of Beaconsfield). There is Kempe glass of 1890 and 1902. In a wooded setting near the river is Bridgefoot House, a three-storeyed, early Georgian house in yellow brick with red dressings, with elaborate wrought-iron railings and gates, the home of the architect G. F. Bodley at the turn of the century. Across the village green from the church is the timber-framed Swan Inn with a long range of old brick buildings to its north. Up Bangors Road (towards Iver Heath) is the early 19th-century yellow-brick Iver Lodge and then Coppins, former home of Princesses Marina and Alexandra. 1 km further west is the splendid baroque brick, late-Wren style, Iver Grove, built 1722, rescued from near collapse by the Ministry of Works after the Second World War. At Richings Park, to south-west beyond the leafy Grand Union Canal, is the 18th-century Thorney House and a simple church of 1840. The Park, now largely a housing estate, contained a house of the Bathursts and was a haunt of Pope and other early 18th-century writers.

Iver Heath [15] A large suburban-looking 19th- and 20th-century village formed round a junction north of Iver, with old film studios and pleasant wooded parks. St Margaret's church on the Denham Road is a flint-faced brick building with a short south tower, built by C. Reeks in 1862 in the flush of Victorian expansion. The old Pinewood film studios still stand surrounded with steel hangars and junk, like a bombed airfield, on the edge of woodlands which are part of the County Council's Black Park 'Country Park'. Ratification of the agreements establishing the Irish Free State in 1921 was signed here.

Ivinghoe [12] A handsome village with a large church and good 17th- and 18th-century buildings along nicely enclosed curved streets. It is at the junction of the Upper and Lower Icknield Ways, with another old track through the Chilterns to the south, and was once a small market town. It now suffers the dust and dirt of the nearby cement works and too much passing traffic. There are wide chalk fields, south-east, and orchards to north, but drab houses and petty industries of Pitstone Green encroach to the west. St Mary's church is a large cruciform building of stone. The crossing tower is 14th century but the rest is mainly early 13th century though drastically restored by G. E. Street (1871), who destroyed much 15th-century detail and rebuilt both the porches. The nave has five wide bays, octagonal piers and large stiff-leaved capitals, and is well lit by the 15th-century three-light windows of the clerestory. These replaced a series of rose windows, which are still retained in the transepts. The tower was added about 1340 and given a copper spire later. Roof posts rest on grotesque-headed corbels and have wooden figures of Bible characters with, between them, larger angels with outstretched wings. The pulpit in dark Jacobean oak has a heavy sounding board whose supports are carved with figures in relief, one being of Jesus stepping from a coffin. Lectern and poppy-headed benches (one carved with mermaid and mirror) are 15th century. Internal arrangements were much altered in 1966 when the chancel was made a chapel, the altar was brought under the crossing and organ and choir stalls were moved to the west end. A number of brasses are set in the transept floor; one is of Richard Blackhed (1517) and his wife; those of the Duncombe family of the 16th century were formerly on altar tombs. To the west of the church is the handsome, dark red brick, three-storeyed 18th-century house now used as Youth Hostel and then the Old Town Hall, originally 16th-century timber frame and brick but much altered in 1840 when tall 'Gothic' dormers were added. The Old Rectory opposite the church is another 16th-century building refaced in 18th-century brick, but this is in a delightful Strawberry Hill gothic with a high stepped gable on its east wing. Vicarage Lane runs north-west to many smaller attractive buildings, particularly huddled round the Rose and Crown, but the lane is then spoilt by egalitarian modern housing in geometrical layout. At the end of the village centre Station Road has another handsome group of buildings clustered near the King's Hotel. Ivinghoe Beacon is a bare, sphinx-like hill projecting from the Chiltern scarp. It has an immense view over the clay plain and more intimate views adjoining woods and coombs. These were acquired by the National Trust from the Ashridge Estate in 1926.

Jordans [15] Known worldwide for its Quaker Meeting House of 1688 set in an orchard-fringed valley between the Chalfonts and Beaconsfield. It was built at the expense of Isaac Pennington's widow, following the Toleration Act of 1688, previous meetings of the Society of Friends having been held secretly in houses in the neighbourhood. It is a simple brick building with a hipped roof covering a one-storeyed chamber at the one end and an integral but two-storeyed caretaker's house at the other. Inside it has a low balustraded platform for elders and a timber gallery. In the lawns outside are plain headstones of graves of William Penn (1644–1718), Gulielma Penn, Isaac Pennington and Thomas Ellwood. Jordans Farm is one house where Friends met before the building of the Meeting House. It was a 17th-century building but has been much altered and is now a hostel. The large barn adjoining is said to have timbers from the *Mayflower*. Jordans village is a small 'garden-suburb' designed

Ivinghoe Church, 15th-century poppyheads

by F. Rowntree and begun in 1919, with red-brick Tudorish houses round a 'square' full of birch and Lombardy poplar. There is a pleasant walk to the Meeting House from Gerrards Cross by way of Layter's Green.

Kimble, Great [11] On the Upper Icknield Way, sheltered beneath the Chilterns' beech-wooded scarp with views over the Aylesbury Vale. Clusters of chestnut and sycamore have grown to heal the ravages of post-war main-road widening through the village. The area has been inhabited since Iron Age times and the name is claimed to be a corruption of Cymbeline, British king in Roman times. The church of St Nicholas is of flint with stone dressings, with tiled roofs, parapets patterned in flint and square stones and embattled 14th-century west tower, over-restored externally in 1876–81. Inside are 13th-century arcades

with octagonal piers, early 14th-century chancel arch, and a large Aylesbury-type font with fluted base and foliage-decorated cup. The striking east window glass in blue, gold, mauve and white is by R. Frankland Russell (1844). A framed copy of the report of parish overseers sets out the names of those who, in 1635, refused to pay 'ship money'. It is headed by that of John Hampden, and his trial for non-payment was one cause of the Civil War which so divided Bucks. A mound in the churchyard is an old barrow. Vicarage is by E. B. Lamb (1859), in a red-brick neo-Tudor style. There are small Iron Age forts of Raypit Hill in the Chequers Court estate and Pulpit Hill to the south-east.

Kimble, Little [11] Part of a joint parish with Great Kimble, though the village is distinct and even slightly larger than its neighbour, thanks to its own (timber) railway

station on the Great Western branch to Aylesbury. The church and half the village are on the Upper Icknield Way, in fact close to Great Kimble; the rest, bungalows, telegraph poles and elms, is mainly on the Lower Icknield Way north of the station. The church of All Saints is on a gentle slope above the old road approached through dark, formal, lines of yews. It is small, of flint with nave and chancel and two porches and a west bell gable and mainly late 13th century, though the churchyard approach and the heavy restoration of 1876 have given it the air, externally, of a Victorian chapel. The interior has a pleasanter and more medieval atmosphere with good timber roof and the early 14th century wall-paintings in the nave. These show a finely drawn St Francis preaching to birds; St George and a Doom (on the north); St Catherine, and a slim, dignified St Bernard (on the south). The chancel floor has a

block of 13th-century tiles of Chertsey type with secular scenes—the romance of Sir Tristram—strange in a church. The font is a plain Norman tub and the pulpit has 17th-century panels.

Kingsey [11] A small village islanded in flat land between the Thame and the Cuttle Brook, hence the suffix 'eye' (island). It has a small 19th-century church, one large 17th-century house and a few 19th-century cottages. It was transferred to Oxon. in 1894 but later exchanged for the neighbouring Towersey when the Cuttle Brook finally became the county boundary. St Nicholas's church is an angular rebuilding in vaguely 15th-century and earlier style, at the expense of the Wykeham family of Tythrop, using the stone from a previous church built in 1780. It has a south-west tower with an ill-proportioned broach spire and, inside, a wall monument by

Whitelaw to a Mrs Wykeham (d. 1823) and a Kempe window of 1901. Tythrop, the only large house, is plain, late 17th century, with simple 2½ storey elevations enlivened by colonnaded porches. Victorian accretions were swept away after the Second World War, when the house was restored, and the wealth of internal decoration, the grand 17th-century staircase with balustrades of flamboyant foliage and the 18th-century rococo plasterwork, were saved from demolition.

Kingswood [7] (near Grendon Underwood) A hamlet with a few cottages, the Crooked Billet pub and a Baptist chapel of 1851. Its woods are a relic of the medieval forest of Bernewood.

Knotty Green [15] A pleasant 19th- and 20th-century extension of suburbia from Beaconsfield along the road to Penn, of mainly modest

houses in dark brick between mature garden trees with a simple house by C. F. A. Voysey of 1907.

Lacey Green [11] Strung-out houses on a chalk ridge with a college-style chapel at the centre and a great smock-mill. St John the Evangelist's is a stone-dressed flint church of west porch, nave, apsidal chancel and two stubby transept-like projections. The main body is by J. Chadley (1825) and the chancel was added (1871) by J. P. Seddon in patterns of red and yellow bricks and bright red, yellow, green and blue tiles. In the nave are 29 18th-century armorial shields in stained glass. The windmill is mid 17th century, brought here from Chesham in 1821, and restored by the Chiltern Society in 1972–8. The Pink and Lily pub in Pink Road was a haunt of Rupert Brooke and friends before the First World War. He wrote doggerel here which has been proudly preserved.

Lane End [14] Large village, or perhaps a small town, with towny brick terraces and some rendered flint cottages strewn about bumpy tracts of gorse, bracken and thorn, birch, poplar, beech and ash. It was an early settlement of chair-makers and still retains old workshops, mostly converted to light engineering. The church of Holy Trinity is on the south side of a small rough common off the central crossroads, a largish brick, flint and Bath stone building by J. O. Scott (1878), enveloped in yew trees. It is in a vaguely 13th-century style, with a north tower, heightened and pyramidally capped in 1901. Roof timbers were brought from a 14th-century barn at Bisham. The Clayton Arms is a two-storey colour-washed building of the 18th century and some of the nearby cottages in the centre are of the same period. Most, however, are of the 19th and 20th, unenlivened even by fantasy. Moor Farm, 1 km south, is a late-17th-century house in flint and red brick. Lane End runs south-east to Booker, which has a small airfield for light aircraft, and then merges into suburbs of High Wycombe.

Langley Marish [18] Here a large London County Council estate of the 1950s has been added to suburban sprawl from Slough and a disused wartime airfield to devastate 5 sq km of Middx.-type market gardening land. In 1974 it was banished, with Slough, into Berks. Hidden in all this, however, is one of the most surprising and attractive churches anywhere in the Home Counties. The church of St Mary the Virgin, in St Mary's Road, is between two ranges of old brick almshouses with a few trees and a pub, and just north of Langley Road, which acts as a spine, if that is not too strong a word, to this jellyfish of a town. The church is architecturally chaotic but of attractive variety, with works of most centuries. To St Mary's Road it presents a buttressed and

battlemented north-east brick tower of 1609, while the main body and the south transept are in flint with stone dressings. The Kederminster chapel and porch are in domestic gabled brick. The use of heavier stonework on the main body shows where the church was partly rebuilt in the late 14th century. The nave is mid 12th, and the north aisle late 12th, century. Its original arcade is still represented by one heavy arch piercing the north wall of the nave, but the rest was replaced in 1630 by a colon-

nade of three pairs of Tuscan columns in oak. North of the chancel is a chapel separated by a Decorated arcade. The Kederminster Chapel was added to a south transept in the early 17th century and the former 15th-century porch was converted to an ecclesiastical library which is the chief glory of the church. There is a slender gothic arcade in Coade stone to the transept and chapel added in 1792, and the Kederminster Chapel beyond has a separate screen decorated with obelisks and strapwork across its top and panels painted like marble below, with a diagonal lattice of windows in between. Behind this the chapel is little more than a large family pew but it is covered with decorative panels, many filled with awesome 'eyes of God', and an east end emblazoned with heraldic achievements. From this a door leads into the churchyard and to the Kederminster house in Langley Park, long vanished, but the west door opens into an even more extraordinary room, the Library, decorated with over 250 painted panels in grey strapwork cartouches on black and red grounds, larger panels having plain centres and smaller figures of saints. Just below the ceiling are a series of landscape views of Windsor Castle and other places. The chimneypiece has a magnificent frieze and overmantel framing Kederminster Arms. The library itself contains 250 Latin works and a book of herbal remedies by the Kederminsters. The collection includes the illuminated mid-12th-century 'Kederminster Gospels', now on loan to the British Museum. The church also has Royal Arms of 1625, an ogee-headed rood screen, a carved pulpit of 1609, and a number of monuments to Kederminsters of 1599 and their successors of the 18th and 19th centuries, the Harvey family. In the churchyard's south-east corner is the grave of the artist Paul Nash (d. 1946) beneath an inscription 'Whatever things are lovely, think on these things'. The five-gabled almshouses were founded by the Kederminsters in 1617. The slightly larger range to the north was founded by Seymours and built near the end of the 17th century. In Langley Park the present yellowish, ashlar-faced house was built for the 3rd Duke of Marlborough by S. Leadbetter about 1755. It is about 1 km north, whereas the vanished house of the Kederminsters was nearer the church, perhaps in the moated site east of Middle Green. 'Marish' is not a misspelling of Marsh but a corruption of Marisco, the name of early manor-holders.

Lathbury [5]

In meadows and trees across the Ouse from Newport Pagnell. A short stone-walled lane leads from farm buildings on the main road, past a few brick and stone houses, to a stone church and a stone house near the river. The church of All Saints has a battlemented low west tower, aisled nave and lower chancel, built mainly of limestone but with ironstone battlements and gargoyles and ironstone patches in the limestone that give it the friendly but alert look of a good springer spaniel. The body is 9th century but little of this save a windowhead above the south arcade can be seen, since so much has been rebuilt. However, the bowing of nave walls betrays the narrow nature of the 9th-century walling. The south arcade is late 12th century, though the south aisle was rebuilt about 1300. Its massive central pier has a square capital carved with dragons. The north aisle was added about 1340 and the chancel and chancel arch were rebuilt about the same time. The double-basined piscina with trefoiled arches and the sedilia are late 14th century. The black-and-white marble floor of the chancel is an unusual late 17th-century memorial to a child of Sir H. Andrewes, whose family and descendants held the manor from the late 16th century to the present. The ashes of one descendant, Baron Uthwatt of Lathbury—known to town planners for his Commission's report on land compensation problems—are buried in the chancel. Lathbury Park, the plain but handsome L-shaped stone-faced house of 1801 by the river, replaced the Manor House rebuilt by the Andrewes in the mid 17th-century. The only other house of interest is the Rectory, in early 18th-century chequered brick.

Latimer [12]

Tiny village in the upper Chess valley. Part is whimsical 17th- and 18th-century cottages round a tiled pump on a triangular green in the side valley leading into Herts., and part Victorian romantic park, house, and church on a hill with views over both valleys. In the park is Latimer House, the former house of a branch of the Cavendish family, Lords Chesham, and the site of a house where Charles I and Charles II stayed. It is on the crest of the swelling parkland hill with the River Chess below dammed to make a long tree-fringed lake, and was rebuilt by Blore in 1863 as a large Tudor-styled mansion of red brick with stone dressings. It is now a college of the Ministry of Defence. The nearby church (St Mary Magdalene) was rebuilt earlier, in 1841, for the 1st Lord Chesham, but this in turn was rebuilt by Sir George Gilbert Scott in 1867 in red brick with a small, spired turret, angular and ugly. The main interest of the interior is in memorial windows to the Cavendish family by Powell, Clayton and Bell, Woodridge and Kempe. More attractive to look at is the former Rectory, which is in 18th-century red-and-grey brick with red-brick fringes to windows. Latimer is named after the family which was granted the manor by Edward III and, like Chenies, it was originally called Isenhampstead. The two villages have a largely common landscape with pretty walks between.

Lavendon [2]

The most northerly parish in the county, 80 km from London and in character more of Beds. and Northants. than Bucks., with its wide fields and old stone buildings. It has a main-road feel to it, thanks to lengths of red-brick houses at unexpected places along approach roads and traffic on the dog-legged street pattern which makes the place seem larger, dustier and redder than it should be. The church of St Michael is noisily placed between two bends at the centre. It is of stone with an unbuttressed west tower, early 11th century at its base but with embattled 15th-century top, the nave and chancel of the early 11th century. The arcades are late 12th century and have sturdy round pillars, square abaci and unmoulded pointed arches. The south arcade has grotesque heads on the corner of the abaci. There is a bearded 14th-century head on a bracket in the chancel and four brasses dated from 1654 to 1690. Good mid-19th-century glass. Up a cottagey lane to the north is the site of Lavendon Castle—extensive earthworks of a motte and three baileys now occupied by a stone farmhouse. To its east is Uphoe Manor House, a much-altered 17th-century stone building in a moat. Near Warrington is Lavendon Grange, a stone house of about 1625. This is within the site of a Premonstratensian Abbey, founded in the 12th century and suppressed in the 16th, of which only traces of a moat remain.

Leckhampstead [5] An isolated leggy village of four different 'ends', with buildings in limestone, brick, half-timber and thatch or tile. The church of the Assumption is in the middle, near a stream and a disused mill. It is of stone with a west tower, 13th century at base but embattled 15th century on top, and a body with considerable Norman remains. These include a 12th-century arcade and two doorways. The south doorway has shafts whose capitals have carved birds diving earthwards. The tympanum, decorated with intertwining dragons, does not fit and may be older. The chancel has Decorated piscina and sedilia. Nave arcades bear traces of 13th-century paintings in which it is possible to read 'Hic sedet Isabella'. The 12th-century font was recut in the 14th century and given carved panels of Jesus on the Cross, St Catherine, Jesus and Mary, roses and a dragon. There is a large recumbent knight in early 14th-

century chain armour and a brass of Reginald Tylney (d. 1506). The cottagey white-painted Manor Farmhouse south of the church is of the 17th and 18th centuries and is approached by a bridge of three stone arches. At South End is the stone and tiled 17th- and 18th-century Home Farm with an arched fan-light to its central door.

Lee (or **The Lee**) [11] Small village on sinuous lanes, with a well-planted triangular green and much-altered manor house and two churches in one churchyard. Not far away are larger, more mundane settlements of small houses and bungalows which make Lee Common and Ballinger Common. Intervening land is filled with beech and yew woods more typical of Chilterns proper. The Lee itself has a curiously suburban air, but this is due less to the incursion of bungalows than to insensitive alterations to the manor, and oversensitive attention to other houses around. In part also, to the new church of St John the Baptist. This was built by Augustus Frere in an Early English style but in soapy red brick and was extended and embellished in Edwardian style by S. F. Prynne in 1911 for the Liberty family, the silk-printers and Regent Street furnishers, who then lived at the manor. The old church is still there, hidden behind the nave of the new. It is a simple stone rectangle with tiled roof containing nave and chancel, with heavy buttresses at the corners and a prominent porch. It has a three-light 13th-century east window and piscina and sedilia 'borrowed' by the new church and then replaced here by the Libertys. Beyond, at the Church Farm with its nice barns, one is back in the country. The Manor House has long historical associations, particularly with Plaistows whose memorials can be seen in the old church, and with the more recent Libertys but is otherwise of little interest. On a bend in the road south is a staring-eyed,

wooden figure of Admiral Howe, formerly the figurehead of the 1860 ship of that name. It was set here by one of the Libertys while other timber from the ship was used in the rebuilding of the Regent Street shop in the 1920s.

Lillingstone Dayrell [4, 5] Has no village, just a pub and a few cottages on the Towcester Road and the church and chief house in park-like fields. The church of St Nicholas is of grey stone with 11th-century nave and 13th-century west tower and chancel. North aisle added by G. E. Street (1868). The tower has a flat top with roof tight against the belfry windows and only just clearing the high tiled roof of the nave. The south porch has stone tiles, not commonly used in Bucks. The chancel is dominated by the centrally placed tomb chest of Paul Dayrell (d. 1571) and his wife. He is in knight's armour and their ten children are on the sides of the tomb, which is seen before the altar, framed by the depressed 11th-century chancel arch of large unmounded stones. The sanctuary has some 13th-century embossed tiles and on the south the plain tomb chest of an earlier Paul Dayrell (d. 1491) and his wife with two finely drawn brasses. There is also a headless brass of a late 15th-century priest. The church was extended, restored and given expensive woodwork, tiles and stained glass by G. E. Street in 1864 and later. Lillingstone House in the adjoining park is early 19th century, of yellow brick. The old Manor House was closer to the church. Tile House, 2 km away and bordering the park of Stowe, is large, of red brick, gabled and turreted neo-Elizabethan; Old Tile House in the same park is a more sober brick house dated 1693, but still using English bond. At Chapel Green on the Northants. border was another medieval church, later converted to cottages. This disappeared in the extension of a war-

Lillingstone Lovell

Roger Hunt (d. 1473), Thomas Malyn (d. 1536) and John Uvedall (d. 1611), and memorial tablets to Sir William Prichard (d. 1704), founder of adjoining almshouses, and to Thomas Uthwatt (d. 1754). Between the church and the Manor House are almshouses built for Sir William Prichard. The dwellings are of single storey but have a raised two-storey centre which acted as a school house. The ends and the raised centre have double-curved gables and the central door has a shell hood. The Manor House is of $2\frac{1}{2}$ storeys in creamy limestone, glowing after its recent restoration, five bays wide with a central pedimented and pilastered central doorway. Symmetrical stone stable ranges frame the approach from the west. The Grand Union Canal sits quietly in a cutting between the church and some old manorial fishponds north of the house. Great Linford Wharf still has picturesque stone warehouses and pub.

time airfield which is now the Silverstone motor-racing circuit, largely in Northants.

Lillingstone Lovell [5] A church and a few houses along a stream but on high ground. (Though on the Northants. border it was a detached parish of Oxon. until 1844.) The church of the Assumption forms a nice group, with its former Rectory, a Georgian stone building on the edge of pastures. It is largely Early English and Decorated, with a south porch of 1639, but was over-restored in 1891 when internal plaster was scraped off. It has an early 13th-century west tower with a saddleback roof. In spite of the 19th-century restoration the interior retains 18th-century box pews, a two-tier Elizabethan pulpit, 17th-century communion rail and reredos panels with the Lord's Prayer and Creed between Corinthian columns. There are 13th-century piscina and sedilia in both north and south chapels, two brasses of the 15th

century and one of the 16th, and a monument to a Mrs Wentworth (d. 1768), an urn on an obelisk in white and pink marble.

Linford, Great [5] The most attractive village in the Milton Keynes New Town; it is being preserved as such. Stone, brick, tiled and thatched cottages lead to a formal group of stone church, stone manor house, stables, barns and almshouse—an island of picture-postcard scenes in many hectares of raw new housing. St Andrew's church has an embattled west tower and Decorated windows. It is an early 14th-century limestone building but was stuccoed over in Georgian times. It retains the simple pulpit, box pews and panelling, the widened chancel arch and the occasional round-headed windows—features added in the early 18th century which were left when the church was re-gothicized in 1884. It has no east window but there are two Kempe windows on the south side. There are brasses to

Linford, Little [5] At the beginning of this century nothing but a small 13th-century church in the park of large 17th-century house watered by a spring on the slope above and almost surrounded with Ouse water meadows. Now the large house has gone, water meadows are laid waste as gravel pits, the spring has been culverted and large new housing estates, escaping from the Milton Keynes New Town across the Ouse, cover part of the park. The church is still a charming example of a simple 13th-century country church: of rubble with limestone dressings and some clunch, of nave and chancel, with original twin bellcote over the triangular gable end of the nave. The interior is slightly eccentric as one arcade is of two 13th-century bays with circular piers and the other of three 14th-century bays with octagonal piers. Chancel and north aisle were largely rebuilt by the Knapp family (of the Hall) in the late 19th century. Knapps are commemorated by a number of wall tablets, including two of the late 18th century by R. Westmacott Sen. The Hall was demolished in the 1950s and replaced by a small neo-Georgian house with porch and windows too big for its pretensions.

Linslade [8] Transferred to Beds. in 1965, since it had by then become the railway-end of larger Leighton Buzzard across the River Ouzel. Old Linslade is still a small place near river and canal, secluded by the Midland Railway viaduct on the present Bucks. border. It has a few old houses, such as the red and grey brick 18th-century Manor House, and its original parish church of St Mary. This is of mixed limestone and ironstone of 12th-century origin, as can be seen in the chancel arch and the circular font with its frieze of grotesque figures, but was converted by later additions and alterations with indifferent Decorated and Perpendicular details. It was expensively restored in 1898 but gradually ceded its functions to the larger red-brick church of St Barnabas, built in Linslade New Town by B. Ferrey (1848).

Little Brickhill, *see* Brickhill, Little

Little Hampden *see* Hampden, Little

Little Horwood *see* Horwood, Little

Little Ickford *see* Ickford, Little

Little Kimble *see* Kimble, Little

Little Linford *see* Linford, Little

Little Marlow *see* Marlow, Little

Littleworth [14/15] (near Burnham) A small settlement on the edge of clearings in the beech-wood country near Burnham, round a rough wooded common. It has an appropriately named and friendly pub, The Jolly Woodman; a small 19th-century church; a few cottages; a primary school, and a lodge

Great Linford

to Dropmore Park. St Anne's is a small flint church with brick bands, tile-hung bell-turret and timber-framed west gable in a 14th-century style by William Butterfield (1866). A north transept was added in 1877. Inside are a frieze of red and grey bricks, a scissor-braced roof and an east window by A. Gibbs (1866). Oak Lodge, near the primary school, is of timber and a 19th-century mixture of re-used antique carvings. Dropmore House, to which it led, is hidden in trees and security fences and is in the parish of Taplow.

Long Crendon [10] A large picture-postcard village on a rise. Really a collection of 'Ends', so called in this part of Bucks. because they are groups of houses and cottages which have grown up away from the through-ways of the place (as at Haddenham), the people who lived in them being engaged in small industries or other self-contained occupations with no need for constant contact with the

outside world. The best parts are tied together by a winding High Street, which gives the 'Long' to the name and is lined by tight groups of colour-washed and tiled or thatched cottages. The Manor of Crendon, later divided into three, was given by William I to Walter Giffard, afterwards Earl of Buckingham. He made Crendon his chief manor and the centre of a great park for 'beasts of venery' on the edge of Bernewood Forest. He is supposed to have built a castle on Cop Hill. The 3rd Walter Giffard founded the Augustinian Abbey of Nutley (now Notley) in 1162, and the family founded the predecessor of the present church. In medieval times the place was much more important as a market town and wool trade centre. The Court House, close by the church, was the Staple Hall for the storage of wool. Crendon was also a centre of lace-making, like many N. Bucks. villages, and, from the 16th century, an important needle-making centre. The needle-makers did not adopt machinery, and the trade migrated to Redditch in the mid 19th century, though specialized types, such as sail-making needles, were still made here till the end of the century. The Court House has a limestone ground floor and oversailing timber upper floor of one large room and one small room under an open timber roof. It was restored by C. R. Ashbee before its acquisition by the National Trust, and was the first building to be acquired by the Trust (1900). St Mary's church is an imposing cruciform building in grey stone with tiled roof. It has prominent Perpendicular crossing tower and a pleasing air of solidity with consistent design in spite of its long history. The nave arcades and south aisle, the crossing and the lower part of the central tower, the north transept and the chancel were rebuilt in the 13th century. The north aisle was widened and the north transept extended in the 14th. The latter was given a window of five ogee-headed lights and a ten-spoked wheel, a pattern adopted in 19th-century restoration for the chancel's east window. South porch was added, south transept extended and south aisle windows rebuilt in the 15th century and the chancel roof of arched and wind braces was added in the late 15th century, though this was plastered over in Queen Anne's day and then uncovered again in 1928. The west porch and the upper stage of the tower were added in the 16th century. Screens to the transepts and the communion rail are 17th century, the font is a late 14th-century octagon, and there are 14th-century tiles from Penn in the sanctuary, some plain black and some with yellow slip on red ground. One is decorated with a rabbit. Though burials are numerous and account for many uneven floors in the church, monuments are comparatively few. There is a brass to John Canon (d. 1460) and his wife, with half life-size figures on the nave floor, but the only grand monument is that to Sir John Dormer (d. 1626) and his wife (d. 1605). This has recumbent effigies, the knight in armour and the lady richly dressed, between pillars of black marble supporting a shallow arch and pediment. Much blue and light-red work is scagliola (plaster imitating marble). It is thought to have been designed by the Johnsons of Southwark because of similarities to their work at Wing. South of the church and approached by an avenue of elm and yew is the site of the oldest manor, marked by a modest 17th-century stone Manor House. Outside the yew-framed western gate is the Court House. From here the High Street starts its winding course past a series of attractive, often much-restored cottages, and farmhouses. The best of these (nearly all are delightful) are Madges on the north-west, and the Vicarage and Thompson's Farm on the south-east. Near the Square there is a Victorian school (now library) in red brick and a group of inset houses of the 1950s, not so agreeable. Long Crendon Manor is down Frogmore Lane beyond the Square. It has a 15th-century stone gatehouse on the street and through this, in a courtyard open to the west, is the main house, partly of stone and brick and partly timber-framed. The centre, which has a fine timber-roofed Hall, and the east range, are 15th century, while the range to west of the Hall is 16th. The stature of the house was much improved by Philip Tilden, who from 1920 on rebuilt the central bay of the Hall as a main entrance as well as the courtyard stair-turrets, and made other additions and embellishments, including 15th-century woodwork from Kent and later work from Oxon. It is now difficult to untangle old from new but together they make picturesque architecture which cannot be surpassed in the county. At Lower End is another collection of old houses, as attractive as most in the High Street.

Longwick [11] A ribbon of development joining several farms, a number of modern houses, a few dissenting chapels and one nice pub, The Red Lion. There is no church; the parish church is at Ilmer.

Loudwater [14] Is the eastern tail of High Wycombe. The valley bottom is full of furniture factories, paper mills, motorway viaducts and small houses overlooking a once pleasant valley. Made a separate ecclesiastical parish in 1866, but as early as 1788 had its own brick church. St Peter's retains the original plain rectangle with its two hipped-roof extensions housing little columned galleries inside. A chancel, in an insensitive gothic style, was added by G. H. F. Prynne in 1903.

Loughton [5] A scattered village with patches of bad development but mainly attractive clumps of stone and old and new brick and timber buildings. The church of All Saints is central and commanding for it stands on ground above the twisted local lanes. It has a pleasing texture of limestone rubble outlined in stone dressings. Its heavily battlemented west tower is crudely but endearingly buttressed, with one of the buttresses, added in the 19th century, running right across the Perpendicular west window. The interior is mainly Perpendicular in style. The roof has moulded beams and carved bosses. There is a small brass to an early 16th-century priest and a 17th-century painting of Jesus at Emmaus attributed to a 'Gonzales'. Near the church are a late Georgian three-storeyed house with a Tuscan porch, and a Regency stuccoed house. The Manor House and some thatched and heavily buttressed cottages are half a kilometre west, facing a green hidden from the rest of the village by willows along a little stream. The main house is stone gabled, of early and late 16th century with a two-storeyed porch.

Long Crendon: the Court House

Among the modern ribbon development along Watling Street are two 18th-century inns, The Talbot and The Fountain, but both have been much altered.

Lower (or **Nether**) **Winchendon**
see Winchendon, Lower

Ludgershall [7] A remote and curiously spacious village spread out round a square of lanes with wide grass verges, in flat country. There are small groups of old buildings round the church, and on Salter's Lane on the route to Wotton. Up to the mid 19th century it must have looked the unfinished

medieval settlement of limestone and timber-framed buildings which it basically was. But then came the railway with a station (now gone) and there followed intemperate infilling right down to the 1960s (and unfortunately latterly under the county's planning control). The infill is mostly housing, but a chapel of 1844 rebuilt in 1904 and a memorial hall of 1923 do no more credit to the place. St Mary's church is an untidy-looking but nicely textured building of limestone rubble with stone dressings, once plastered over. It has a squat tower, low lead roof to the nave and steeper and

higher tiled roof to the chancel, and a prominent porch. It looks mainly Decorated but has its tower partly embedded in an earlier nave. Inside are a wide early 14th-century chancel arch and piers in the nave decorated with heads and busts. One on the south side has jovial peasant faces and interlinked arms (like ones at Bloxham, Oxon.). The font is of simplified Aylesbury type with a fluted base and bowl banded with beads. The plain tomb-chest in the chancel has three brasses commemorating Anne Englishe (d. 1565) and her daughter and granddaughter. George Grenville, Whig Prime

117

Ludgershall

Minister 1763–5, is buried on the south side. The Rectory has a neat 18th-century front to a lower, L-shaped, 17th-century building. Other good buildings are Small Farm, formerly the Five Bells Inn, which has lath and plaster infill to a 16th- and 17th-century timber frame, Petty's Farm on the Green and Kingham's Farm in Salter's Lane.

Luffield Abbey [4] A small, almost uninhabited, anomalous parish in the tip of the county against Northants. Most of the parish, with the site of a Benedictine priory founded in the 12th century and suppressed in 1494, is in Northants., and under the Silverstone motor-racing circuit. (*See also* Lillingstone Dayrell.)

Magiovinium [8] (near Fenny Stratford) A Roman staging-post identified in the Antonine Itinerary as being between Watling Street and the adjoining River Ouzel, i.e. close to Fenny Stratford in the parish of Little Brickhill. The site of a Roman fort of Claudian times (early 1st century) has been found

adjoining the route of the A5 diversion constructed to avoid Fenny Stratford.

Maids Moreton [4] Now more a pleasant suburb of Buckingham than the independent medieval village of a few years ago, for it has been joined to Buckingham by the planned expansion of the latter. Modern development is indifferent in design but in light brown brick and tiles which are melting rapidly into maturing gardens. The old village has a few pleasant grey stone houses and old cottages, and an exceptional church. St Edmund's is in limestone rubble with ashlar dressings with some roughcast, with lead roofs, all of the mid 15th century, and is one of the most homogeneous churches in the county. It was founded by the generosity of two Peover sisters (hence the Maids in the name) in 1450 and has an embattled west tower with deeply recessed windows, a wide aisle-less nave with large three-light windows, a chancel with five-light east windows filling the whole wall and two generous porches. Yet the interior,

owing perhaps more to whitewash and the varnishy smell of Victorian woodwork than to the brightness, lacks medieval atmosphere. There is much worth seeing: the elaborate sedilia with vaulted canopies; faded 16th-century wall-painting of the Last Supper; late 12th-century font with leaf band (only relic of the older church); the altar table dated 1623 with urn-shaped legs and dragons; and fragments of old glass. The most pleasing architectural details are the elaborate fanvaults over the west door, the vestry and over both porches. The north porch is additionally decorated with its own battlements and gargoyles. Outside, the churchyard too has lost atmosphere and looks suburban; too many gravestones have been tidied away in favour of roses.

Marlow [14] The happiest town in Bucks. in an amphitheatre of chalk hills running down to a wide reach of the Thames; a popular place of residence in 18th, 19th and 20th centuries, dramatized by its tall, stone church spire and the towers of its bridge above a roaring weir. The

church and bridge are both early 19th-century rebuildings of medieval structures which were for centuries isolated from the market area of the town on higher ground where the road from Reading to Wycombe, the High Street, met the road from Henley, West Street. Both these streets have splendid 17th- and 18th-century buildings. The cult of the picturesque, the increasing habit of seeking country retreats, then the coming of the railway from Bourne End, led to the filling of the river bank with miniature estates which joined the church and the bridge area to the market area, then spread on to the surrounding hills. All Saints, the parish church, is of light brick with red dressings, built by C. F. Inwood in 1832 with vaguely Perpendicular windows and gaunt porches. It was embellished by G. E. Street, who rebuilt the chancel in 1876 and replaced the internal galleries with nave arcades (1882). The slender crocketed spire was added by J. O. Scott. Inside, the chief monuments are from the older church on the site. There is one to Katherine Willoughby (d. 1597), which has small, facing, kneeling figures; one to Sir Miles Hobart (d. 1632), with a bas relief of the coach accident in Holborn in which he died; and a tablet to Richard Davenport (d. 1799) by Nollekens. There is also a tablet to Sir William Clayton of Harleyford (d. 1834) by R. Westmacott jun. The graceful suspension bridge with its twin towers was built by W. T. Clark in the same year and was so much admired that he was asked to build others: one at Budapest, which is much loved, and the bridge at Hammersmith, which is not. It replaced an old timber bridge which was on the other side of the church and had been approached down St Peter Street. St Peter's Street is twisting, picturesque, and more domestic than the straight

Marlow Place (*top*);
the High Street (*bottom*)

Marsworth

wide High Street. It leads from a number of neat Georgian and early Victorian houses by the river up to the intertwined Deanery and Old Parsonage, the former a red-brick three-storey house and the latter hiding, among 18th-century alterations, a medieval house part stone and part timber-framed with a 14th-century hall. St Peter's (R.C.) church, externally a somewhat clumsy essay in flint with north-west tower and broach spire is by Pugin (1848), paid for by the Scott Murrays of Danesfield, Medmenham. Internal detail and the adjoining school were also designed by him. Marlow Place, the grandest building in Marlow, was built in 1720 by Thomas Archer for John Wallop, Earl of Portsmouth, in red brick. Its central section has an elaborate doorcase and a wide pediment supported on giant pilasters. Further pilasters on the corner have capitals decorated with leeks. The house is too closely adjoined by a lumpish brick cinema. High Street leads north, wide and handsome, from the Causeway and the line of the present bridge, to the Market

Place passing the fine 18th-century End House, Brampton House and the Brewery Offices, and narrows slightly as it converges on the Market Place where the old Town Hall, now the Crown Hotel (a building in coursed stone by Samuel Wyatt, 1809), looks down the street. In the centre of this little triangular space is a stone obelisk of 1822 put up by trustees of the Reading and Hatfield Turnpike Trust. The trust improved the road via Henley so as to shorten the journey of Cecils from Hatfield to the spa at Bath and the road consequently became known as the Gout Road. West Street is part of this route and for nearly 1 km westward has an almost unbroken line of houses of charm and interest on a long gentle curve, a continuous pleasure to the eye. T. L. Peacock wrote *Nightmare Abbey* at no. 47. Further on, at Remnantz, a large early 18th-century house in yellow and red brick with canted windows, was the Royal Military College from 1799 to 1811. The long curve ends at Western House, dated 1699, with a shell hood to the door and, in its gardens, a pretty, pyramidally

roofed gazebo which marks the reverse bend in the street. Almost opposite is the grammar school founded by Sir William Borlase in 1624. The oldest portion in flint and brick has a projecting three-storeyed and gabled section over the main porch but has been extended in imitation in both 19th and 20th centuries. In a cottage with Georgian gothic windows (no. 104), Percy and Mary Shelley lived in 1817–18 and here Mary wrote *Frankenstein*. Down by the river is Court Garden, former Council Offices, in a pretty park, and there are some other old buildings along the road to Wycombe east of the Square, though most have given way to indifferent post-war buildings. In Trinity Road is the flint church of Holy Trinity by Sir G. G. Scott (1852), interesting only for the interior decoration of the chancel and for the reredos in alabaster, Caen stone and coloured mosaic.

Marlow, Little [14] A pretty group of stone church, brick manor house and pub and brick or timber cottages round a triangular grass and lime-treed space, wide Thames

Medmenham

meadows. The latter are neglected here and cut up by a large 'water-treatment station', which blocks the way to the willow-fringed river. But the village can still be reached by a footpath along the north bank from Bourne End. The church of St John the Baptist is in rough-plastered flint and has 12th-century origins, but details of most other ages. There are mid-12th-century south transept arch, late-12th-century chancel arch, Geometrical chancel windows, 14th-century west tower, 14th-century arcades and dormer windows in the nave which are 1902 replacements of original 17th-century dormers. There is an altar tomb with brass to Nichol Ledwich (d. 1430); an architectural monu-

ment, pilasters and gable, to James Chase (d. 1721); and fragments of 15th-century glass in the south chapel. The east window is by Heaton & Butler (1866). The large Manor House, behind well-weathered brick walls, has an 18th-century front and 17th-century gables. Inside is a staircase with arched screens to its hall. At Abbey Farm towards Wooburn was a Benedictine nunnery of which little but some 13th-century masonry incorporated in the Farm is left.

Marsh Gibbon [7] Mixed stone, brick and tiled cottages with a stone church and two stone manor houses, above the wide flat fields at the headwaters of the River Ray. It

is on the Oxon. border and feels more Oxon. than Bucks. in character. The marshy origin of the name is obvious: the Gibbons were holders of the manor in the 13th century. The village lost in recent years the great elms which gave the place its friendly, sheltered unity. St Mary's Church is of a cream-grey stone and brown tiles with an irregular silhouette of square embattled tower, shallow lead roofs to nave, aisles and transepts and a high-pitched, tiled, chancel roof. It is mostly 13th century. Capitals in the transepts have well-cut stiff leaves and stiff angels' heads. Perpendicular windows were added to the clerestory and a big Perpendicular window with panel tracery in the south transept. Major alterations were made in 1880 when the tower was rebuilt, with un-Bucks.-like pinnacles to its corners, and an aisle was added. Inside are simple 17th-century benches, a medieval stone coffin lid with foliated cross, a late Victorian reredos with Last Supper complete with food and pots, and a stained-glass east window of 1892. The major Manor House, near the church, is in a nicely textured stone. The four-gabled east front is early 17th century but masks a large section of mid-16th-century building with a two-storeyed bay window. A second manor, called Westbury, has another 17th-century stone house.

Marsworth [11] A village for narrow-boat lovers, at the junction of the main Grand Union Canal with its Aylesbury branch, and with the River Ouzel and the Tring reservoirs which feed its top levels. Canals and humped bridges have somewhat disjointed the village, as dead elms have disjointed the landscape of ploughed fields. The church of All Saints, the only building of consequence, is near the centre of the old village. It is of irregular plan and silhouette of mixed flint and clunch, part chequered. It has been badly treated but retains more interest and atmosphere than many which have been well maintained. The north side of the church, the present nave and chancel, was built in the 14th century as extension to an earlier church. The present south aisle and south chapel are on the lines of this church and were rebuilt in the same century. Then, in the 15th, the north side was widened to make the present nave and a tower was built at its west end. The church was, however, a poor one in a poor parish and was not improved by the botched repairs and alterations in 1828 and 1854. It was largely through the work of Vicar F. W. Ragg, from 1880 to 1905, that the church was saved from collapse. With the help

of his wife and local labourers he undertook a long and total restoration which, with what Pevsner calls 'proud and naïve ostentation', included building a new east window, remodelling the south chapel, redecorating the chancel, underpinning the tower, making chancel and other walls safe and jacking up the nave roof by a metre. Much detail, for instance in the chancel arch, was carved by Ragg's own hand. The present pulpit was set on a large 14th-century capital carved with angels and leaves, left over from this work. Monuments in the church include a brass to N. West (d. 1586), which is a re-used brass of a late 15th-century German priest and the tomb chest of Edward War, Serjeant-at-Law (d. 1586), which is decorated with allegorical reliefs and marked (north side) with a brass plate showing him on his death bed and signed 'Epiphanius Evesham'. The Wests lived at a manor house of which only the large moat adjoining Marsworth Great Farm survives. There are other attractive timber-framed farmhouses and cottages on Church Lane, which leads down to the canal junction. The Tring reservoirs are partly in this parish, though mainly in Herts., which makes a deep incursion north into Bucks. to the west of Marsworth. They now form a world-famous bird reserve which can be observed from the canal towing path and surrounding banks.

Meadle [11] An Aylesbury Vale hamlet in the large parish of Longwick with Ilmer (though closer to Monks Risborough than to either of the latter) made up of brick and tile or white paint and thatch cottages. Wooster's Farm has a large barn of cruck construction, rare in Bucks. John Nash the painter (1893–1977) wrote the first *Shell Guide to Buckinghamshire* here in 1936.

Medmenham [14] A Thames-side village with expensive houses in small riverside parks but with some

older flint, timber-framed, brick and mixed cottages on the lane which runs from the former ferry by the Abbey to the chalk slopes beyond the Henley–Marlow road. By the road is the church of St Peter, of flint and clunch with a chequered chancel and a plastered embattled west tower, overlooked by a beech-clad chalk scarp. There are traces of 12th-century work in the north and south doors but little of architectural interest. The stained glass in the east window is by Willement (1845), and there are modest monuments to Robert Scott (d. 1808), signed by R. Westmacott, and to J. M. T. Ritchie (d. 1940), with a bronze portrait by Kathleen, widow of Captain Scott. H. W. Caslon, last of a line of famous typefounders, is buried in the churchyard (1874). The church was expensively restored in 1839 by the Scott Murrays of Danesfield, who later paid for the new R. C. church at Marlow. The church and the small timber-framed Manor House are embowered in beech and yew but, seen up Ferry Lane, are dominated by the angular house and barns of Lodge Farm on the hill above. This farmhouse is 17th century, flint-faced with red-brick dressings and has tall gabled windows; its brickwork seems to have fascinated Pugin who copied some in his R.C. school at Marlow. Ferry Lane leads pleasantly down to the heavily hedged and fenced Medmenham Abbey, site of a Cistercian Abbey founded in the early 13th century. Of the latter only one pier survives above ground. The present house is partly of 1595, partly 18th-century gothic, but largely late 19th-century additions and alterations by F. H. Romaine Walker. Of this the 16th-century range overlaps the cloister and church of the abbey. 18th-century gothic additions were made when the house was rented by Sir Francis Dashwood of West Wycombe and used for meetings of the Hell Fire Club. Signs of their moral lapses translated into architecture were

122

◁ **Milton Keynes New Town:**
Fullers Slade near Wolverton;
(*and bottom*) the centre

Nash village centre ▷

swept away when the late Victorian stone gothic wing was built. The picturesque ruins still to be seen are of the 18th century, though mostly built from old material on the site. Adjoining the Abbey Park on the east is that of Danesfield, the home of the Scott Murrays, patrons of Pugin, and here Pugin made alterations and additions to the former house on the site. This was swept away for a huge 'Tudor' stone building of two courtyards, gatehouse and other towers, built for the railway king, Robert Hudson, by Romaine Walker in 1900. House and grounds and a further area of parkland north of the Hen-

ley Road are occupied by the Ministry of Defence. East of Danesfield is Wittington, almost contemporary with Robert Hudson's Danesfield, but in a very different William and Mary style, by R. Blomfield.

Mentmore [8] An estate village of brown cottages along a green with elms and chestnuts and the park of a grand Victorian mansion approached by wide chestnut and Wellingtonia avenues. The great house is a pastiche of the Elizabethan Wollaton Hall, Nottingham, and its towers are an important landscape feature seen

for miles floating like a mirage above its tree-capped hill. It was built in 1854 by Sir Joseph Paxton and his son-in-law, G. H. Stokes, for Baron Meyer de Rothschild, youngest of the three brothers who built in Bucks. Like Wollaton, it is in fine Ancaster stone and has similar angle towers, though with even more ornate Jacobean detail, and Paxton's modern improvements of copper casements, plate glass windows, central heating and his own ridged glazed roofing over a central Grand Hall, 15 m by 12 m in plan and 12 m high. Thick planting was done on the side of the hill from which the house rises, to give a background to distant views of the house, and most of the 3 km-square park was drained to nearly a metre deep by hand digging and steam ploughing before further landscape works were undertaken. Of the house Lady Eastlake said 'I do not believe that the Medicis were ever so lodged at the height of their glory'. Meyer was a great collector of French furniture but had no hesitation in having Louis XV commodes with marble tops drilled to take taps and converted to guest-room lavatories. Gladstone's daughter was rather shocked to find an absence of good books and only a few 'indecent' French novels. Meyer's only child married the 5th Earl of Rosebery, who shared with Meyer a passion for racing and carried on the stud at Crafton. The house remained in the Rosebery family till recently and its contents were dispersed in a splendid sale in 1977, after these and the house had been offered, at a price, to the nation. The Park is still pleasant, the fringes arable, the home section meadow, and the gardens modest and of little interest. The parish church of St Mary is tucked into the

north-east side of the Park. A late Norman building in an orange ironstone with grey stone dressings, it was over-restored by G. H. Stokes, who rebuilt the chancel in 1858. Inside it has a 19th-century whitewashed purity and an east window by Kempe of 1905. Almost lost in trees on the east side of the park is the handsome small Manor House of 18th-century brick.

Middle Claydon *see* Claydon, Middle

Milton Keynes [5] A small village in the flat clay fields of the Ouzel valley of whitewashed and brown brick cottages with some thatch, a good Decorated church and a handsome rectory. Largely because of its modesty it was chosen to give its name to the largest New Town in the county on whose edge it lies. The Keynes name is that of the family who held the manor in the

13th century, and was pronounced 'Kaynes' until the New Town came. The church of All Saints, the Rectory and most of the pleasanter cottages are up the cul-de-sac to the north of the attractive whitewashed and thatched Swan Inn. The church is in coursed limestone, has a chancel arch of about 1200 but looks, otherwise, all Decorated in style with flowing tracery and decorative mouldings which make it the best small church of this style in the county. The porch, which has side openings with little columns and traceried head, and the inner doorway, which is decorated with a line of ball flowers between the arch and the drip moulding, are especially good. The tower on the north side forms a transept; the south parapet has grotesques and gargoyles. Inside the nave is wide and well-lit from big three-light windows; the chancel has piscina and sedilia with ogee

arches on shafts and the north chapel has its own piscina and sedilia decorated with more ball flowers. There is Powell glass of 1864 in the chancel, a brass of 1427, and a handsome Royal Arms. Other fittings dating from heavy Victorian restoration are gloomy. The Rectory, opposite, is a handsome early 18th-century red-brick building. In its predecessor Francis Atterbury, Bishop of Rochester and political cleric, was born in 1662. The New Town has dealt gently with this pleasant village, adding to its centre only low mono-pitched bungalows and a community hall which have helped to make it feel even more homely.

Milton Keynes New Town [5] This was intended to be a new city by the end of the century and still could be if population and resources grew rapidly again, but it is more likely to remain a loose federation of Bletchley, Stony Stratford, Wolverton, New Bradwell and a number of old villages, with rather isolated housing estates scattered over the designated area of some 8,900 hectares. An attempt is being made to pull together the many existing settlements by providing one main shopping area half-way between Bletchley and Wolverton with 9,000 square metres of new shops together with a 'leisure complex', law courts, police headquarters, large new offices and also its own main-line railway station. Much of the central spine of shopping and a large lump of projected offices have already been built. The rest of the 'city' is designed to remain in discreet lumps with little green belts between, threaded with traffic routes and swaddled in trees. Much of the new design in the area seems bright, some brash and some even silly (see, for exemple, the Willen pumping station, Bletchley 'Leisure Centre' and street lighting at Wavendon Towers) but the New Town's designers are inventive. Their landscape design, and, still more, its execution deserve special praise and will make the area much more attractive, whether it is fully built-up or not.

Missenden, Great [11] Has a long High Street between steep beech woods ·and water meadows along the infant Misbourne but has been expanded into a little London suburb by the Metropolitan Railway, which reached here in 1892. The main street is still crowded with interesting buildings but the one large house, of Missenden Abbey, is isolated in trees and meadows at the south end, while the village church is now more isolated, cut off by a bypass on a little platform above the valley to the east. Missenden Abbey was founded by William de Missenden in 1133 and survived till 1534. The decayed estate was acquired by a London ironmonger, James Oldham, in 1787, who built a

Venetian-style house which he then converted to neo-Gothic with castellated walls and little castellated central pediment. The whole is now gloomily cemented over. This is on the site of the Abbey cloisters and incorporates two of the walls of the cloister, as well as a 15th-century roof (in the upper floor of the east range) of the Abbey dormitory. The church of SS. Peter and Paul is of roughcast flint with an oblong west tower in squared stone which looks down on the Abbey. Tower and church are long and low and were over-restored in 1900. The chancel has 14th-century piscina, sedilia and niches and a blank arcade on the north wall with detached shafts about 2 metres off the ground. The roof braces in the nave are carried on stone angels. The font has a Norman scalloped base but 15th-century cup. There are two 15th-century brasses and a number of tablets to members of the Bois and Dormer families: one to Lady Bois (d. 1638) by Nicholas Stone has a purely classical pedimented frame. In the High Street is a classical Baptist church, rebuilt in stucco and flint in 1838, a number of pleasant late-17th- and 18th-century houses in grey and red brick, and a brick library with steep mono-pitched roofs and internal timber lining by the County Architect (1970). At the south end of the village is the County Secondary School, completed in six months in 1955 with steel-framed assembly rooms and brick classrooms, whose simplicity has been lost in later additions.

Missenden, Little [14] A prize beauty spot of a village in the Misbourne valley. In spite of being in 'Metroland' it has been bypassed by both railway and main road and saved from over-development. Brown brick houses and grey church, with beech, yew and garden trees are among water meadows with watercress and hazel hedges. The church of St John the Baptist is charming and

historically interesting but architecturally modest and retiring and almost in the garden of the manor houses. It has an Anglo-Saxon core with unmoulded chancel arch south arcade cut with unmoulded arches in the 12th century and north arcade built a bit later in the same century. The chancel is largely 13th century with a three-lancet east window. The north chapel was added in the early 14th century and timber south porch in the 15th. The exterior of the south aisle was rebuilt in brick and a dormer window added to the nave in the 18th century. A new vestry is to be added on the north side with a steep hipped roof with stucco finish between stone quoins and Georgian windows, designed by Q. Terry (1977). Inside are attractive odd views, through the rough arcading, of nave roof timbers and 13th-century and later wall paintings uncovered in 1931. The most complete is the late 13th-century figure of St Christopher with the Child Jesus and fish around his feet. The font has a simplified Aylesbury pattern with fluted base and tub decorated with leaves. The Manor House is mainly Jacobean and has a fine staircase of that time. The south front to the house was added in the late 17th century. Missenden House is in red and grey brick, dated 1728, with canted bay windows and broad central door. Little Missenden Abbey is a picturesque neo-Tudor house by W. H. Seth-Smith.

Monks Risborough *see* Risborough, Monks

Moulsoe [5] A small village with some timber-framed thatched and cob cottages with steep roofs near the church and, beyond, some less attractive later houses in brown brick. From the church porch one can look over many kilometres of Northants. and the Ouse valley with fields of rape and hedgerows with dying elms. The church of the Assumption is large for this small place. It is in a yellowy limestone rubble with stone dressings and has a west tower, with Decorated flowing tracery at the middle stage and Perpendicular battlements, and Decorated nave, aisles and chancel. Inside, the screen is part 15th and part 19th century, with an ogee-headed entrance and there are early 16th-century brasses of a man in armour with figures about half life size, a French bronze tablet to the 2nd Lord Carrington, Lord of the Manor (d. 1868), and an alabaster tablet to Lady Carrington (d. 1879). In its churchyard is a late 19th-century enclosure with iron grilles for Carrington graves. On the London Road the tall, gaunt house, called Moulsoe Buildings, has one-storey wings curving up to a narrow main body, all of red brick.

Mursley [8] This was an important little market town in the 13th century; it is now a rural, fairly open village, with a medieval church at the centre, a cream-painted water tower dominating the north end and radio masts the east side towards the historic house of Salden. The church is of limestone rubble and the older cottages are in black timber frame with white plastering and occasional thatching. The more modern are in red brick. The church of St Mary is in a cul-de-sac crowded with incongruous, suburban-looking, upright houses. It has a stumpy west tower of 14th and 15th centuries, but the exterior looks otherwise Victorian from its extensive restoration in 1867. The nave and aisles are mainly 14th century but the chancel and clerestory were rebuilt in the Victorian restoration. The chief interest of the church is in its Fortescue monuments. Sir John Fortescue (1538–1607) was a distant relation of Queen Elizabeth, became her tutor and later amassed a fortune as Chancellor of the Exchequer. Much of this was spent in building a grand house at Salden. His monument is in a recess on the north side of the chancel and has

kneeling figures in painted alabaster. Below this is the black marble table tomb of his wife Cecilia (d. 1570), with a brass depicting her in rich brocades. Their son, Sir Francis, has an early 17th-century monument with kneeling figures on the opposite side of the chancel. East of the church is the Manor House, whose 17th-century chimneys stick up in clusters above its 18th-century, chequered brick frontage. The former, nearby 17th-century Mursley Hall was the home of the pill-manufacturer Thomas Beecham from 1881 to 1892. He left it to his conductor grandson who lived here for a short time after his marriage. The Fortescues' Salden House, where Sir John entertained Queen Elizabeth, is now represented only by part of the red and blue brick east wing which is built into the present Salden Farmhouse and approached by a long farm-track. It was built at the end of the 16th century round a courtyard with main fronts nearly 60 m long. The Fortescue titles became extinct in 1729 and the house was demolished in 1743. Traces of the terraces, marked by great yews, and fishponds are round the now isolated farmhouse.

Nash [5] A small village in Whaddon Chase hunting country, with a few old cottages, a small church and an early Baptist chapel, on a dog-legged pattern of old lanes. Buildings are of stone or brick and timber frame with some thatch but mainly tiled roofs. The church of All Saints is small with nave, chancel and bellcote, in a light brown stone with lancet windows (stained glass in those to east and west) and a long barrelled roof, designed by G. E. Street and built 1858–62, largely at the expense of the Cavendish family of Thornton Hall.

New Bradwell *see* Bradwell, New

Newport Pagnell [5] An old market town at the confluence of the Ouzel (here called the Lovat),

with the Great Ouse in the north of the county. It was, as Betjeman and Piper in their Bucks. guide of 1948 said, a 'small Midland town'. Indeed, it grew up along river and road communications which ran east and west and was bypassed by the London-orientated canal and railway. It was only with the coming of the motorway, and refugees from London and Milton Keynes, that the town took off to expand like other towns this distance from London. This expansion has distorted its former east to west pattern into dog-legged forms outlined with boxy shops, factories and houses with flat roofs, garish fascias and infill panels which subdued the mellow brickwork and older shop-fronts of the town. In spite of these changes, however, it keeps its small market-town air in the High Street, from the former Town Hall (on the west side) past the church tower (which dominates the east side) down to the stone bridge over the Ouse, and even in parts of St John Street and Silver Street which run off south towards the M1, London and Milton Keynes. Historically the town was important only in the Civil War, for occupation by Royalists in 1643 threatened Parliament's links with the north and had to be removed by a large force under Essex. For the following three years it was garrisoned strongly under Sir Samuel Luke, the original of Samuel Butler's *Hudibras*. The High Street has pleasant but not exceptional buildings. The former Town Hall looks its part though it was originally a British school. It was built in 1845 in yellow brick with a wide pediment supported by giant pilasters. No. 84 is probably the best individual house. It is in red brick with stone quoins and a fanlight and shell hood to its door. The Swan Hotel to the east has a stucco front of the early 19th century disguising its earlier origins, for it keeps its Jacobean staircase. Opposite are three buildings which illustrate the attractive variety of the street: no. 38, having exposed 15th-century timber framing; the White House, simple early Victorian with upper oriel window; and Barclays Bank, red-brick gothic of 1870. The High Street takes a sharp bend when it reaches the narrow lane to the church, which at this point is hidden by a foreground of low buildings, and is carried round the corner by the white-faceted front of an old ironmonger's shop. The street continues down to the stone-arched bridge over the Ouse of about 1810. Coming back from the bridge the church tower rises splendidly above the little 18th-century houses (and some nasty replacements) on the south side of the street. Set back from these is the second best looking house, later a county library, in late-17th-century red and grey brick with giant pilasters and heavy parapet. The church of SS. Peter and Paul is on a slight ridge above the High Street, between the latter and the River Lovat or Ouzel. Its graveyard has a long yew-lined terrace stretching north across a little iron bridge to a low tree-covered mound at the junction of the rivers, all that is left of the Paganells' Castle. The path back along the Lovat affords a sunny view of the church, battlemented and pinnacled all round. 'Very fair and like a cathedral' said Pepys of it in 1668. Fair it is outside and in and the most attractive large town church in the county. The early church was cruciform with a central tower but in the rebuilding of the 14th century the central tower was removed. The present broad west tower was built in the mid 16th century, while the pinnacles all round the parapet were added, with other alterations such as the rebuilding of the south aisle, by J. Savage in 1827. The north porch is of two storeys but the south porch and doorway have, in arches and blank arcading, the best Decorated details. Inside the church is long and wide, clear and bright with nave of six matching bays and

clerestory. The roof was rebuilt, keeping the 15th-century wooden figures of apostles, in 1934. The roof boards were painted a dark red, the bosses gilded, the 1870 chancel screen regilded and small Victorian Arms above the chancel arch repainted in bright red, white, blue and gold under the direction of Laurence King in 1957. Only new conical lampshades spoil the redecoration scheme. The chancel is somewhat obscured by the bright chancel screen and the resited altar but this is the weakest feature of the church, in spite of an east window designed by Street. The church is not notable for its monuments. There is one late-14th-century brass and in the churchyard is the tomb of J. A. Hamilton (d. 1788), with an inscription by Cowper, the poet of Olney. There are still a few pleasant buildings in streets running south from the High Street but the most notable structure can be seen from the churchyard. This is the Tickford Road Bridge over the Lovat, an exciting cast-iron bow of 1810 with delicate, decreasing circles in the spandrels and the oldest cast-iron bridge in the country in full use. In Tickford, near the Ouse, is a small wooded park which is the site of a Benedictine Priory founded in the 12th century by Fulk Paganell whose family gave their name to the town. A few monastic fragments are built into the present house whose garden contains an 18th-century stone obelisk and a grey brick gazebo by the river. New buildings in the town are generally depressing but there is a creditable Telephone Exchange in brick and slatehanging of 1968.

Newton Blossomville [6] A stone cottagey place in trees and stone walls along the south bank of the River Ouse, almost as pretty as its name, which it took from the Blossomvilles, Lords of the Manor in the 13th century. St Nicholas's church is by the river, behind a little green and almost lost in farm buildings. It is of grey stone with

lead and tiled roofs and has a narrow embattled west tower with higher stair-turret, nave, north chapel and chancel. The nave is of the beginning of the 14th century, the chancel was extended and north aisle added in mid 14th; the north chapel rebuilt in the late 14th and the tower and south porch added in the early 15th. Inside are an octagonal 15th-century font, a late 17th-century pulpit, 14th-century glass fragments in north aisle, an east window by Kempe and a wall tablet by Andrews of Olney, friend of Cowper, of 1793. Cottages and gardens here are pleasant but not of architectural importance. Newton Park farm buildings cover the site of the formerly important Manor House. Away from the village the land slopes up to seemingly endless, treeless, heavy clay fields.

Newton Longville [8] Was an important medieval village and still has a great many old cottages scattered in its modern housing estates. It is now somewhat overshadowed, metaphorically, by its large neighbour, Bletchley, and, more literally, by large brickworks between the two. Its second name derives from its double connection with Longueville in Normandy, for its manor was given to the Norman Abbey of that name by Walter Giffard who was also Earl of Longueville. There was indeed a Cluniac cell, later a priory, on the present manor house site from 1150 until its suppression in 1415. The church of St Faith is on the edge of the former priory precinct, now the centre of the village. It has an embattled west tower, embattled parapet to its nave, long chancel roof and generous Perpendicular style windows, and a harmonious silhouette and form which owes much to work by the patrons, New College Oxford, in the mid 15th century. The interior is, however, disappointing for it was zealously and tastelessly restored in 1881–91 leaving little to admire but some spirited carving of animals and foliage on capitals of the late 12th-century arcades. The 14th-century figure of St Faith, which was previously in a niche on the outside wall above the east window, has been brought in recently from local weather and sulphur dioxide. The present Manor House south of the church is an H-shaped building, mainly in brick but with a stone base and stone quoins, which has a 16th-century core but much addition of the 17th century and later alterations, luckily screened by trees from church and roads. The Old Rectory across the Stewkley Road is a handsome, square, three-storey, late 18th-century building with traces of its 16th-century predecessor. It has generous arch-headed windows to the ground floor of its garden front. Of the remaining old cottages there are still nice groups at Moor End down the Stewkley Road and at Westbrook End to the southwest which are divided by hectares of modern housing. The Westbrook End group, in spite of much 'improvement' is still remarkably picturesque in colour-washed brick and thatch.

North Crawley [6]

A compact place on the Beds. border with an east to west spine of stone and brick cottages along a little ridge and a tiny square north of its church, which is almost hidden behind yew trees. The church has that rare dedication to St Firmin found in only one other place in England, and is largely of stone, with embattled tower and higher stair tower. The base of the tower is early 13th century, the upper part 14th century. The south aisle and a west extension of the nave were built in the late 13th century and the chancel rebuilt as the gift, recorded in an inscription outside the east window, of Peter of Guildford in 1294. The north arcade is early 14th century, but aisles were remodelled and clerestory added about 1460 when the church was reroofed

throughout with moulded ribs and bosses. The rood screen with its open tracery and fan-vaulted canopy painted with figures of 16 saints and prophets is also of the later 15th century. There are some linen-folded bench ends and an octagonal and castellated font-cover of 1640 but the main interest of the interior is provided by the Georgian restoration which gave it a set of box pews, its pulpit and its painted panel of Royal Arms. There is a brass to Dr Garbrand (d. 1587), a well-known preacher and son of a Dutch bookseller in Oxford. Other medieval building has been destroyed by several fires and the street has only a few 18th-century stone cottages and a number of mid-19th-century brick ones, together with some later infilling. Older buildings are outside the village. Crawley Grange to the north-west is a large E-shaped house of late 16th century with a stone base and stone dressings. At Little Crawley is Moat Farm, a 16th-century timber-framed house with wattle and daub infilling, on a stone base. It has been much altered in later centuries but is still entered by a little bridge over its moat.

North End [14]

An 'end' of Turville, though separated by 3 km of fields and woods from that village. It has a long, largely overgrown, common with scattered 16th- and 17th-century cottages, usually second homes or modernized, but still picturesque. North End Farmhouse, hidden in trees near the junction of roads from Turville and Turville Heath, is a 17th-century building refronted in early 18th-century flint with brick dressings and a tall central door.

North Marston [8]

On a little hill commanded by an important church overlooking great clayey pastures. There are half-timbered, thatched and tiled cottages round the hill and a long High Street bordered by strips of green stretches away to the north-west. A great fire

of 1705 swept away most pre-18th-century buildings and outside the church the village now has little of interest. The church of St Mary, however, makes up for this. It owes much to the miracle worker John Shorne, rector 1290–1314, whose relics were the subject of popular pilgrimage in the 14th and 15th centuries. He is famous in fable for having confined the devil in a boot, a feat which gave rise to Jack-in-the-Box toys and many Boot inns. More usefully he struck a chalybeate spring in the hillside (now covered) which was found good for eye-infections. Pilgrims contributed to the beautification of his church. It has a plain battlemented west tower, north aisle and arcade of 13th century; south aisle part 14th- and part 15th-century rebuilding and, its particular glory, the wide Perpendicular chancel and south chapel with an added two-storey vestry and priest's room, embattled and pinnacled. The nave was improved later. The clerestory with four-light windows was added, new roof erected with oak brackets carved with angels playing musical instruments and the nave parapet was embattled. The chancel was given niches, now empty, and piscina and sedilia with projecting rib-vaulted canopies and choir stalls carved with poppy heads and misericords. A shrine with Shorne's relics was set up in the chancel and his statue was placed in a niche in the south aisle but the relics and shrine were removed to Windsor in 1480 by jealous clerics and not returned until the relics had lost their appeal. Of the church's quieter times there are a simple monument to John Virgin, rector (d. 1694), with a painted hand pointing to the floor and inscription reading 'He lies dust downe thare' and there is a brass to Richard Saunders, physician to Queen Elizabeth I (d. 1602). The chancel and the south chapel were restored for Queen Victoria by M. D. Wyatt in 1855 as a thanksgiving for the bequest

Olney

made to her by J. C. Neild, a miserly London solicitor who owned property in the village. He left her his whole fortune, estimated at a quarter of a million pounds. Queen Victoria was much pleased and used most of it to buy the Balmoral Estate.

Notley Abbey [11] (near Haddenham) A house on a monastic site on the north bank of the Thame. The Abbey, earlier called St Mary de Parco, and later Nutley Abbey, was founded by Walter Giffard, 1st Earl of Buckingham, for Augustinian canons in the mid 12th-century. With Missenden Abbey it was one of the most important religious houses in the County and grew in wealth and prestige almost up to the Reformation, since it became, in the 15th and 16th centuries, a place of correction for other monks—e.g. from Missenden—who had become corrupt. The most important is the Abbot's lodging, which forms the greater part of the present house.

This is part 15th century and part early 16th, the work of Richard Rydge, last Abbot who left his name on some panelling (since removed to Oxon.), and includes the Abbot's Hall, Parlour and Solar, and a connection to the cloister range. The church lay on the north side of the cloister and of this only piers of the crossing and the south-east corner remain. The church seems to have had a 12th-century nave nearly 35 m long, early 13th-century aisles, chancel and sanctuary nearly 36 m long (rebuilt in the early 14th century) and a crossing tower rebuilt in the 15th. Some graceful 13th-century arcading from the Abbey refectory is incorporated in the later buildings, as are some doorways. On the gentle slope above the Abbey is a large square stone dovecote of the 14th century which is still a prominent feature seen across the valley from the Aylesbury Road.

Oakley [10] The old verse 'Brill on the Hill, Oakley in the Hole' puts it

in its place in water meadows between Brill and the remnants of Bernewood Forest on the Oxon. border. It is a medium-size village with houses of all ages and types down to council houses in Cornish concrete. The church of St Mary, the only building of much importance, is on a bend in the main road, of grey stone with red and grey roofs. Its low early-14th-century west tower has a bold stair-turret with a conical cap. The north windows and the gracefully reticulated south window in the deep south transept are Decorated and below the latter on the outside wall is a wide cinquefoil-arched recess for a tomb. The incongruous concrete and wood porch added in 1960 has now been reduced to plain and inconspicuous ugliness by the weather. Inside, the five-bayed north arcade has both circular and octagonal columns and there are piscina and 14th-century coffin lids decorated with crosses in the north aisle. The interior is otherwise dull. The adjoining Rectory is simple

Olney

Georgian and the only large dwelling, Oakley House, in Warminghall Road, is of brick, with stone dressings and square panelled chimneystacks, dated 1660. Many local farmhouses and cottages are in Flemish brickwork. In one was the hideout in 1963 of the Great Train Robbers of Cheddington.

Olney [5] A small, warm, stone town with Northants. character, dominated by a Northants.-type spire. It is full of memories of the poet William Cowper and his friends, though better known today for its Pancake Race on Shrove Tuesday. It is set in a bowl of gentle hills at a bend in the Ouse and, unlike most towns, all its approaches—even the northern—past its incongruous boot factory are pleasant. That across the river towards the high church tower and steeple is splendid. The spine is the main road from Newport Pagnell to Wellingborough, which bends violently after crossing the bridge, opens up briefly into a wide, triangular Market Place and then takes a more placid course up the wide High Street. The bridge itself (strictly in Emberton parish) is an 18th-century stone structure. Its central arches are segmental with rusticated voussoirs and the wing-walls of its approaches curve outwards as though to welcome visitors. Good stone houses start as soon as the bridge is crossed, the best being Bridge House, which backs on to a long-established tannery (last sign of the leather and leather-goods trade which once sustained the town); Courtney House, whose late 18th-century front screens an older building; and no. 2 Bridge Street, of the 18th century, which backs on to the churchyard. The church is down Church Street, to the right, past the early-18th-century stone Vicarage, which was the home of John Newton and Thomas Scott, and, for a time, of Cowper. The church of SS. Peter and Paul is large, about 50 m overall, with a west tower and spire, nearly 60 m high, and one of only two medieval spires in the county. It is all of the 14th century and has tall windows with flowing tracery. West galleries were installed in the 18th century and removed later but more dramatic changes were made in 1807, when, to pay for repairs and save expense, the clerestory, timber roof and lead coverings were removed from the nave and a lower plaster ceiling substituted. The interior is wide and still well-lit but the proportions inside and out, for the nave roof is now lower than the chancel, have been spoilt, while stonework inside has been left as unnaturally rough as a 'ranch-type' bungalow (of which there are samples outside). Early 20th-century timber roofs over the aisles are better. The wide chancel arch gives a fine view to the east window with its little knot on top and five lights filled with glass by Holland in 1870. The north-west and south-west low side windows have decent glass of 1973, but the north aisle memorial window to Cowper with its gambolling hares is not worthy of its place. Cowper's connection with Olney is owed to John Newton, curate-in-charge from 1764 to 1780, who befriended Cowper and his protectress Mrs Unwin and found them a house here to which they moved from Huntingdon. This is an early 18th-century red-brick house on the south side of the Market Place. It stands out thin, tall and red in otherwise low and grey buildings. At its back is the modest summer house where the poet studied and behind was a path across a little field to Newton's House, the Vicarage. Newton was a former slave trader and has left an excellent diary of his early life. He became a notable preacher and filled the

church to overflowing. With Cowper he produced the 'Olney Hymns' of which his best known are 'Glorious things of thee are spoken' and 'Amazing Grace' and Cowper's 'O for a closer walk with God' and 'God moves in a mysterious way'. Cowper suffered prolonged fits of depression and it was then that villagers gave him the pet hares of which he wrote to Coleridge and Lamb. Otherwise, as he said, 'occurrences here . . . are as rare as cucumbers at Christmas'. Newton left for a popular London parish in 1780 and Cowper moved to Weston Underwood in 1786. His house in the Market Place has much of his furniture and, with the summer house, is now a Cowper museum. Newton was followed here by Thomas Scott, the 'great commentator', and part of the north aisle was restored in his memory by his grandson George Gilbert Scott. The graves of John and Mary Newton, brought here from London in 1893, are in the churchyard, together with many tombstones by their friend James Andrews, the local sculptor who taught Cowper to draw. Beyond the churchyard on peaceful Ouse meadows is the much-altered 18th-century mill-house, all that is left of the long established mill on this site which was for so long another prominent landmark in the town. Set back on the west side of the Market Place is a Baptist chapel of 1893. This was founded in 1694 and has a graveyard crowded with simple old stone memorials. North of this is the High Street proper, wide and particularly distinguished by having two almost unbroken lines of decent stone houses. The more important, e.g Olney House and Clifton House, are at the south end, but there are pleasing groups all the way to its end, where there is a curious group of red-brick houses and an Edwardian boot-factory, now a book warehouse. At Asfurlong, near the road to Bedford, parts of a Roman building, where 3rd-century coins and pottery and a

bronze Mercury were found, were long visible.

Olney Park [2] (near Olney) A tiny parish with a tiny population in the northern tip of the county. It was formerly an 'extra-parochial' area and only made a separate parish in 1861. It once belonged to the Duchy of Lancaster and was emparked in 1374. Olney Park Farm, the only dwelling in the parish, is a 17th-century stone house much altered.

Oving [8] A little square of roads on a limestone hill in a huge area of gently swelling clay. The village has spread out towards Whitchurch but the church and Black Boy Inn, which are on the western edge with a wide view as far as Buckingham, seem the natural centre of the village. The only large house looks southward to the distant line of the Chilterns. All Saints Church has a plain 15th-century tower and mainly 13th-century nave, south aisle and high chancel. The aisle chapel was added in the early 14th century, the nave roof with its arched braces and carved bosses and the clerestory in the 15th and a small north transept in the late 19th. South and east chancel walls were rebuilt in 1867 in an extensive restoration of the church by G. E. Street which left the interior a little hard and unfeeling. There is a simple 15th-century chancel screen and four knobbly bench ends in the south aisle, an ogee-headed tomb recess in the south wall and a fragmentary 15th-century painting of Christ with tools of trade, a warning against working on Sunday. The 17th-century timber-framed and brick-filled Black Boy Inn and the 18th-century, mixed brick and stone Rectory make a group of picturesque variety with the church. Oving House, the principal dwelling, faces away from the village. It is an early 17th-century stone house, remodelled in 1740–43, extended in the late 18th century and given an internal flourish in the mid 20th. The north front is of stone. Here two projecting gabled wings were given half-sided parapets and circular windows in 1743. At the same time the south side was extended out and given a stuccoed, brick-pedimented, front. To the east new two-storeyed stables with a cupola were added. All this was for Charles Pilsworth, an ambitious local lawyer who married one of the Tyringhams of Lower Winchendon, became M.P. for Aylesbury and died childless. He had ambitions for elaborate decoration of the interior but only completed the intricate plasterwork of the drawing-room ceiling. Work in the same style was completed in other rooms by Felix Harbord (1955).

Owlswick (in Longwick-cum-Ilmer parish) [11] A hamlet of brick and tiled cottages with a tiny green and the Shoulder of Mutton pub in big flat fields north of Princes Risborough. Bruce Bairnsfather, best-known comic artist of the First World War, lived here.

Padbury [8] A village of 16th-, 17th- and 18th-century cottages, some early Victorian, a few Edwardian villas and a grey stone church, lining a shallow cleft in a slight clayey, once elmy, ridge. The original backbone of the village is still called Main Street and runs gently south-west from the top end of the village where the church stands across the main Buckingham road. The pattern of the village was distorted by the turnpike which cuts off the church end of the village leaving it as a modern 'end' containing the church, the manor house, two large Edwardian houses and some recent infill. St Matthew's (or the Church of the Nativity) is of stone with a square 15th-century tower decorated with 18th-century 'chimney pots', a low pitched lead roof to the nave and a steeper tiled roof to the chancel. The tower is enclosed in the body of the church, embraced between extensions to the narrow (mid-13th-century) north aisle and the wide (late 13th-century) south aisle, which were made in the 14th and 15th centuries. The clerestory to the nave has—that feature of some N. Bucks. churches—circular windows, but on the north side only. There are early 14th-century wall-paintings of the life of St Catherine on the north wall and some fragmentary figures on the south arcade. There are attractive and picturesque cottages along Main Street, particularly in the little hollow behind the school and around Old End at the lower end of the village, some thatched, some half-timbered, some painted black-and-cream and some cream, but none of special architectural interest. South-west of the village, near the little River Lovett, is an earthwork of uncertain date known as Norbury Camp.

Pednor [12] (near Chesham) A few old houses on a chalk ridge west of Chesham. The principal house is of the 16th century, round a courtyard which incorporates a barn some 20 m long.

Penn [14] A large, well-preserved and reasonably well-contained, village of brick and tiled houses in beech, sycamore, ash and garden trees with an old church built along a gently sloping high ridge. The view from the church tower is said to be the widest in the county but views from the village road are confined to glimpses north of beech woods and occasional longer views south over the Thames valley. William Penn of Pennsylvania was proud of his connection with the village, and four of his grandsons are buried in the church, but he was only distantly related to the Penn family which held the Penn Manor (and adjoining Beaumond Manor at Penn Street) from the 13th century till 1731, when, on the death of Roger Penn, County Sheriff 1706, it passed to the Curzons of Kedleston and so to the present Earl Howe. Holy Trinity church in limes and large yews has a somewhat gloomy face to the village street, of rough-cast flint tower and nave and brick chancel, in perpetual shadow. It has a gayer and more varied, domestic, sunnier side to the flowery graveyard and its long views south. It is mainly 13th century but with few structural features of interest, though the 15th-century woodwork of the roof, with tie-beams on arched braces resting on stone heads, is better than average for a small church. The chancel and the south chapel were rebuilt in brick with some old stonework in 1736. Inside are plaster walls and ceilings, 18th-century pews, and 18th-century pulpit with spiral stair rails (from the Curzons' chapel in London). Also a large late-15th-century Doom painting on oak boards with red, orange and yellow figures, interesting rather than good. Monuments include a floor slab marking the grave of William Penn, grandson of Pennsylvanian Penn, some 16th-century brasses and many Penn and Curzon memorials, including two by Chantrey with medallion portraits. There are also a number of hatchments, and Royal Arms of Queen Anne. The more interesting village buildings are scattered round the church. Opposite are late 17th-century almshouses, spoilt by some weak modern extensions, and the early 19th-century whitewashed Vicarage. To the south is the late 17th-century The Knoll, which has a heavily modelled cornice. Along the street are more old brick houses with neat gardens and 20th-century neighbours dressed up to look even older. There is little industry now but medieval tileries of Penn were famous and their tiles used at Westminster, Hampton Court and Windsor palaces.

Penn Street [14] Has a tidy rectangular village green connecting a furniture factory and some villagey cottages to a tidy suburban north end with a tidy primary school (by County Architect 1960). The tall spire of Holy Trinity church stands out above beech and oak and ash woods which screen the west side of the village. It was built for the first Earl Howe by B. Ferrey (1849) of flint with stone dressings, cruciform in plan, like his church at Brockham, Surrey, but with a taller octagonal tower and tall spire. The approach to the church is now obscured by Victorian rhododendrons and laurels and 'Welcome' notices, though the church is usually locked. Inside is a copy of Raphael's *Transfiguration*, formerly the altar-piece of the Curzons' chapel in London. Penn House is the home of Earls Howe and Curzons and has 17th- and 18th-century parts obscured by later additions, but the Penn Manor, which was the former residence of Penns, was at Penn. Beaumond End, with its pretty, brick and flint but somewhat suburban, cottages in trees to the north of Penn Street, commemorates the manor of Beaumond which was held with Penn by the Penn family, from the 13th to the 18th centuries, when both passed to the Curzons.

Pitchcott [8] Consists of a farmhouse, a few white cottages and a grey Victorian-looking church on a hill top overlooking the Vale of Aylesbury. It is in heavy clay, mainly pastoral country, with no important houses. St Giles's church, small of grey stone with tiled roof, has a plain 15th- and 16th-centuries tower, 12th-century nave and early 13th-century chancel. There are two lancets in the chancel, of which the south-west has a stone book-rest. The church was over-restored in 1864 and no old wood was left. The adjoining Manor Farmhouse dates back to the 17th century, and probably earlier, but its architectural interest has been cemented over.

Pitstone [12] Has an old village, 'Church End', with an isolated church on the edge of high open treeless Chiltern fields, with a few cottages and terrace houses, and, on the valley floor at Pitstone Green

Pitstone

(along the road to Ivinghoe and threatening that village), a large estate of red-brick houses. The two parts are separated by the giant chalk and clay pits and the buzzing factory and smoking chimneys of the Tunnel Cement Company which now envelopes the old village and has spread along and across the Herts. border. The church of St Mary on its windy hill feels, like the Pitstone Windmill, more of Ivinghoe than of modern Pitstone, and, like the windmill, is redundant and unused. It is large for a small place

and mainly Perpendicular in feeling, with a tall battlemented tower and an east end extended and north arcade renewed in the 15th century. The plan is eccentric: both tower and chancel are off the centre line of the nave and the chancel is sharply skewed to north. The capitals on the north side of the latter have bold stiff-leaved foliage, the font is of Aylesbury type, with fluted bowl and cable moulding and arches to the bowl, the pulpit with tester is Jacobean, the box pews are later 17th century and the communion rail with delicate twisted balusters is 18th century. The small brass of a lady in early 14th-century dress is probably the oldest brass in the County. Above the chancel arch is a large area painted in 1733 with Royal Arms, Commandments, Creed and Lord's Prayer. Its Parsonage is a yellow-brick house with heavy barge-boarded gables built in 1856 by G. E. Street. Pitstone Windmill, in fields towards Ivinghoe, is an early type of post-mill with timbers dated 1627 and 1749. It was badly damaged by a freak storm in 1902 but has been carefully restored in National Trust hands from 1963 onwards and is now a tourist attraction. On the scarp above were Neolithic flint mines.

Poundon [7] A small place of mainly red-brick houses climbing, up a clayey slope, to the masts and stays of a radio station on its hill top. There is no church and the only large house is early 20th-century neo-Georgian.

Preston Bissett [7] A small village with colour-washed brick or grey limestone houses and cottages and some later red or pink brick council houses in large clay fields bared by the loss of its former elm-trees. The church of St John the Baptist, in the centre of a triangular pattern of village lanes, is of silvery grey stone with lead roofs. Its low 15th-century west tower looks even lower, thanks to the addition of a 19th-century clerestory to the nave. There is much flowing tracery, particularly good in the east windows of chancel and aisles. The inside is dull, due to too much scrape and cement but there are still two enjoyable items: the crude beasts supporting the chancel arch (the northern points a large bottom into the chancel) and the crocketed ogee arches over the sedilia. The stuccoed neo-Tudor Rectory is dated 1840. The White Hart and the Old Hat are picturesque old pubs.

Prestwood [11] A suburb of nowhere, on flattish chalk hills of houses and bungalows set with garden trees between remaining areas of Chiltern woodland. The ecclesiastical parish was formed in 1852 from parts of Great Missenden and Hughenden but the area had already been given its handsome church in 1849. Holy Trinity church is by E. B. Lamb in his individual Decorated style. It is flint-faced and tiled, with nave, chancel and western bellcote and is, itself, almost hidden in trees. It has wide nave arcades—whose original piers were of clunch and burst under the weight—tall narrow chancel and baptistery arches, and odd roofs. The adjoining Vicarage in flint but with some tile-hanging is also by Lamb. Among the many undistinguished brick and tile 20th-century houses is 'Cherry Cottage' in Green Lane, home for many years of the 1st Earl Attlee, Prime Minister 1945–51.

Princes Risborough *see* Risborough, Princes

Quainton [8] Is large and spread out on an H-shaped pattern of lanes which are outlined with old, mellow, red-brick cottages on the green slopes of Quainton Hill. The latter rises behind the village to a height of 187 m above sea level, the highest point near the centre of the county. The cross bar of the pattern is the thin sloping green which is also the centre of the village and is dominated by the forbidding, plain, brown brick tower, of a disused windmill. The mill, of six storeys and over 30 m high, is dated 1830 (though parts are probably older), and was restored, though without sails, in 1976. On the Green just below is the stone block and shaft of a 14th-century cross, where funerals from outlying places waited for the rector to conduct them to the church at the east end of the village. Cross Farmhouse is in chequered brick with a carved stone panel dated 1723 over the nine-panelled central door, and was built by Justice Dormer for one of his daughters. From here the best street runs eastward, following a gentle curve between pleasant buildings to terminate, visually, on the church tower between the Rectory on the upslope and the Winwood almshouses on the downslope side. The church, St Mary and the Holy Cross, is of stone with tiled roofs and looks mainly Perpendicular in style. It has an embattled tower, early 14th-century nave, late 14th-century chancel and 15th-century north chapel, aisle windows and south porch. The southeast window has an angle piscina rare in the county. The chancel was rebuilt and the reredos and sedilia designed by William White in his extensive restoration of 1877. A low screen to the north aisle incorporates late 15th-century painted panels showing four saints, which were formerly part of the rood screen. The simple octagonal font is of the same date. But the chief interest of the church is in its monuments and particularly those of the 17th and 18th centuries. There are brasses dated from 1350 to 1593. That to Margery, wife of Sir Ralph Verney (d. 1685), describes her as daughter of John Iwardby 'Lorde of this Towne' and shows her and her children approximately half life-sized. On the north side is a heavy black sarcophagus on claw feet, inset in pilasters and pediment of grey and white marble, signed by Giacomo Leoni. This is to Sir Richard Pigott of Doddershall. On the same side is a monument to Lettice Coote (d. 1693), perhaps by William Stanton, who designed and signed the monument on the west wall to Susannah Dormer (d. 1672) and her husband Sir John (d. 1675) of Lee Grange, which has busts and a large inscription plate. On the south side are a wall monument with coloured kneeling figures to Richard Brett (d. 1637), one of the translators of the Authorised Bible, and a table tomb to Richard

Winwood (d. 1689) and wife. He was the founder of the adjoining almshouses and is shown life-size in plate armour and wig with his wife. The monument is signed by Thomas Stayner. The two most imposing monuments are under the tower and are to Dormers. That on the south is a tablet and urn to Fleetwood Dormer (d. 1632) set inside a much larger wall monument to John (d. 1679) and another Fleetwood Dormer (d. 1696). Opposite is that to Robert Dormer, Justice of the Court of Common Pleas (d. 1726) and his wife and son, who died just before the father in 1726. It has dramatic figures of the dead son on a sarcophagus with his weeping mother kneeling beside it and his father in wig making a

sorrowful gesture towards him. Winwood's almshouses alongside are dated 1687. They are of dark brick of one storey and have dormers in alternating large and small gables, two porches with Dutch gables and groups of tall chimneys. Opposite is the Rectory, a 16th-century building refronted in red and grey brick in the 18th century and given outer canted bays and a three-bayed centre capped with a gabled dormer. Many houses leading back to the Green have timber frames and some are still thatched. Houses round the Green, apart from Cross Farm already mentioned, are not of architectural importance, but at Magpies Cottage, George Lipscombe, author of an authoritative *History of Bucking-*

hamshire (1847), was born in 1773. North-east of the village is Denham Lodge, 17th-century stone and brick, which seems to have been part of the Manor House of the Winwoods. It is surrounded by a moat with a little single-storey gatehouse commanding the old bridge across it, and old brick walls along fields to the north which formerly enclosed its deer park. The Dormers' mansion was next to Grange Farm on the road to the Claydons but was destroyed in the 18th century. Here there are a 16th-century timber-framed and brick-infilled barn with a massive queen-post roof, fishponds, and fragments, in the present farmhouse, of this important manor which had belonged, before the Dormers, to Thame Abbey. Alongside, the grass-grown track of the former railway to Verney junction leads down through banks and gorse to Quainton Road Station, where, on the former Great Central and Metropolitan Railway lines, there is a young railway museum busy restoring and maintaining vehicles of the age of steam. In clear weather, it is worth climbing from the village to the top of Quainton Hill; from here the whole of Bucks. north of the Chilterns, together with distant Shropshire hills, can be seen.

Quarrendon [11] (near Aylesbury) A vanished village in meadows just across the Thame, outside Aylesbury. It has a few late 13th-century stone fragments of the parish church of St Peter and, alongside these, the site of the Lee family mansion. Here Sir Henry Lee entertained Queen Elizabeth I in 1592 and in the church was his handsome but now vanished monument. That of his wife was taken to the parish church at Aylesbury. Around both churches

◁ **Quainton**: Winwood monument, detail

Quainton: Justice Dormer monument ▷

Radclive: 14th-century glass

are traces of trenches and low earth banks which were gun ports for the defence of Aylesbury during the Civil War. The Christian martyr St Osyth was born in the village in the 7th century.

Radclive [4] Little more than an old stone church and old stone manor house in oak and dying elm in the Ouse valley. The church of St John the Evangelist has an embattled tower and tiled roofs, an early 12th-century south doorway ornamented with zigzag mouldings above stiff-leafed capitals, and a chancel arch with toothed ornament. The rest is mainly Early English but the medieval feel was removed in a drastic restoration by J. O. Scott in 1903. There remain a few bench ends with poppy heads

in the porch, an early 17th-century communion rail, some hat-pegs (a rare survival) of the same date, and fragments of 14th-century glass showing a worried Virgin and Child and a cheerful apostle under golden canopies. The manor was part of the endowment of New College, Oxford, who owned the Manor House until 1965. The house, in a bend of the Ouse south of the church, is largely 16th century and has a timber frame fronted with stone, three large gables on the east front and square chimneys set diagonally. A large wing was demolished in 1621 but it still has its Elizabethan hall screen with panelled arches on stone columns, a staircase with pierced-panel balustrading and 16th-century panelling and fireplaces.

Radnage [14] A parish of many 'ends': Bennett End, Church End, The City, Sprig's Alley and Town End. The church of St Mary is on a steep slope backed by beech woods, adjoined by the yew hedges of the 18th-century rectory and which, with a small 16th-century cottage just below, makes a pretty group. It has a core of flint rubble with limestone dressings and is covered with an orangey-grey plaster which is peeling, though not unattractively, to reveal flint and even brick patching beneath. Its simple central tower is the most notable feature inside and out and its thick walls sharply divide the chancel from the nave. Nave, chancel and tower are of the early 13th century but the nave was lengthened, its walls raised and reroofed and the south porch added in the 15th century. The interior is chalky white and simple, so that the tall tower arches and the nave roof of tie-beams and decorated arched braces speak for themselves against the plain tapering plastered walls. There are traces of 13th-century figures painted on east and north walls. The pulpit is late 17th century and the simple font may be pre-Conquest. It was dug up in a neighbouring field. The views from the churchyard over little fields to more beech woods are attractive. The other 'ends' are uninteresting, or even irritating, interruptions in pleasant Chiltern scenery. The largest is The City, a collection of bungalows and cottages, along twisting lanes east of Stokenchurch, made pretty in spring by suburban garden trees.

Ravenstone [5] A stone village of Northants. character with church and almshouse at the top end and a village street winding down through thatched ironstone cottages. The Finch monument in the church is worth a special visit. All Saints Church is on a little hill within the site of a priory of Augustinian canons. Of this parts of a large moat and some fragments of

Radnage in its Chiltern setting

building are incorporated in the adjoining Abbey Farm. The church has a severe silhouette with a plain, square-topped, unbuttressed, 13th- century tower and low lead-covered roofs. The chancel is 13th century; herringbone masonry can be seen in its west wall. The south arcade is late 12th century. The south aisle was extended the length of the chancel with mullioned and transomed windows in the 15th century and now forms the memorial chapel of the Finch family, who were Lords of the Manor from the late 16th to the 20th century. The centrepiece of this chapel is the memorial to Heneage Finch (1621–82), 1st Earl of Nottingham, Lord Chancellor to Charles II. This is a large four-poster in black-and-white marble

with white curtains looped back to black columns to show the Earl in white, reclining on a black marble slab. Below is a long Latin inscription describing his ability, discretion, honesty and generosity, though it does not say that he asked for the hanging of John Milton on the grounds that Milton had been Latin secretary to Cromwell. The portraits and drapes are lovingly carved, perhaps by Joseph Catterns. Finch restored his church, built the elaborate screen with twisted balusters around the south chapel and presented the grand two-decker pulpit. He also gave to the village the Finch almshouses, which are reached through ball-capped gate piers on the church-yard edge. They are two simple, single-storey rows in chequered

brick. There are many stone cottages and houses in the village and of these the best are farmhouses: those of Northend Farm, which is in rubble, stone and thatch, and Home Farm, which is in coursed rubble.

Risborough, Monks [11] Owned by monks of Canterbury Cathedral before the Norman Conquest. Until the First World War it was a small place isolated by fields from its sister Princes Risborough but it is now a large residential suburb of the latter, joined by the Icknield Way. The medieval parish church and some picturesque cottages are hidden in a lane north of this. St Dunstan's church is a flint and stone building with a west tower in knapped flint with a square stair turret. The exterior of the body of the church is mainly the Victorian flint of Street's restoration of 1864, but the windows are genuine rich Perpendicular, large in the chancel and in the north transept. The arcades with octagonal piers are 14th century but the church is more interesting for its fittings than for its general effect. There are a late 15th-century rood screen with nine of its original painted panels remaining, some carved bench ends, brasses of 1431 and 1460, fragments of medieval glass, and a Norman font with fluted base and banded cup. In the recreation ground across a stream north of the church is a 16th-century square stone dovecot with lantern; to the south a row of exceptionally picturesque, timber-framed cottages.

Risborough, Princes [11] A small medieval market town, in the mouth of a great gap in the Chiltern Hills caused during Ice Ages, surrounded by large residential estates of the 1930s and 1950s. It was once called Great Risborough and got the name 'Princes' from its connection with the Duchy of Cornwall. Like Wendover (which sits in the next gap in the hills) it has an S-shaped pattern of main streets which give attractive views to and along the Chilterns scarp. The best view is that of Whiteleaf Cross seen above cottages in Bell Street, but Risborough is otherwise unluckier than Wendover, for its former pattern of close-lining small cottages has been torn to tatters and the partial infill which has been done is generally inappropriate. Betjeman reasonably called it 'untidy Metroland' for it is dependent on a (Western Region) railway line to London and has been badly treated. The chief focus of the place, the little Market Square, is, however, pleasantly varied with low buildings with neat doorcases and gables surrounding the central Market (or Town) Hall built in 1824. This has a square brick core

topped by a little roofed clock-turret and with timber pillars all round supporting lean-to roofs, a squashed and anglicized pagoda. It makes a nice centre and turns the eye down Church Street. Here, past Dutch gables and lots of bright new paintwork, are the principal buildings, the church and the Manor House. St Mary's church, in a red-wood and yew-covered graveyard, is faced in smooth flint and stone. Its most prominent feature and indeed the most prominent feature of the town is the recessed spire on the west tower which was built by J. O. Scott in 1908. The rest of the church is basically 13th- and 14th-century work but was so extended and restored by Arthur Blomfield in 1868 as to look entirely of that date. Inside, too, it looks all Victorian except in a corner of the south aisle where there are windows with triple lancets embroidered with Purbeck marble shafts, piscina and sedilia, and four gaping ogee-headed tomb recesses. The panelled early 17th-century pulpit is one other relic of the older building. Beyond are earthwork remains of a castle of the Black Prince, son of Edward III. The Manor House is on the town side, a two-storey building of five bays in red brick. The Church End frontage is late 17th century with windows separated by broad brick pilasters, approached through its original gate-piers and ironwork and a narrow formal front garden. On the garden front it is picturesquely gabled. Inside, the main staircase has a square open well and strapwork balustrades. National Gallery pictures were stored here in the Second World War. It was given to the National Trust by Mrs C. Rothschild in 1925 and is regularly opened to the public. High Street, south of the Market Place, has pleasant 18th-century houses with some good doorcases. It is continued north by Duke Street, in which is the R.C. church of St Teresa, the boldest symbol of the 1930s expansion of the town. It is in a

gloomy, dark brown brick, with a prominent tiled dome and a triangular plan with an apse on each side, designed by an Italian architect, Rinvolucri (1938). There are exhilarating walks on the hills to Saunderton, Pink Hill and Whiteleaf.

Rowsham [8] A roadside hamlet on the way to Wing with a few timber-framed and red-brown brick cottages with disused chapels.

St Leonards [11] (near Cholesbury) A shapeless settlement of little houses in scattered groups on the high chalk-lane. The place still looks unfinished, the more so as it has been fossilized by Green Belt controls. But these should, at least, give native oaks and chestnuts time to soften the effect of unfortunate building on its landscape. The church of St Leonards, the only building of much interest in the place, is an ancient chantry chapel of Missenden Abbey but was ecclesiastically in the parish of Aston Clinton (5 km to the west), until 1860. Set in holly and yew, it has white cemented walls enclosing an old timber frame supporting nave and chancel under one tiled roof, accented only by the bellcote over the west end. Its body is probably 15th century but needed considerable rebuilding after Civil War damage and was heavily restored in 1845. There are two monuments by Nicholas Bigee inside, carved of chalk rock. These are to Seth Wood (d. 1717) and to his son General Cornelius Wood (d. 1712), the latter having trophies and cherubs sitting on cannon balls. There are Royal Arms of 1963 over the south door, a copy of Botticelli's *Virgin and Child* in a circular frame and modern glass in the south-east window of the nave. Hen Grove, one of the larger houses in the area, is a simple neo-Tudor brick building by Morley Horder (1910).

Saunderton [11] A hamlet in a

Heneage Finch monument, **Ravenstone**

damp hollow with beech and dying elm at the foot of the Chiltern scarp, only just clear of the bungalow fringes of Princes Risborough. The old parish was a long thin one, typical of many on the fringe of chalk downs, and stretched from Longwick out in the Vale of Aylesbury 9 km south-east to Bradenham in the heart of the hills. It was united later with its southern neighbour Bledlow. St Mary's church is still the centre of the present hamlet and is dedicated additionally to St Nicholas. St Nicholas's was another medieval church, now lost,

and the amalgamation indicates the shrinkage of the medieval settlements in the parish which are represented now only by the small group at Saunderton itself, by Frogmore Farm to the west and Home Farm to the south, with almost nothing on, or near, either of the ancient Icknield Ways which cross the parish. But the former, isolated, picture-postcard quality of the little group of church, ponds and farm buildings has been destroyed in the last few years by the erection of a blotchy brick block in front of the church, filling of

adjoining ponds with motorway spoil and the fencing of the remaining pond with green plastic mesh. The church itself has little interest inside or out except an attractive silhouette. It is of flint with nave and chancel under tiled roofs and a timber belfry over the west end. The timber frame of the belfry can be seen inside together with an inferior Aylesbury-type font and a screen made from 14th-century tracery. The body is mainly 13th century, but was largely rebuilt by J. S. Alder in 1891. Church Farmhouse, which has the remaining

141

duck pond, has been tidily restored but its farm buildings and functions removed. Frogmore Farmhouse to the west has a 16th-century timber frame and a fine seven-bay barn. Near the Three Horseshoes (towards Risborough), a 2nd- and 3rd-century Roman villa was excavated in 1927. Finds are in the County Museum at Aylesbury.

Sedrup [11] (near Hartwell) A hamlet of farm and former farm labourers' cottages in brick or wichert with tile or thatched roofs round a small rough green on the Hartwell–Stone parish boundary. It is a settlement mentioned in Domesday and looks unchanged for centuries.

Seer Green [15] A collection of red-brick commuter houses and bungalows in cherry trees and old orchards, served by its own railway station. It was made an ecclesiastical parish (out of Farnham Royal) when the little church of Holy Trinity, a flint and stone building of nave, chancel, bellcote and lancet windows, was completed in 1847.

Shabbington [10] A small, low-lying village on a bend in the River Thame with views of the Chilterns across willows and wet meadows. Buildings are of all ages, styles and materials set at odd angles which are accentuated by the angular street pattern, so that the sober but regularly set new houses near the church look doubly out of place. St Mary Magdalene's on the lane to Thame, is an aisle-less stone church with tiled roofs and a low embattled 15th-century tower sagging to the west and supported by heavy buttresses. The body is 11th century, to judge from the herringbone laying of some of the rubble, but doors and windows, outside the upper stage of the tower, are mainly 14th century. Inside are 15th-century piscina and low side window to chancel and a panelled hexagonal pulpit dated 1626. The churchyard has friendly carved limestone gravestones. The School

House near the church has a neat grey 18th-century frontage to a 17th-century rear and a schoolroom with a big gothic window.

Shalstone [4] Grey and creamy stone cottages with tiles and some thatch and slate, a grey Victorian-looking church and a neat Georgian stuccoed manor house, along a narrow winding lane overshadowed in trees, near the Northants. border. The church of St Edward the Confessor was largely rebuilt by G. G. Scott in 1862 when its tower was given a trefoiled parapet and the staircase a spirelet while, inside, the south arcade was 'improved' with extra naturalistic foliage and sprigs of yew on the capitals. The north arcade is still 15th-century work but the north aisle was rebuilt early in the 19th century. The walls inside are creamy yellow and there is a brightly painted iron screen under the tower. There is a brass to Susan Kyngeston (d. 1540), a mid 18th-century portrait bust and inscription plate to a Mrs Purefoy, and a number of tablets to other members of the Purefoy family, holders of the Manor for many generations. The two best tablets are, however, to Mary Howes (d. 1828) by R. Westmacott sen., and to Geraldine Jervoise (d. 1852) by R. Westmacott jun. Shalstone House, the tidy five-bayed, cream-stuccoed, 18th-century house opposite the church is on the site of the older manor house of the Purefoys and the park has, in two long tree avenues, relics of its earlier formal planting. The Manor Farmhouse by the church is a more rambling, irregular, two-storeyed 18th-century stone house with pleasing rubble stone barns. At the north end of the village are new houses in artificial stone which would have looked more 'in keeping' if built of brick.

Shenley Brook End [5] Originally just an 'end' of Shenley (see Shenley Church End) but is now divorced by parish and district boundaries.

Mainly indifferent cottages are lined out along roads leading from a narrow central green and along the line of the Brook. The only historically interesting building, the 16th- and 17th-century L-shaped Westbury Farm, which is part timber-framed and part brick, lies to the west, away from roads.

Shenley Church End [5] Shenley Church End and Shenley Brook End are over a kilometre apart and have no middle. Church End is in Milton Keynes District, though just outside the New Town area, and has an architecturally important church on a little hill and buildings of mixed styles and materials. St Mary's church, sadly disused since 1973, is surrounded by trees and fenced in by the tall yew hedges of its former rectory. It is large, cruciform and of brown iron stone, while most of the village is of grey stone or red-brown brick, with a big embattled central tower. The latter seems too large for the church because the chancel roof is not of the height intended. The chancel has late 12th-century pilasters and stone corbels for a vaulted roof which was never completed. The south arcade has short late 12th-century circular piers while the north has 14th-century octagonal piers and double-chamfered arches. The chancel has a 19th-century rood loft and the wall above the crossing arch is stencilled in a tile-like pattern. Together these features give a Victorian unity to the interior. The chief monuments are those to Thomas Stafford of Tattenhoe (d. 1607), which has an alabaster effigy, in armour and ruff, semi-reclining above kneeling figures of wife and children in high relief, surmounted by a framed inscription plate, and to Edmund Ashfyld (d. 1577). The latter has a sarcophagus behind columns of porphyry and jasper supporting an open pediment, a composition spoilt by the central column. The Rectory is a neat, late 18th-century, brick house with arched windows and a splendid cedar. The other side of the church is a large timber-framed L-shaped farmhouse and down the village street are the Stafford almshouses (founded in 1654 by the son of Thomas Stafford, a plain stone row with heavy tiled roof and dormers. To the west of the church are medieval earthworks and moats. One has a mound called the Toot, presumably the bailey of a small medieval castle, and the other encloses the 3-hectare site of the early manor house pulled down in 1724. On the west side of these is the principal house of the village, in early 19th-century stucco, approached by an avenue of lime trees.

Sherington [5] A fair-sized village, full of stone houses and farm buildings and brick bungalows and trees placed in a square pattern of lanes joining a number of old 'ends': Church End, Crofts End and the High Street. Church End has a group of stone farms overlooked by the grey stone church on a little hill to the north-east; the pubs and few shops are on the main road (the High Street) on the south-west. The approach to the church is by a lych-gate overhung with obscuring chestnut trees. But away from the gate the church dominates the village and is a landmark for many miles around; it can be seen up the Ouzel valley south of Newport Pagnell and from the hills around Woburn. The dedication to St Laud (or Lo), a little known 6th-century French bishop, is unique for it is the only church in the country so dedicated. Its imposing central tower was started in the 12th century and was raised in the 13th and 15th. To support these additions the north and south walls of its base were thickened, making the crossing narrower and the interior somewhat meaner, but relieving arches were added on the outside of the upper storey which make a special decorative feature of the tower. It

was finally capped with a little lead spirelet. Extensive alterations were made to nave and aisles in the 13th century and appear to have been part of an unfinished scheme for rebuilding the whole church, but the chancel remains eccentric in plan and meaner than nave and aisles. The nave was further improved by the addition of a 15th-century clerestory and west window of five lights. The font is also of the 15th century and has somewhat worn figures of saints under ogee arcading. There is an interesting open area outside the church with fine stone farm buildings which would have made an attrative 'square' but has been spoilt by the incursion of brown brick bungalows and garages, widened road and open flower beds on the lane to Croft End. Beyond the bungalows the village improves. The former rectory, a stone building dated 1607, contains a handsome 18th-century staircase. Then in Croft's End itself are The Laurels, a 17th-century stone house with coped gables and irregular chimney stacks, the Congregational chapel of 1822 in chequered brick neatly pedimented, and, finally, the Manor House, a painted stucco, early 19th-century, rebuilding with a large moat and stone farm buildings. The High Street has a number of pleasant stone cottages and the colour-washed brick of the late 18th-century Swan Inn. North of these from its north end is a pleasant view right to Church End which looks quite independent on its hill. Sherington Bridge, which carried the Newport Road across the Ouse to the south, is a five-arched 18th-century stone structure with rusticated pilasters above cutwaters.

Simpson [5] A tiny green, odd thatched cottages and timber-framed houses and a grey church, islanded between the Ouzel and canal. It was formerly isolated in heavy clay fields but is now in a sea of New Town estates though pre-

served as a special suburb by the diversion of through traffic. The medieval church of St Thomas is still its natural centre. A cruciform stone building, its central tower is so narrow that it looks like part of a building toy, popped down over the wider nave and chancel roofs. Its lower part is late 13th century and the major part of the church was built around it in the early 14th. Inside is the unusual roof of the nave which has tie-beams and two tiers of wind-braces, exposed by the removal of plaster ceilings in 1904. There are painted Royal Arms above the chancel arch, two fonts (the older disused 15th century) and a monument by John Bacon to Sir Walden Hanmer (d. 1783), which has a black marble obelisk rising to the chancel roof, and a mourning Justice with scales. The L-shaped Manor House is late 17th century but was refronted in buff brick in mid 19th century.

Skirmett [14] A hamlet in the Hambleden valley. There is a mid 19th-century church, a simple heavily tiled box with flint walls, lancet and buttresses now converted to a dwelling, and a group of neo-Georgian boxy houses which are out of place in this settlement of colour-washed, timber-framed or plain brick cottages.

Slapton [8] Small, rather suburban-looking, between the River Ouzel and the Grand Union Canal. Indifferent post-war housing along its many-angled street has destroyed its villagey feeling and hidden its church but there are still wide views over broad meadows to the long line of the Chiltern Hills. The parish church, of Holy Cross, is behind houses and trees in a chalky limestone, rendered over, with an embattled west tower, chancel rebuilt and faced in brick in the 19th century, and lead roofs. It has fine early 14th-century arcades and clerestory, a 12th-century font and brasses of 1462, 1519 and 1529. The much-altered Carpenter's Arms at the village centre has a genuine 16th-century timber frame. Horton is partly in this parish.

Slough [18] Throughout its short history, has been a main-road place. Its centre was and is the junction of the road to Eton with the old Bath Road at the west end of the present main shopping street, which is secluded from through traffic by an expensive desert of new roads and car-parks. There are still traces of the late Georgian coaching houses, along the Bath Road, but its religious centre was away at Upton on the road to Datchet, and Slough was for some centuries simply part of the parish of Upton-cum-Chalvey. Now Upton is almost unknown outside the locality, its church is neglected and its traffic simply local. The greatest changes in the place were triggered off by the coming of the railway in 1838 which ran parallel to the Bath road and a little north. A station was planned at Slough from the first, though it was to serve Eton rather than Slough, but senior Etonians successfully fought to prevent a station being built here which they claimed would whisk boys off to the vices of London. The railway overcame the problem by stopping trains at Slough but without benefit of station. Etonians then dropped their opposition and the first station was built here in 1840. A line was later built from here to Windsor, avoiding Eton. The rapid development of Victorian Slough, with distinctive upright red-brick villas, followed and this can still be seen in the area north of the High Street, though much has been swept away. Farther out, off Stoke Poges Lane, is the most important old house in Slough, the 17th- and 18th-century brick Baylis House, built at the end of the 17th century for a Dean of Windsor. It was extended later for the Godolphins of Eton, whose dolphins can be seen on its wrought-iron gates. The stables with Tuscan colonnade and lantern were added, for the younger Godolphin, by John James in 1735. This house was isolated in fields when built. The Bath Road area was, however, growing in importance even before the coming of the railway and a new neo-Norman church dedicated to St Mary was built on the Windsor Road in 1835. It was rebuilt in 1876 by J. O. Scott though the tall spire with flying buttresses and pinnacles on its north-west tower was only completed in 1912. It is in an Early English style, but in red brick with dressings and odd details in stone, darker brick or flint. Windows by Kempe and four lancets in the west filled with glowingly coloured abstract patterns by A. A. Wolmark of 1915. The Victorian-looking factory by the railway with three-storey brick front and castellated and turreted tower at one end, was built for Horlicks Malted Milk in 1908, apparently in imitation of its American parent factory. Another Victorian church was built at Chalvey, Slough's western suburb, in 1861 by G. E. Street, with large nave and small chancel in flint with brick bands, but the explosive expansion of Slough started with the development of the Industrial Trading Estate out to the west of the station (which was rebuilt in French-chateau-style in 1882). This was the site of the War Department central motor depot at the end of the First World War and was re-used from 1920 by the Estate Company, first for the disposal of war-surplus stocks and then as home for the many new industries growing to meet demands for consumer goods in south-east England. The lengthy and apparently piecemeal development of this 600-acre site on what had once been market garden land caused much heartache, particularly to users of the Great Western Railway on their journey to countryside further west. The many factories built by the Estate Co. were generally small, symmetrical and identical and the ensemble was boring rather than ugly. The Company deserves credit on the social side as a pioneer of industrial health. Its community centre with common welfare and recreation facilities was built on the Farnham Road in 1936. Later industrial buildings, e.g. the Berlei, Aspro and I.C.I. Paint factories and offices are more free in design but no more attractive. Contemporary architecture in other fields was almost equally boring, even the Town Hall in Bath Road by C. H. James of 1935, to say nothing of the hectares of new housing, and there was little improvement till the mid 20th century when the Law Courts (1957) and the Central Library (1972) were built by the County Architect. Other redevelopment, particularly north of the High Street, where Victorian houses have been swept away for new car-parks and bus station, has been fresh but irritatingly jazzy. Nevertheless Slough is no uglier than large parts of High Wycombe, the industrial estate at Marlow, parts of Chesham or even parts of Windsor. One item of curious interest which should not be overlooked near the Town Hall is a tiny hill with thin worn trees on one side. This is 'Montem', an ancient tumulus which was the site for some centuries of the Montem (or 'Ad montem') ceremony, by which Eton schoolboys held up travellers on the Bath Road and extracted money from them to send an already well-heeled senior boy to Cambridge University. When this became popular and less scrupulous pickpockets arrived from London to take part, the ceremony was stopped by the headmaster of Eton (1864). All this ignores Upton, where there is still the most interesting building in Slough, the church of St Lawrence, in trees and modern houses at a busy crossroads. It is an almost perfect Norman parish church though wastefully extended with a large new south aisle by B. Ferrey in 1851 since the church was almost unused

Grand Union locks at **Soulbury**

in 1850 and is little used again today. It is in brown puddingstone with rough flints and clunch quoins and tiled roofs. The chancel is 12th century with rib-vaults painted black, red and yellow, and much ornamented with zigzag mouldings—the south aisle is in flint. There are monuments to Bulstrodes and to Sir William Herschel (d. 1882), astronomer to George III. The Herschels settled at Slough in 1786 and Sir William and his son Sir John made many of their notable discoveries here. Their house, near Windsor Road, was destroyed in the 1960s but the park laid out for them by Paxton in the

mid 19th century has been preserved by the Corporation.

Soulbury [8] A hill-top village of great variety whose gently winding streets are suffering from increasing traffic generated by the New Town to its north. All Saints church commands most of the village from its open churchyard on the hill top, now the crowding elms have gone, and looks down over small meadows to the ring of old farmhouses and cottages round the base. It is built of a red-brown ironstone obscured by rendering. Its simple 12th-century nave and chancel were extended by aisles

and the chancel was rebuilt in the mid 14th century. In the early 16th the nave arcades were rebuilt, the nave was given a clerestory and new roof supported by carved angels holding shields, and the west tower was battlemented. The font is 15th-century octagonal and trefoiled but has been recut. There are two early 16th-century brasses (in the nave) and a number of monuments of the Lovett family of Liscombe (in the chancel). The earliest is a brass to Robert Lovett (d. 1491), which has a small figure of a knight in armour, brought from Biddlesden Abbey after its demolition in 1704. The monument to Sir

145

Robert (d. 1643 buried at Sparsholt, Berks.) and Lady Lovatt (d. 1699) has kneeling figures in armour and in black robe and farthingale. That to Robert Lovett (d. 1699) and to his first wife and two children is a rare and provincial work by Grinling Gibbons. It is in white marble and has a large urn on a large sarcophagus decorated with cherubs, obelisk and flower friezes. Eleanor Lovett (d. 1786) has a reclining figure in Coade stone. Across the road east of the church is a short lane of dark brick houses. On its corner is Lovett's school, dated 1724. It is a two-storeyed block with dormered attics and, though now a private house, retains its two hooded doorways. Outside is a large block of millstone-grit which is claimed to have magic powers. It was left by the last glaciation of England very near its southern limit. None of the other individual houses deserves special note but there is a pleasant group round a small green at the north end of the village. About 2 km south is Liscombe Park, the home of the Lovetts for five centuries. It is a red-brick mansion round a courtyard open to the south and looks late 18th century, as most was refronted in 1774 when the centre was given a castellated pediment and square turrets and the corners were given little round turrets. Behind this much is of the early 17th century with some chimneys late 16th century. The east wing incorporates early 18th-century stables with rusticated niches and blank oval windows; on the south side is a detached medieval stone chapel with early 14th-century pattern windows. In the Ouzel valley is Chelmscott Manor, a large modern-looking house which encloses another 14th-century chapel. The Three Locks on the Grand Union Canal near by were built in 1800 to drop boats 6 metres on their journey north. The picturesque group of locks, humped bridges and New Inn are enlivened by brightly painted narrow boats. (For Stockgrove, in the north-east tip of Soulbury parish, *see* Great Brickhill.)

Stewkley: the west door...

Speen [11] Another large suburban village on another Chiltern ridge.

Stantonbury [5] (near New Bradwell) Sometimes called Stanton Low, a parish on the north fringe of the Milton Keynes New Town. The medieval settlement, and a previous Romano–British village, was at the north end in the flat fields and gravel pits traversed by the sinuous Ouse. Large housing estates on the New Town now fill much of the rising clay slopes to the south. The name 'bury' is a corruption of Barre, or Barry, the Norman family holding the manor after the Conquest. The church of St Peter was founded in A.D. 950 but it was isolated for some centuries and its parish functions eventually transferred to New Bradwell church in 1909. An earlier attempt to transfer these functions resulted in the embarrassing invalidation of over a thousand local marriages. The principal remains of its long decaying ruins—an elaborately

...and the chancel

moulded chancel arch with carved piers and capital—were transferred to the New Bradwell church in the 1960s.

Steeple Claydon *see* Claydon, Steeple

Stewkley [8] A thin village with one main street, linking, along 3 km of a gentle ridge, a wide variety of buildings of many different dates. It is visually untidy and its red and red-brown brick Victorian and later villas make one overlook the grey church which is the finest Norman building in the County

and one of the best in England. St Michael's is near the centre of the village, behind yew hedges and in a churchyard beset with yew. It is largely 12th century and one of only three in the country which have retained their original plan. It was carefully restored in 1862 by G. E. Street who tactfully resisted a commission to add transepts or aisles. It has nave, squat central tower, chancel, south porch of 1867 (replacing an earlier porch) and a detached shed-like vestry of 1910. It is of mixed limestone and ironstone, with tiled roofs, whose steep

pitch was restored by Street. The west front is the most commanding external feature. It has an arcade of three arches, the central forming the west doorway and being recessed with three rows of zigzag course which runs right round the church, bending gently over openings. The north door has double chevron mouldings on single shafts. The tower has a pattern of interlaced arcading with zigzag moulding and, until 1964, had 16th-century pinnacles and a spirelet which gave it a monumentality now lost. Inside, the chancel arch has two orders of zigzags and one of beakheads. The chancel itself has a stone vault with broad rectangular ribs decorated with bands of lozenge. The stone roof which it supported was replaced with lighter brick in 1844 and plaster-work was then stencilled in red and black. It is strange that this village with its splendid church and many attractive old buildings did not become treasured like Haddenham or Long Crendon. Of course it had no railway and when its straw-plaiting industry collapsed (and that was a poorly paid cottagey business) no light engineering moved in to make it prosperous. But whatever the cause, 19th- and 20th-century developments have been poor and ugly. The more attractive old buildings are scattered along the street and include Sycamore Farmhouse, with 16th-century timber frame and 17th-century barns; Dovecot Farm, with 16th-century timber frame; Manor Farmhouse, with 16th-century timber-frame and diagonal chimney stacks, and a nearby octagonal brick dovecote which has diapered brickwork and pilasters, moulded brick cornice and a little lead cap to its tiled roof. The dovecote is said to contain 800 nests. At South End on a gable can still be read the words 'Stewkley God Help Us', a relic of the local battle against the possible establishment here of a third London Airport which would have required the removal of the church and most of the village (cf. Cublington and Wing).

Stoke Goldington [5]

Another near-Northants. village of stone cottages, some white and some colour-washed, strung along a street which winds gently up a valley northwards to reveal the church and Church Farm isolated by fields against a background of woods. St Peter's is of grey stone with battlemented tower, 12th-century nave and two aisles of the 13th and 14th centuries (the south extending the length of the chancel), under roofs of lead and tile. The interior is light and wide but over-restored and the nave roof is plaster-ceiled above the tie beams. There is Kempe glass of 1902 in the east window, a plain Norman tub font on a moulded base, Royal Arms of William IV on a painted panel, 18th-century panelled pulpit and a wall monument to Thomas Hodgkins (d. 1720) with an inscription plate framed in Sienna marble and an urn in a broken pediment above. Church Farm incorporates parts of the former manor house and is of coursed limestone rubble with an old tiled roof, with an eight-light mullioned window facing the church. The village street in the valley below has a single-storeyed stone school of 1837 and a stone Congregational chapel dated 1819. From the school Ram Alley runs to a little knot of thatched stone cottages, a separate 'end' now less isolated by the building of over-urban council housing near by.

Stoke Hammond [8]

A large village, south of Bletchley, with the church and the more attractive part of the village on a lane, off the Linslade Road, which loops up the hill to the church, thatched half-timbered and dark brick cottages in pretty gardens. St Luke's church is approached through an over-pollarded lime avenue and between yews and Wellingtonias which are starting to overwhelm the south end of the churchyard. To the north

it is open and from here new estates in the New Town can be seen stretching out towards it. The church is of ironstone with grey limestone dressings and has a cruciform plan with simple embattled central tower, early 14th-century chancel and transepts and most windows of the 15th century. There is some 15th-century glass in the north of the nave with figures of prophets and some aggressive 1931 glass in the east window. There are also small carved Royal Arms, a 14th-century font, communion table dated 1619, a pillar almsbox dated 1618 and a tall late 17th-century wall monument to the Disney family. On its west side is the 17th-century old Rectory of grey brick with red dressings. At the junction of the village lane with the main road is Tyrells Manor Farmhouse, a handsome early 18th-century brick house with moulded cornice and an attractive Edwardian porch with twisting balusters, the centre of a flourishing dairy farm in the Ouzel meadows.

Stoke Mandeville [11]

A large suburban village tributary to both London and Aylesbury, with its own Metro station. It is now best known for its hospital for paraplegics to the west although that is more in Aylesbury than Stoke. The village has a few old houses and is still centred on a crossroads alongside the present St Mary's church. This is a building of flint with red-brick and stone dressings and a south-west tower which also acts as porch. It houses the 15th-century octagonal font and the late 16th-century marble monument to three children of Edmund Brudenell, with the effigy of a reclining girl and two swaddled babes brought from the old church of St Mary's. The site of the latter, now little more than brick and stone foundations, is 1 km south in meadows, where adjoining earthworks represent the site of the ancient manor house, now also gone. In the fields between old and new is Stoke

House, a red-brown brick house with red dressings, built in about 1700, and one of the best of its time. It is of two storeys and has eaves carved with egg and dart moulding and two carved porches of which the main one has a shell hood and elaborate garland of flowers. West of the central crossroads is Moat Farm, an L-shaped, 16th-century, farmhouse. This was the property of John Hampden and it was the 'ship money' tax on this property which he refused to pay in 1635.

Stokenchurch [14]

A large village near the crest of the Chilterns which carries on a long tradition of chair-making. The centre is a large rectangular green, the medieval church is tucked away on the north side and small groups of houses and an old pub are in islands in the middle. A lot of the older buildings still look slightly temporary, as though, having squatted here (which they did), they might be told to move on again. The church of SS. Peter and Paul is mainly 13th century of flint, partly plastered over, with a low slate-hung tower, and with one good 15th-century window in its lower stage. The north aisle and belfry were added in 1893. In the chancel are brasses of two knights, died 1410 and 1415, with inscriptions in French. On the green is the King's Arms Hotel, a 20th-century replica of its 18th-century predecessor, and an Italianate Methodist chapel of 1893. On the axis of the Oxford Road, to the north-west, is the Post Office Tower, a cylinder of concrete 100 m high crowned with radio dishes. It is the most prominent landmark on the Chilterns and can be seen across the plain from Oxford and beyond. Fringes of Stokenchurch are unattractive but in the beautifully wooded valley to the south-west are the charming 17th- and 18th-century Wormsley Farm and Wormsley House, the former of flint with brick dressings and the latter in brick with pretty porch and fan-light.

Stoke Poges [15] World-famous for its 'country churchyard' immortalized by the poet Thomas Gray (1716–71) who wrote his 'Elegy in a Country Churchyard' here. Stoke is now a large suburban area north of Slough but more a suburb of London than of Slough whose encroachment it (or the masters of the old manor estate and of Stoke Place) successfully resisted. So there is still an occasional illusion of country between the very ordinary village of Stoke and the large town of Slough in spite of the expensive detached villas which line Stoke's roads. The church of St Giles is in Stoke Park, the park of the medieval manor, south of the village. The curious parish name arose from the marriage of a 12th-century Bucks. knight, Robert de Pogies, to the heiress of the Manor, a Miss de Stoges. The church is approached through a lych-gate down a long graveyard decorated with yew and cypress, from which it looks a huddle of old gables against the trees that screen the Manor House. It is of flint with puddingstone and clunch, with a south chapel in brick, an irregular plan developed over several centuries. Nave and chancel are basically 12th century, the north tower, south aisle and sanctuary are early 12th century, the north aisle is late 14th and the south, or Hastings, chapel is mid 16th century. The timber south porch and nave roof are 14th century. The church is rambling and unimpressive, though friendly inside, and its chief interest is in its fittings. These include the rare bronze base of a late 15th-century altar cross (in the sanctuary); a canopied 14th-century niche over an unmarked tomb; brasses to Sir William Molyns (d. 1429) and his wife and daughter, with half life-size figures; and a tablet to members of the Penn family who were buried in a vault under the church. The first was Thomas Penn (d. 1775), the second son of William Penn of Pennsylvania, and the last was buried in 1869. Stained glass includes some 17th-century heraldic work and a curious medieval Italian cyclist. Gray is buried, with his mother and aunt, in a grave marked with a simple slab just east of the south chapel but he has a large and less appropriate monument in a little field outside the church gate. This is a huge stone sarcophagus on a pedestal inscribed with verses from the 'Elegy', designed by James Wyatt for John Penn, in 1799, as a landscape embellishment for Stoke Park (*see* below). South of the churchyard is a 'memorial garden', a burial ground with flower beds in place of grave stones, which is becoming a popular park with a 20p entrance fee. The Manor House, home of Poges, Molyns, Hastings, Cokes and Penns, is in thick trees near the church but has been reduced to its mid 16th-century central core in red brick and Tudor chimneys which enclosed the Hall where the Chief Justice Coke entertained Queen Elizabeth I in 1601. Here too, in the mid 18th century, Lady Cobham, widow of the first Viscount (*see* Stowe) entertained Gray. Thomas Penn, who bought the manor, thought the house and site too modest and built the house now known as Stoke Park and used as a magnificent Golf Club. This has a white-stuccoed square core, three storeys high, designed by Robert Nasmyth, which was translated into a Palladian building from 1795 on by James Wyatt. He added low wings and Doric porticoes round the base and put a drum with delicate composite columns, leaded roof and pilastered lantern, over the centre. Grounds landscaped by L. Brown with a lake in 1771 were re-worked by Repton at the end of the century and it was then that Wyatt embellished the Park, building an arched bridge over the lake, a 20-metre-high pillar to Coke and the Gray memorial. The latter was designed to be seen from the house and the former Rectory near the church was demolished for this purpose, and replaced by a castellated and cemented brick building north of the Park. Wyatt also built the south lodges with their Doric porches and attractive iron gates. Stoke Place, the other important estate, is at Stoke Green to the south-east. The house is of brick with a late 17th-century core and 18th-century wings and is in grounds laid out by Brown in 1771. Gray wrote his 'Elegy' and his 'Ode on a distant prospect of Eton College' (where he had been a pupil) when staying from 1742 to 1753 with his mother and aunt at the modest West End Cottage 1½ km north of the church. This is now incorporated in the later and larger Stoke Court.

Stone [11] At the crossing of the turnpike road from Aylesbury to Oxford with an old route from Bishopstone and the Chilterns to Waddesdon. At first sight it seems an east to west main-road place dribbling with bungalows and petrol filling stations, to end abruptly at a mental hospital, but off the main road is an attractive village lining the route to the Chilterns. Its centre is the church of St John the Baptist which is on a sandy hillock (partly artificial), approached by an avenue of pines and surrounded by a south-sloping graveyard overlooking old farmhouses and the edge of the Vale of Aylesbury. The church is cruciform, of limestone rubble with stone dressings, with a 14th-century west tower which has a 19th-century, tiled, saddlebacked roof, late 12th-century nave and north arcade and 13th-century chancel and transepts. There is a 12th-century south door with shafts and zigzag moulding, within a 14th-century porch. The church has been over-restored so that it feels scrubbed neo-Romanesque instead of genuine. The 12th-century font is, however, delightful in spite of some restoration. It is a large cylindrical tub decorated with interlocking beaded bands enclosing symbolic animals and

Stone: the font

rosettes, with one large panel showing human beings subduing dragons. One of the dragons has his tail knotted to indicate that he (symbol of evil) has been subdued by the Trinity (represented by human figures and other symbols). It is contemporary with the body of this church (late Norman) but appears to have come from Hampstead Norris (Berks.) by way of Lewisham in 1843. There are small

brasses of 1470 and 1520 to members of the Gurney family, who lived at Stone for some centuries. The mental hospital retains much of its Victorian buildings in red-brick Italianate designed by T. H. Wyatt and D. Brandon in 1850 with a separate large chapel in 13th-century style by Brandon, but has been continuously extended. The latest additions, including a handsome glass boxed boiler

house, are by Gollins, Melvin and Ward. (*See also* Hartwell and Sedrup.)

Stony Stratford [5] A market town consisting of a long straight street (the Roman Watling Street) and a hidden market place, which has never quite prospered in spite of its many coaching inns such as the Cock and the Bull, site of many tall tales. It was incorporated with

150

Wolverton in 1927 and put in the New Town of Milton Keynes in 1967, both moves which reduced its identity. Much of the old town was destroyed by fires in 1736 and 1742, the latter taking most of its main church, but there is a pleasantly compensating consistency about the main street which has a large number of good Georgian house fronts even when masked by later shops and, of course, the attractive fronts of the Cock Hotel, which has a main entrance flanked with fluted columns and friezes with beautifully carved garlands, and of the Bull Hotel next door. The present parish church is St Giles's, in a cramped position on the south side of the High Street. It is of stone with a somewhat weak west tower which was almost entirely rebuilt by F. Hiorns in 1776 in his own gothic style. His entertaining apsidal chapel with flamboyant windows was unfortunately rebuilt in 1923 and the east end obscured in 1905 by a clumsy oak chancel screen by G. F. Bodley, an otherwise sensitive architect. Internally it is still worth a glance for the little forest of Hiorns's columns in the nave. At the east end of the town is St Mary's church, a straightforward 'Early English' essay by G. G. Scott with nave, bellcote and apsidal chancel and north aisle of 1864. Down Church Street is the pleasant Market Place away from the central street which is still noisy with traffic, in spite of bypass and motorway. Here, in a medley of buildings from the 17th to the 20th centuries, is another attractive library by the County Architect. This one is of 1975, externally in brick and white rendering. Between the High Street and Silver Street, which connects the south end of the Market Place, is Cofferidge Close, a new shopping centre, surprisingly good-looking for such a development, all in brick with well-detailed landscape work, the whole designed by the New Town Corporation's staff. Silver Street leads to Horsefair Green, a

Stony Stratford: inn signs on the Holyhead Road

second secret market place now given up to grass and lime trees. It has a Baptist church founded in 1657 but rebuilt in 1823. The old parish church of St Mary Magdalene is represented only by the medieval tower standing behind no. 98 High Street.

Stowe [4] On account of its beauty, historic interest and integration of landscape and build-

ings, the most important place in the county. It is a princely palace set in a garden of international importance which is not only beautiful but is unique in illustrating the whole range of 18th-century English landscape garden history. From the late 17th century to the end of the 18th it was a forcing house of new design in buildings and gardens on a grand scale; it has survived unspoilt because by 1800

Stowe: the entrance bridge and one of the Boycott pavillions

major tree-planting was coming to maturity and the interest of the owners of the Park was turning to other pursuits. In 1680 Sir Richard Temple, the 3rd Baronet, built a new house, a little north-west of the older family house and its walled garden, on a ridge facing the tower of the medieval Buckingham church 4 km south-east. It was a red-brick building with stone quoins and hipped roof in a Wren manner and most is still buried in the present house. Temple then set about landscape improvements. He planted an avenue across the Home Park towards Buckingham and laid out formal parterres south of the house. These cross the line of the old gardens at an awkward angle (110 degrees) because he was loath to sweep them away and he then made their conciliation to the fashionable symmetry of the times harder by planning an avenue of

limes west of the house on the old line. The 4th Baronet was more determined. He was a successful general and courtier and with his own means and those of his wife, daughter of a rich brewer from Stoke Poges, set about lifelong rebuilding of both house and gardens. For their design he employed Vanbrugh, a fellow member of the Kit Kat Club, who added a tall portico to north and south of the old house and low service courtyards to east and west, in line with the house. Now Earl Cobham, he continued after Vanbrugh's death, sometimes with help from other architects, and piled masses of brickwork on the low service wings left by Vanbrugh. The south front now looked more like a street than the palace intended, but he was succeeded by his nephew Richard Grenville of Wotton Underwood, later Earl Temple, a more gifted

amateur architect and a pioneer of the neo-classical school. He designed, with some help from Kent, the garden buildings known as the Grecian Temple and the later Temple of Concord and Victory, and employed three architects to design a grander south front to the House. The last of these was Robert Adam, called in 1770. Adam's design was executed up to *piano nobile* level but was altered again by Cobham's talented cousin, Thomas Pitt. Pitt retained the flat pavilions of Adam's design but raised their height, extended the south portico forwards, made the Venetian windows square headed under relieving arches and carried Adam's 'antique Ionic order' right across the design. The south front was completed in 1775 and the loss of Adam's refinement was made up by Pitt's boldness. The less interesting north side was

Stowe: the south front

being transformed meanwhile. Ionic colonnades were built to enclose the forecourt, the old brickwork was stuccoed over, an attic added and crowned with vases. The interior was, however, still in confusion and was not completed until the inheritance by George Grenville, later Marquess of Buckingham, and the end of the century. The interior is still of much less interest than the exterior, which is, as landscape historians have pointed out, really the grandest garden ornament in the park. This is particularly so now that the house is used as working parts of the present public school. Two rooms are, however, special: the Oval Hall, with its pink columns, its frieze by Valdré and coffered dome, and the Gothic Library, on a lower floor, put in by Soane in 1806. Work on the landscape kept pace with major changes to the house.

The 1st Lord Cobham had employed Bridgeman. Bridgeman overcame the problem created by the awkward diagonal lines of the Park by making it a feature of his grand design. His deliberately assymetrical plan used slanted views and triangular woods and, by introducing the ha-ha (or sunken fence) made the surrounding country part of the park. He still made certain formal features such as the Octagon Lake and his concepts were a half-way house between the formal gardens of the 17th century and 'Landscape' of the 18th century. Gibbs and Kent decorated these works with many new temples and Kent then took up where Bridgeman had left off, to create first in the 'Elysian Fields' south-east of the House and then in the 'Grecian Valley' to its northeast a new and more intimate landscape where hard edges were blur-

red by irregular planting and straight lines were removed or blurred. Conversion of the Octagon Lake into a less formal lake was his. Capability Brown worked here from 1740 to 1751 before leaving to work on his own, and executed many of Kent's designs. He went on, with Lord Temple's encouragement and simultaneously with the enlargement of the house, to increase the scale of the Home Park and open up wide vistas in its centre. At the end of the 18th century the work was largely completed, the trees were maturing and, as Laurence Whistler says, it then went aesthetically to sleep. The Temples, now Dukes of Buckingham, turned to other things; they were bankrupt by 1848 when the House was the subject of enforced sale. A number of tenants followed until in 1920 it seemed that the House would be

demolished for want of use. But a new school was founded which took over house and grounds in 1923. The house did not suffice for the fast-growing school which needed new buildings. Clough Williams Ellis built an extension to the Orangery in 1923, a new gymnasium in Adam style north of the house in 1925 and a new boarding house on the lawn to its south-west. Sir Robert Lorimer followed in 1927 with a large chapel, the most monumental of the new buildings ever provided by the school, where he fitted the interior with 16 giant columns taken from Kent's Temple of Concord, and furnishings from the Temples' old chapel in the house. The latter included panelling, pulpit, Royal Arms of Charles II and west gallery, which had originally been carved by Michael Chuke for a Grenville House called Stowe in Cornwall. Then a number of other boarding houses were added, then an art school, hall and headmaster's house (1955) in increasingly forward positions and backward designs. We must be grateful to the school for saving the noble house from total destruction in the 1920s, but it has not been without cost. The house is in school use and rarely open to the public but the gardens and garden buildings are often open, as they have been since the early 18th century. Visitors will find it rewarding to read first the guide to the gardens by Whistler, Gibbon and Clarke. The motto of the family of Lord Cobham and Earl Temple was 'Templa quam dilecta' and the family delighted in providing more temples in their park than there are anywhere else in the country. The house may be of more interest to architectural historians but the park and its temples are of greater international importance and a delight to all. It is generally approached from Buckingham by the 3 km avenue of beech which ends at the Corinthian Arch nearly 20 m high designed by Thomas Pitt in 1767. From this there is a distant

view of the south front of the house, across the lakes and up the lawns to the portico. But the road does not lead straight on to the house and curves off west before reaching the Corinthian Arch to run round the Home Park to join the Oxford drive south-west of the House. The latter runs straight to the house across the Oxford Bridge of stone arches by Gibbs (1761), between two pavilions designed by Gibbs with pyramidal roofs (but later tamed with shallow domes) and up an avenue of limes to the north court of the house. Here is a statue of George I on a little mound and a distant view 1 km north of a 30 m obelisk to General Wolfe (1759). Ideally one should go through the house to the south portico to enjoy, at one gasp, the view over the huge lawn stretching down to the lakes, between the two Lake Pavilions on the far side and up the hill-slope to the Corinthian Arch beyond, a softened version of the late 17th-century classical vista. Whistler suggests that visitors with time should visit first the Grecian valley to the north-east but, if time is short, should make a tour first south-east through the Elysian Fields and then in a clockwise direction round the eastern (Octagon) lake and back between the lakes to the college chapel and the south-west corner of the house. Visitors who need to see the principal garden buildings in the least time can, however, include them in one irregular anti-clockwise circuit starting at the south portico. From here they are in order: The School Shop, a domed building built as a menagerie (1781); the Rotondo, an open circular temple by Vanbrugh (1719). This was the focal point of the old geometric gardens and of Bridgeman's design. It was given a shallower dome by Borra in 1752 to make it less dominant in the smoother and more open landscape of that time; the Temple of Venus (beyond the lower, sailing, lake), a large pedimented alcove, originally painted with erotic pictures. The

design is attributed to Kent (1732); the Lake Pavilions, built by Vanbrugh in 1717 but rebuilt more widely apart in 1764. There is a fine view of the House from here; the Octagon Lake—the upper of the two large lakes—was laid out by Bridgeman and softened later by Kent and others to take its present informal shape; the Congreve Memorial, on an island in the Lake with a monkey holding a mirror, by Kent (1736); the Temple of Friendship, south-west of the Octagon Lake by Gibbs (1739). It was dedicated to the Whig opposition of that time which included the elder Pitt. It has been badly damaged by fire; the Palladian Bridge—the little valley running north of the Octagon Lake was laid out by Kent from 1755 onwards; the Temple of British Worthies, a semicircle of niches by Kent (1733). Niches contain busts of Queen Elizabeth I, Bacon, Shakespeare, Hampden, William III, Locke, Newton and Milton by Rysbrack, and King Alfred, Black Prince, Gresham, Sir J. Bernard, Drake, Raleigh, Inigo Jones and Pope by Scheemakers; the Doric Arch (to west of Elysian Fields, 1768); it frames a view of the Palladian Bridge and of the mock Stowe Castle east of the park; the Temple of Ancient Virtue, a circular temple by Kent (1734), which was the terminal of Bridgeman's 'great cross walk' on the line of the older gardens. It is now an important feature of the Elysian Fields; the Church of the Assumption, hidden from the house in trees on the west side of the Elysian Fields; it is the last relic of the medieval village of Stowe which was damaged in the Civil War and largely removed to the present hamlet of Dadford, north of the park, by 1740. It is a modest, mainly 14th-century building of roughcast stone with a west tower, aisled nave, chancel and north chapel. It contains a defaced 14th-century effigy of a civilian, brasses of 1469 and 1592 and a white marble effigy of Martha Penyston—née Temple—

◁ **Stowe**: the Gothic Temple and its evening shadow

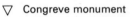
Stowe: gate into forecourt   Doric Arch ▷

▽ Congreve monument   Palladian Bridge △

Stowe: the Temple of British Worthies, and detail

(d. 1619), as well as tablets to later owners of Stowe. The church was little used by the Grenvilles who had their elaborate chapel in the house and their principal internments at Wotton Underwood. Capability Brown was married here in 1744; Grenville Monument, a Roman-type monument of ships' prows projecting from a column in the Elysian Fields east of the church (1747); Shell Bridge, by Kent, leads across to the east side of the Elysian Fields; the Gothic Temple, a red ironstone triangular building with two turrets, a tower and a picturesque silhouette, by Gibbs (1741); the Queen's Temple, hidden east of the Elysian Fields, by Gibbs (1748) and altered in 1773. It has a pedimented portico and encloses a 4th-century Roman mosaic found at Foscott. It is now the school music-room; the Cobham Monument, a tall column east of the Queen's Temple, capped originally by cupola and statue, in total 35 m high. It was struck by lightning in 1957 and cupola and statue were replaced by an urn. The Coade stone lions at its base are by Valdré; the Temple of Concord and Victory, north of the house. This is based on the Maison Carrée at Nîmes. It was designed by Kent but finished by Borra (1764). Sixteen of its columns were removed by Lorimer for use in the school chapel; the Grecian Valley, a dog-legged valley nicely seen north-east of the Temple of Concord, by Kent just before his death in 1748; the Bourbon Tower, an ironstone keeper's lodge designed by Vanbrugh as an eyecatcher east of the park; Stowe Castle—five towers disguising two cottages, another Vanbrugh eyecatcher east of the park. The principal buildings on the long approach from Buckingham have already been mentioned and should not be overlooked.

Swanbourne [8] A place of stone houses, and black-and-white cottages in high hunting country,

exceptionally rich in trees, which afford glimpses of attractive buildings or pleasant scenery around. The central point is St Swithin's church, in smooth ashlar limestone rather lacking in texture since its restoration in 1863. It has a battlemented west tower with an unusual stone face to its clock, 13th-century chancel and an internal five-bay arcade with three lancets on the east wall and a double piscina, a 13th-century south doorway and 14th-century windows. The west gallery built in 1936 has Royal Arms across its front and the north wall has traces of late 15th-century painting supposed to represent the soul before and after death. The Manor House (west of the church) is a stone, gabled and mullioned Elizabethan building once owned by the Fortescues and later by the Fremantles. Deverell's Farm (to the south-east) is another stone house with mullioned windows and is dated 1632, and to its south-east is the Old House, which has a 16th-century timber frame infilled with brick but extended in the 18th century. There are other old timber-framed and brick buildings north of the church in the area known as Smithfield End and a row of old black-and-white cottages in Nearton End, which looks a separate village, on a lane south of the Mursley Road. Near the Manor House, and often confused with it, is Swanbourne House, of plain 18th-century stone and now a preparatory school. It was the home of Elizabeth Wynne, one author of the Wynne Diaries. She married Captain Thomas (later Admiral) Fremantle at the Hamilton's house at Naples in 1797 and has left accounts of the Hamiltons, Nelson and many contemporaries.

Taplow [14] A patchy parish with a clot of small houses, bungalows, shops and Skindle's Restaurant on the Thames bank near Maidenhead Bridge and an old village on a rise away to the north-east.

Between river and village are large houses not always worthy of their grand wooded sites. The former medieval church was in the grounds of one of these, Taplow Court—a large, angular neo-Tudor house of 1855 with sharp gables and pointed turret. A Saxon tumulus in its grounds adjoins the church site. The new church is 1 km east on the far side of the village. This is St Nicholas's by Fellowes Prynne (1912), in a Decorated style with a sharp copper spire over a west tower, and a stone rood screen incorporated in its chancel arch. The building replaced an early 19th-century brick church. There are two interesting memorial brasses brought from the medieval church, one mid 14th century with 30 cm figure of N. de Aumberdene, which is the oldest brass to a civilian in England, and the other with half-size figures to a brother, sister and half-brother of the Manfeld family (1455). In Rectory Road, the spine of the village, is the elegant early 18th-century Elibank House, with a pedimented central bay, and to the south is Taplow House, of 1751, but altered by Basevi in the early 19th century to look a castellated cottage. The road bridge at Maidenhead is wholly in Berks. but the Taplow railway bridge is half in Bucks. It has two elliptical brick arches with 40 m spans about 7 m above river level, built by Brunel for the London–Bristol railway in 1838; it appears as the foreground of Turner's painting *Rain, Steam and Speed*.

Tattenhoe [8] Only 3 km from Bletchley but feels the most remote place in the county. It is still, as Betjeman and Piper said in 1948, 'what Bucks. must have been like in Cowper's day'. A medieval church sits in yew and scrub and the overgrown fishponds of a long-gone mansion, connected with the outside world by a muddy track across flat fields past still remote cottages. St Giles's church is part rubble and part plastered and within the moat of the former house of the Stafford family (see Shenley Church End) which was a ruin by mid 18th century and now shows only its earth banks. The church consists of nave and chancel in one rectangle with wooden bell-turret over the west end. It was built in 1540 partly from the ruins of the former Snelshall Priory in the parish of Whaddon. The font has a 13th-century oval base and shafts (presumably from Snelshall) but 19th-century bowl. The church was restored in 1892 but is now disused.

Thornborough [8] A spread-out village away from main roads but with a complicated pattern of lanes along brooks lined with ash, willow and vanishing elm, and greens bordered with limestone or colour-washed cottages, church and farm buildings. St Mary's is on the south side of the greens though central to the village. It is of limestone rubble, partly rendered, with lead and tiled roofs, and an embattled west tower of three stages which seems tall against a modest nave. The latter has 13th-century arcades and 15th-century windows. The chancel is late 13th century and the south porch was added and most windows were enlarged in the late 15th century. The interior has been cream-washed and naïvely decorated during this century. It contains a converted Georgian barrel organ, a brass of William Barton (d. 1389) and his wife with one-third life-size figures and a wall tablet to C. Wodnoth (d. 1778). Thornborough Manor, behind stone walls under which a brook disappears to reappear near the church, is of the late 17th century but has been much altered, while the Old Manor House, for centuries the property of Magdalen College, Oxford, is a two-storey Elizabethan stone house with a small 17th-century addition yet incorporating remains of a 14th-century Hall. Alongside the Buckingham–Bletchley road is the old

Thornborough Bridge, the sole 14th-century bridge in the county. It is not much more than 3 m wide with six low arches, of which three are pointed and ribbed. There are two Roman burial mounds near by, of which the 1st- and 2nd-century contents are in the Cambridge Museum of Archaeology. On the Ouse north of the village is the late 18th-century stone Mill House.

Thornton [5] Northants.-looking stone farmhouses, church and a large house hidden in a wooded park near the Great Ouse. The church of St Michael and All Angels is approached through the park by an avenue of pines and is of rough limestone with lead roofs and an embattled west tower. It has a sawn-off east end, for the chancel was pulled down about 1780 and the present east window was stuck in the former chancel arch. The arcades are 14th century but the north aisle and much else was rebuilt by John Tarring in 1850, though he retained the box pews, the two-decker pulpit and the squire's pew. There are mid-15th-century alabaster figures of John Barton in armour and his wife and brasses to Robert Ingylton (d. 1472) and his granddaughter Jane St John (d. 1557). The adjoining Thornton House incorporates part of the medieval manor house, but was rebuilt and enlarged by John Tarring at the same time as the church, for the Hon. Richard Cavendish. It is rendered neo-Tudor with an entrance stair tower and stair-turret, gabled wings and a great dining hall based on its medieval predecessor. The Ouse was dammed to make a sinuous lake alongside the great lawn leading to the house. The Home Farm west of the park is a picturesque jumble of stone buildings while Thornton Hall, 1 km south-east, is a modest but elegant red-brick Georgian with pedimented doorcase and canted bay windows, and views over the Northants. border.

Tingewick [7] A stone village of rather dusty cottages along the heavily used Buckingham Road, but picturesque along the parallel Upper Street. The church of St Mary Magdalene is on a little hill north of the Buckingham Road, overlooking meadows leading gently down to the Ouse beyond. The churchyard is entered under a huge chestnut tree framing the view of thin embattled west tower, low mean nave and odd detached-looking, taller, chancel. The interior is eccentric, scraped and characterless with an over-restored late 12th-century north arcade with chevron mouldings and a south aisle and arcade rebuilt in 1851. On the north wall of the chancel is a brass to Erasmus Williams (d. 1608), which shows a kneeling figure with moon, books, instruments and painting materials, symbols of his interests and attainments and signed R. Haydock. The nearby Manor House is of 18th-century rubble stone. Lindale, in the main road, has an elaborate 18th-century pattern of chequer bricks but most adjoining cottages are timber-framed, plastered over. Upper Street has more attractive groups of stone and thatched cottages, notably the late 17th-century row of cottages, nos. 5 to 7. Tingewick Mill on the Ouse has a three-storeyed stone mill and two-storeyed cottage with the site of a Roman villa not far east.

Turville [14] A picture-postcard little place deep in a dry Chiltern valley, of brick, or flint, and tile, or half-timbering and thatch, cottages. Its centre is a little triangular green which has a friendly colour-washed brick pub with a thorn tree mushrooming like an umbrella on the east and the grimmer looking, Victorianized, church on its west. St Mary's is scrubbed flint outside and set against gloomy pine and larch but is bright and friendly inside. It is entered by a simple, early 13th-century, south door,

Twyford: detail of the south doorway

facing a blocked Norman door on the north, into a simple nave with steep, open king-posted, early 14th-century, roof. The west tower and chancel arch are of the 13th century. The only major alteration after these was the addition of a short north aisle in brick in 1733, used as pew for the Lords of the Manor and separated from the nave by simple classical oak screens. It contains the standing memorial in varied marbles to William Perry (d. 1740) of Turville Park and his family. The font is a plain Norman cup. The large stone coffin under the tower was dug up from the church floor in 1900 when it was found to contain two skeletons, an example of not-uncommon medieval economy. Stained glass includes pieces with armorial bearings of 16th, 17th and 18th centuries with one recording a late 16th-century marriage in which the bride's surname has been erased. A lunette in the nave has a delicate white hand and lily by John Piper, commemorating the beautification of the church with the proceeds of the sale of the chapel at ease at Turville Heath in 1975. The adjoining old vicarage is of knapped flint and brick with flint decoration and steep gables. Council bungalows in School Lane, which were rightly castigated by critics in 1957 for their alien siting and design, have now been mellowed by time, garden trees and hedges. All these are overlooked by the smock-mill in arable fields at the top of the valley's north side. Its dark brick base, white timber upper stage, black cap and white sails have recently been restored. The parish has a curious S shape, jammed between the Oxon. border and Fingest and Ibstone. A large part of the village, including all the houses on the north side of the street, is in Ibstone parish. Turville Heath is a wide, largely overgrown common with houses scattered around between trees but has the two best houses in the parish. These are Turville Park, a stuccoed classical

Turville church and mill

Turville church

building built for William Perry in the early 18th century, and Turville Grange, another early 18th-century house but in grey brick with red dressings with decorative brick eaves and handsome adjoining farm buildings. South End, towards Fawley, is a tiny settlement with some 16th- and 17th-century cottages, mostly 'improved', round a small common. (*See also* North End.)

Turweston [4] A village of silvery limestone cottages along a terrace above the River Ouse which, with the great brick viaduct of the former Great Central Railway, separates it firmly from Brackley, Northants. The church of the Assumption is at the north end of its sinuous lanes. It is somewhat forbidding externally, thanks to G. E. Street's tall saddlebacked west tower of 1863 and his overall stone refacing of the rest, but is interesting in showing work of most centuries from the 12th on, and for its 19th-century furnishing of altars and carved stone reredos which make it a monument to Victorian Tractarianism of 1863. The main body is 12th century, as can be seen in the chancel arch and north arcade. The south arcade with round arch at the east end and later pointed arch to west is of the 13th century. The chancel is mid 13th century; both aisles were rebuilt in the 14th century and the east window in the 15th. In the chancel are a 14th-century ogee-headed niche; 13th-century piscina and brasses, a one-third life-sized figure of a 15th-century priest and (smaller) figures of Thomas Green (d. 1470) and two wives. In the north aisle is a wall monument to Simon Haynes (d. 1628), which has small figures kneeling on blue cushions with golden cherubs above. There are New Testament scenes by Willement (1851) in south aisle windows and an east window by O'Connor of 1870. The modest 16th- and 17th-century stone Manor House has 17th-century staircase and overmantels, and Turweston House is more formal, early 18th-century, with pedimented central bays, in a small park bisected by the Ouse. The Manor Farmhouse is dated 1634 but has been much altered.

Twyford [7] A small village in a large pastoral parish, up a dead end cut off by the old Great Central Railway line. The church of the Assumption is at the lower railway end, with its Vicarage and the Red Lion pub. It is a grey stone building with embattled west tower, two aisles and an embattled chancel. It is assymetrical in plan as the 13th-century north aisle is only 2 m wide while the mainly 15th-century south aisle is more than twice this width. In 15th-century rebuilding of the south aisle the Norman south door was replaced. This is ornately decorated with a thick band of zig-zags on the inner order, beasts on the shafts, beakheads on the arch, and stars on the jambs. Some 12th-century carving is also re-used on the 13th-century chancel arch. The nave roof with its cusped king-posts and queenposts, the fragment of chancel screen and the 22 plain poppy-headed benches are all 15th century. There is a late 13th-century Purbeck marble effigy of a crusader in the south aisle along-side a large table tomb with a brass to Thomas Giffard (d. 1550) in Tudor armour. The last is a re-used brass of William Stortford, Treas-urer of St Paul's Cathedral (d. 1416). There is a wooden panel framed in columns and pediment to Richard Wenman (d. 1572) and an elaborate monument with black columns, pediment and cherubs to the 1st Viscount Wenman (d. 1640). The Vicarage is largely 17th century but still includes parts of an early 15th-century hall and solar. Twyford Lodge (half a kilometre south-west) is on the site of the van-ished mansion of the Wenmans.

Tylers Green [14] Medieval tiles were made here and at adjoining Penn from clay on the Chiltern plateau. It is now a place of Vic-torian and Metroland cottages, nearly joined to High Wycombe by large estates on the west and north but just saved by belts of beech. Newer houses are largely to the west of the big rough open space called Tylers Green; a more attrac-tive group of older, mellow brick, houses are round a smaller Y-shaped open space with a duck pond, called simply the Green. There are just enough to justify making a 'Conservation Area'. The church of St Margaret is between the two greens; it was built in 1854 and the place became a separate ecclesiastical parish (at the expense of Penn and the centreless parish of Chepping Wycombe) only in 1863. The church, by R. Brandon, of flint with stone dressings and lancet windows, has a south-east tower of flint with a timber bell-chamber and pyramidal roof added in 1890. The chancel was lengthened in 1934 and furnished in light oak con-trasting with the dark Victorian nave. Near the Green is Rayners, a large house in a red-brick neo-Tudor style built in 1847 for Sir Philip Rose, friend of Disraeli. New buildings were added by Eastwick Field for the London County Council when it was converted in the 1960s into a school for the deaf.

Tyringham [5] A small parish (even with Filgrave) in the Ouse valley facing Gayhurst. There is no village of Tyringham, just an his-torically important mansion designed by Soane and a Victorian church, in a park in a loop of the river. The church of St Peter is east of the house and luckily screened by trees, since it is so out of harmony with the spirit of the house and park, which have a noble simplicity lacking in the church. Keeping only the embattled west tower, it was rebuilt in a knobbly near-Arts-and-Crafts-style gothic by E. J. Tarver in 1871. It houses brasses to an armed John Tyringham of about 1490 and to his daughter Mary (d. 1508) who married a Catesby of Astwood. The Catesbys, like the Digbys of Gayhurst, were impli-cated in the Gunpowder Plot and involved the Tyringhams by meet-ing here. There is a much later monument to William Praed, the London financier who built the present Tyringham House, and this has a lunette with a low relief of a canal barge and lock to illustrate his interests. At the west end is a war-memorial by Lutyens (1921). The principal monument of Tyringham is Soane's work for Praed. This included entrance gate and lodge south of the river, the great bridge over the river and the mansion and stables which 'en-gaged a large portion of six of the most happy years of my life', from 1792–97, as Soane himself recalls. Praed had married a descendant of the Tyringhams and engaged Soane to remodel the earlier house before deciding instead to demolish and build again. Soane's house is of pale yellow ashlar of two main storeys with attic and basement, rectangular in plan with a shallow bay on each of the principal fronts. The south-east bay has thick Ionic columns supporting an entablature which is carried right round the house. The lower storey was designed with heavy horizontal rustication and only bands of Greek-key decoration between it and a plainer upper storey. Inter-nally the house was centred around a vestibule leading to an inner hall which had a ribbed dome open to the floor above, a prototype of Soane's later work for the Bank of England. The interior was, how-ever, drastically altered and the exterior modified for the Ameri-can–French couple, the Konings, by G. F. Rees from 1909 onwards. They spoilt the balance of the house by simplifying the decoration of the lower storey and enriching the upper, notably by the addition of a little dome over the central skylight. The Konings later employed Lutyens to provide a water garden and two temple pavi-

Tyringham: Soane's bridge

Entrance gate: **Tyringham**

lions, which are attractive in their own right but incongruous additions to a Soane masterpiece. North-east of the house are the stables designed by Soane. These incorporate a tall stone doorcase with the Arms of the Tyringhams, a relic of the older mansion here. The lodges and the Soane Arch are across the river, strictly in the parish of Lathbury. They are simple in design with Soane's 'trademark' of incised lines and round-headed alcoves, an introduction to the noble bridge which crosses the Ouse in one high sweep of ashlar stone with rusticated archways, a wide string at road level and semi-circular niches in the abutments.

Upper Winchendon *see* Winchendon, Upper

Upton *see* Slough

Waddesdon [8] A plum-coloured model village in a rich, improved, landscape overshadowed by the Rothschild chateau on the wooded hill to its west. St Michael's is still the church of the small medieval village which grew at the foot of Lodge Hill on the junctions of roads to Bicester, Quainton and Long Crendon. Of the old village little but the church and the nearby 17th-century Bell Inn remains. The church has an embattled west tower, roughcast stone nave, aisles, chancel and lead roofs. The nave was started in the late 12th century and extended in 13th and 14th necessitating the rebuilding of the chancel in the early 14th. The north arcade is Decorated while the three west bays of the south arcade are still late 12th century with fat round piers and scalloped capitals. Three of the piers have curious brackets and two have additional little columns as though to support a stone vault. The clerestory was added in the 15th century. There is a worn effigy of a 14th-century knight and a nearly life-size brass to

163

Roger Dynham (d. 1490) brought from the ruined chantry chapel at Eythrope, showing him in full armour under a triple canopy, also brasses to priests Sir Richard Huntyndon (d. 1543) and Hugh Bristowe (d. 1588). The ornate alabaster pulpit from the Great Exhibition of 1851 was given by the Duke of Marlborough, whose estates of Waddesdon and Winchendon were bought by the Rothschilds. Waddesdon Manor is the French-style chateau on the hill which sticks its turrets through firs and dying elms to bring a breath of Touraine to an otherwise very English landscape. The hill was bare of buildings and trees when bought by Baron Ferdinand de Rothschild in 1874. The top was flattened, a steam tramway built from the railway at Quainton Road

and a team of Percheron mares from Normandy brought in to drag yellow Bath stone for the house on its top and fully grown trees to plant round it. The house has steep roofs, heavy angle towers and turrets and motifs drawn from Azay, Blois, Chambord and elsewhere by the French architect H. A. G. W. Destailleur (1822–93). The east wing was completed in 1880, a morning-room was added in 1889, and a major later addition in 1893. The landscape, with its forest of trees and long curving drives round the hill and other fanciful features such as a menagerie, was designed by the French landscape-architect Lainé. House, grounds and most contents were left to the National Trust by James de Rothschild in 1957 and further contents given to the British

Museum. The collection is particularly notable for its 18th-century boiseries (French carved panelling), Savonnerie carpets, Sèvres porcelain and individual French (e.g. Boucher), Dutch, Italian and English paintings. It has valuable 17th- and 18th-century French furniture, books chosen for decorative rather than intellectual content, and a collection of Arms and Armour made by Dame Alice, Baron Ferdinand's sister, of Eythrope, who inherited Waddesdon.

Walton [5] A village within the Milton Keynes New Town but still isolated in meadows east of the River Ouzel. St Michael's church is almost alone in a yew-treed churchyard to the north-west of the village. It has an embattled west

△ **Waddesdon**: copy of the Apollo Belvedere in the Vatican and one of the six 18th-century terms

Waddesdon: (*above*) centre of the north-west façade and (*below*) the east corner of the house ▷

Tympanum over the south door, **Water Stratford**

tower in limestone with ironstone quoins, Decorated nave and aisles under shallow lead roofs and a steeper and higher tile-roofed chancel. The simple plaster walls inside have texts in childish Gothic letters. There are sedilia in the chancel and a wall monument to Bartholomew Beale (d. 1660) and his wife (d. 1657), paid for by their two sons and a daughter-in-law Mary Beale who was a pupil of Lely and a talented painter. It has two portrait busts in oval medallions between black columns supporting an open pediment. In the nave is a monument to Sir Richard Pinfold (d. 1701) with bust and obelisk, signed by Nollekens and therefore carved in the late 18th century. The

Beales and the Pinfolds lived at the Manor House, a fundamentally 16th- and 17th-century, heavily gabled house with brick chimneys and partly timber-framed. Liberal use of white paint, additions and security guards have made it the G.B. headquarters of an international chemical company. Walnut Tree farmhouse is also late 16th century but with 18th-century additions. North of the church is Walton Hall, a two-storeyed, rendered brick house of 1830. This is the headquarters of the Open University which has added large ranges of temporary-looking buildings without too much taste, but leaving the Hall open to the south.

Walton (Aylesbury) [11] Once a pleasant village on the Wendover Road, it has now been swallowed up in Aylesbury and knocked down for traffic improvements. There are still a few pleasant houses on Walton Road and an angular, ugly, late 19th-century church.

Warrington [2] A small parish with a tiny population and no church, in the northern tip of the county. The former character of hamlet on a twisting road has been filleted by road improvement which has left an old stone farm and odd stone cottages or barns separated on each side. (*See also* Lavendon.)

166

Wendover (*above and below*)

Water Stratford [4] On the gentle northern slope of the River Ouse with a small church, a short string of cottages, some timber-framed, some stone and some brick, and a stone manor house. St Giles's church is raised above the road in chestnuts and sycamores. It has a low, 14th-century, pyramidally capped west tower but was otherwise rebuilt by a local architect, Willmoor, in 1828. Willmoor reused the Decorated windows of the church and the two Norman doorways which have important Norman sculpture. The south doorway has chevrons and plaited capitals and a tympanum carved with a Christ in Majesty within an oval supported by two well-feathered angels in flowing drapery. The lintel has a pattern of delicate intersecting arches. The north doorway, a priest's door to the chancel, is not

so boldly carved and has simpler decoration. There is a lamb and cross in the tympanum and the lintel is decorated with intertwining dragons. Inside is an inscribed wall monument to Mary Franckyshe (d. 1629), who is shown lying in bed, with husband and children kneeling in front. The Manor House at the top of the village street is of stone and tile and dated 1598 but has been much altered.

Wavendon [5] A rather ordinary, though well-treed village, with a Victorianized church, rectory, almshouses, pub and brick cottages, on a little clay ridge below the Woburn hills. The 20th century has added a ribbon of houses where the Woburn—Newport road bypasses the village on the east but there are odd developments spotted right across the parish east to the border with Beds. At Cross End is an early 17th-century manor house. Wavendon House, a large, early 18th-century, cream-rendered house, is isolated further east, while on the east boundary are a number of late 18th-century terraced brick houses which look much more Beds. than Bucks. St Mary's, near the centre of the old village, is of coursed limestone with embattled west tower, high lead roofs to the nave and lower tiled roof to the chancel. Nave and chancel are late 13th century with four-bay arcades with slender pillars, but the clerestory and roofs were rebuilt by William Butterfield and the whole church given an early Butterfield look in 1849. The varied stained glass in purple, red and gold which darkens the chancel was added by O'Connor at the same time. The Parsonage, north-west of the church, was built at the same time by Butterfield with lots of little gothic gables. With the adjoining barn of a theatre, it is the headquarters of a Wavendon Festival run by Cleo Laine and John Dankworth. West of the village is a later 19th-century mansion, Wavendon Towers, which has large additions

Westcott

168

by the Bucks. County Architect and a handsome glass-box by the Development Corporations' architects. These house the Milton Keynes New Town Development Corporation, though the New Town itself stops short just west of the village.

Weedon [8] A complicated place of narrow crooked streets with buildings part stone, part brick, some timber-frame and nogging of varied patterns, winding over a small hill. It is a civil parish but has no church being in the ecclesiastical parish of Hardwick to its north. The central narrow lane called the High Street has the most interesting buildings starting at the crossroads with the Five Elms pub in 17th- and 18th-century red and blue brick, the Wheatsheaf pub with 17th-century timber-frame and brick nogging further north and then the Manor Farmhouse of timber and brick and some cemented stone dated 1649, with a gateway dated 1687 and a barn 1647. A number of the houses have stone bases. West of High Street in a park, is The Lilies, a red-brick mansion with stone dressings rebuilt in 1870. The former house was the home of Lord Nugent who planted an early 19th-century 'circle of friends', trees with stone seats each with the name of a prominent contemporary. From the Five Elms crossroads, where elms still survived in 1978, a ribbon of semis spoils the road to Aston Abbots. A little south of the road is the almost separate hamlet of East End with the most attractive group of old buildings in the parish, of which the chief is East End Farmhouse with its 17th-century timber-frame and herringbone nogging.

Wendover [11] A small market town, prettily set in a gap in the Chiltern scarp so that, from the north, it is framed in rounded hills. Unfortunately, the 17th- and 18th-century centre, which is delightful, has been surrounded with large suburban estates which have spread 2 km into Aylesbury Vale and another 2 km along the scarp towards Halton. It was joined to London, 56 km away, and to Aylesbury, 7 km away, by the Metropolitan Railway in 1892 and now seems a suburb of both. Until 1832 it was a borough with two Members of Parliament, of which John Hampden and Edmund Burke were, at separate times, its best-known. But the town is of little importance now, though it provides a smart address for its residents. The two principal streets are at right angles: Pound Street, running down the line of the Icknield Way into the High Street; and Aylesbury Street, which continues the line north of old routes from London. The parish church of St Mary is, however, isolated nearly a kilometre south in chestnuts, sycamores, limes and yews near the site of the old Manor House. It is approached through a sturdy Victorian lych-gate and a churchyard which has been given a garden-of-remembrance treatment with little tablets stuck like stamps into its flint walls in place of traditional memorials. The church itself was over-tidied by G. E. Street in 1869. It is mainly of the 13th and 14th centuries with a heavily buttressed embattled west tower and spire. Inside it is dark. Arcades of five arches are 14th century; the capitals on the south side are decorated with animals, those on the north with flowers. There is one interesting brass, to William Bradshawe (d. 1537) and his wife. Kneeling children and grandchildren, 32 in all, are set out on the same plate below the parents, in pedigree form. North of the church at the central crossroads is a somewhat graceless red-brick spired clock tower of 1842. From this Aylesbury Street runs tree-lined and wide with handsome groups of buildings on each side. The best of these, Red House, with 18th-century brick front and modelled cornice, and Chiltern House, with 16th-century timber frame fronted with brick on a splayed plinth in 1725, are both on the east side. High Street has most of the shops and is more mixed in quality. The best house here is Woolerton on the south, not far from the clock tower. It has a panelled central door in a doorcase with fluted pilasters and pediment. High Street continues uphill into Pound Street, which has a long row of low brick and timber-framed cottages on the south and Lime Tree House on the north, the latter being an 18th-century house in grey brick with red brick arches to openings. In Tring Road, north-east of the clock tower, is the 15th-century Bank Farmhouse. Outside the town are The Hale, rebuilt in 1743; Manor Farmhouse, with late 18th-century barns; and Wellwick Manor, with tall chimneys of 1616 and good weatherboarded barns of its farmhouse. There are good downland walks to Baccombe Hill (to south-west) and to Combe Hill (to east). The latter, at 257 m above sea-level is the highest point on the Chilterns.

Westbury [4] A compact village in a corner of the county between Northants. and Oxon. with grey limestone church and cottages and some infilling of brick bungalows on a sheltered slope near the Ouse. The church of St Augustine has an undersized, saddlebacked, early 13th-century west tower, a 13th-century chancel and 14th-century arcades, but the south aisle was rebuilt and the whole church overzealously restored in 1863. The chancel was decorated with stencilled designs in 1884 and Kempe windows were added north and south of the chancel but the church is dark inside and dull. The 18th-century stone Manor House near by was almost completely rebuilt with neo-Tudor additions in 1903.

Westcott [10, 11] A little brick village, overlooked from the wooded Lodge Hill of Waddesdon on the east. It was greatly expanded by the Ministry of Defence Rocket

Propulsion Establishment, set up on a wartime airfield, and semi-detached Ministry of Works houses put up for staff. The little church of St Mary the Virgin was provided by the last Duke of Buckingham and Chandos in 1867 and designed by G. E. Street. It is Street's best work in the county and has nave and aisles under one sweeping roof with a central bell-turret, and a lower chancel. Externally it is in stone with tiled roofs. Inside it has an open-framed roof, patterned pale brick walls and short circular piers, massive plain circular stone pulpit, low stone screen and plain glass windows, save for one in memory of the Duke's first wife Caroline (d. 1874). The interior is of satisfying severe simplicity. A school east of the church is also by Street; the rest of the village is very mixed with scattered old cottages and, on the Ashendon Road, West-cott Farmhouse, in 18th-century brick.

Westlington [11] An attractive hamlet in the Vale of Aylesbury and a Siamese twin to Dinton to which it is joined by the small park of Dinton House. It has its own little High Street and small green with cottages and pub in colour-washed rubble or timber frame and brick, with thatched or tiled roofs along narrow twisting lanes.

Weston Turville [11] A large spread-out place, now almost joined to suburbs of Aylesbury, made up of 20th-century infilling with villas, semis, bungalows, petrol stations and D.I.Y. shops, in and between four medieval 'end-ships' along the twisted Lower Ick-nield Way. The endships—West End, Church End, Brook End and Bye Green—each retain a thatched cottage or two and with old trees from former orchards look pretty in spring and autumn. Church End, more hidden in poplar and ash and dying elm to the south, is still secre-

tive and medieval. St Mary's, on the southern fringe, is almost in fields. It is of plastered flint rubble and has an embattled west tower with higher stair-turret, 13th-century south aisle and mid-14th-century north aisle and chancel. The chancel was given a raised open timber roof and the nave its clerestory in the 15th century. These have given the interior a light and spacious look. It has an 'Aylesbury type' font with fluted base and scroll-banded top, part of its 14th-century rood screen, a Jacobean pulpit, fragments of 12th- and 13th-century sculpture, a small museum of the church's history and, the best thing in the church, a delicate 15th-century stained-glass Virgin and Child in the east window. The church was decently restored by J. H. Cox in 1963. On its north side is the early 18th-century, three-storeyed, red and blue brick Manor House which stands in the outer bailey of, and alongside the moat and mount of a Norman Castle. To its north-west is the Rectory, built in 1838 by G. G. Scott in a depressed classical style with coursed flint and red-brick dressings. Manor Farm at West End encloses the hall of an early 16th-century house.

Weston Underwood [5] Was, to the poet Cowper, the loveliest village in England. 'Farewell dear scenes for ever closed to me', he wrote on his cottage window when he left in 1795. It is to Cowper what Stoke Poges is to Grey, but almost unchanged. Walls at the upper, Olney, end and the church at the lower, frame a long curving street of stone buildings, stone walls, grass verge and stone causeway. Its setting on a little hill overlooking the willowy Ouse which 'Now glitters in the sun, and now retires, as bashful, yet impatient to be seen' in meadows 'with cattle sprinkled over' has been well captured by Cowper's poetry. He came here from Olney in 1786 to live in The

Lodge (now 'Cowper's House'), a late 17th-century stone cottage, to be near his friends the Throckmortons. They lived at Weston House, which was pulled down in 1826 leaving a turreted range of stone stables and a modern stone house on the site. The street past the house was then private, and the public road to Olney ran east of the village, but the pineapple-capped piers and the flank walls of the Throckmortons' entrance gates are still across the street and now give the whole village a privileged, private, air. Across the road is the Throckmortons' wood, still called the Wilderness, though it is now part of the adjoining 'Flamingo Tropical Bird Gardens and Zoo' and its 'well-rolled walks with curvature of slow and easy sweep' are now grassy. But they retain the urns and busts of Throckmorton days. One commemorates a pointer with Cowper epitaph: 'Here lies one who never drew/Blood himself yet many slew'. 1 km north along the lane skirting the north side of Weston Park is the Alcove, a small temple at the top of the Park, to which Cowper would walk to admire the view of 'square tower, tall spire' among the 'beauties numberless'. The spire was that of Olney, the tower that of St Lawrence's at the lower end of the village. This church is of stone with slate and lead roofs and an embattled west tower with a little, leaded 18th-century cupola. Most of the church dates from the late 14th-century rebuilding of an earlier chapel by John Olney, Lord of Weston and Olney, who died, according to a brass inscription on the chancel steps, in 1405. There is a damaged brass to Elizabeth Throckmorton (d. 1571), a late 17th-century tablet to more members of the family and a later tablet to Cowper's 'Griggy', the chaplain to the Throckmortons, Dr Gregson. In the generous east window are a number of little 14th-century stained-glass figures; at the top Christ and Two Angels.

West Wycombe *see* Wycombe, West

Wexham [15] The greater part of Wexham is a solidly built-up suburb of Slough and was transferred to Berks. in 1974. On its east side is the parish church of St Mary, a simple, 12th-century, flint building of aisle-less nave and chancel with a weather-boarded bell-turret and little spire over the west end. Beyond in the Green Belt area, still in Bucks., are large ploughed fields, residual elms, walls of old estates and a few brick cottages, reminiscent of old Middx. In Wexham Park is the large Slough General Hospital, begun in 1959 to a plan by Llewelyn Davies, but with largely low buildings and small gardens, by Powell and Moya. The landscaping is enticing to picnickers on warm weekends and more popular than a 'Country Park'. Wexham Street, further north and back in Bucks. again, has a number of old estates and large houses, many used as research establishments. The Cement and Concrete Association has one of these called Wexham Springs, where gardens by G. Jellicoe and Sylvia Crowe have shown what concrete can do in sensitive hands. George Green, on the road from Slough to Denham, was a pleasant Middlesex-type village, until filleted by main road widening. Middle Green, towards Langley, is still a pleasant hamlet of brick walls and old houses, notably the 18th-century three-storey red-brick Manor House, but gravel pits are steadily encroaching.

Whaddon [5] A village on a hill in the hunting country of Whaddon Chase, with a church nicely capping its hill and wide views to the west. It is otherwise disappointing owing to infilling with indifferent red-brown brick Victorian and later housing with little charm or character. St Mary's church is of sandstone with lead and tiled roofs, embattled west tower, 12th-century north arcade, early 13th-century south arcade, capitals decorated with foliage and animals, and 14th-century chancel and north chapel. The font is a 13th-century tub on four shafts. Monuments include a canopied tomb with brass effigies of Sergeant Pigott (d. 1519) and two wives and children, a tomb chest of the 14th Lord Grey de Wilton (d. 1533), who was Lord Deputy of Ireland, and one of the Commissioners who condemned Mary Queen of Scots to death, and a brass to Margaret Missenden (d. 1612) in Elizabethan dress with son depicted as a skeleton. Whaddon Hall, in a park on the north side of the village, is the site of the former Manor House of the Greys de Wilton and later of the Selby-Lowndes family. It was purchased by the grandfather of Browne Willis, the Bucks. historian, who lived there for 56 years making his collection of manuscripts and died in 1760 (to be buried at Fenny Stratford). Lipscombe records the 'magnificence of its splendid staircase', but the present house is a plain rendered brick building of 1820. West of its park was the Benedictine Snelshall Priory whose stone was used to build the church at Tattenhoe. Nothing remains but earthworks. Whaddon Chase is the name given to an area west and south of Whaddon with wide fields, long views and little fox coverts but it originally covered a much greater part of N. Bucks, much of it well wooded. It was given the status of 'Chase', i.e. detached part of a former Royal Forest, by Henry III.

Whitchurch [8] A large and handsome village along the Aylesbury–Buckingham road, on a low ridge with fine views south-west over the Vale. The older part is at the top of the long, narrow High Street which curves gently up from Little London to a junction with the road to Oving and North Marston. Near the top are earthworks of the once important Bolebec Castle, demolished in the Civil War. Castle Lane cuts through its bailey but the mount with masonry traces on top is almost complete and it was from here that Rex Whistler painted his best-known view of the Vale. Between the Castle and High Street is a little tangle of streets enclosing, in Market Hill, a small market place, long disused, surrounded with mixed stone and tile and thatched buildings. In Oving Road, parallel to Market Hill on the north, are two of Whitchurch's best buildings, the 17th-century Whitchurch House which has roughcast walls above a stone base, moulded cornice and diamond-shafted brick chimneys together with a cartouche of cherubs on the street face, and the over-restored 16th-century School House which is roughcast over a timber frame. In the High Street near its junction with Oving Road is the stone-fronted and brick-gabled 16th- and 17th-century Old House with 18th-century brick stables. A little lower down the street is the largely 15th-century 'Priory' which has a stone base and timber frame with brick infill, oversailing upper floors and diagonally placed brick chimneys. It is on the corner of Church Lane and with another old house to the north frames the view of the pale limestone church which has given the village its name (Whitechurch). St John's has a west tower built into its west end with buttresses cut into north and south arcades. It is mainly Decorated in detail but the west door with clustered shafts and foliated capitals is 13th century. The light and spacious interior contains a font on a timber pedestal of 1661, plain benches and poppy heads, a timber poor-box of 1620, large Royal Arms of 1753 and fragments of 14th-century glass. The only memorial of interest is a white marble wall monument to John Westcar (d. 1833) in low relief by J. Gibson, showing that enterprising farmer of Creslow standing in front of a prize bull with woolly sheep at his feet.

Weston Underwood

Whiteleaf [11] (near Princes Risborough) A hamlet with old cottages mixed with inter-war houses along a lane under Chiltern beech woods between Whiteleaf Cross and Monks Risborough. The Red Lion near the middle is an 18th-century red and grey brick pub and there are some 16th- and 17th-century timber-framed cottages, usually with brick nogging but some with flint infill and some thatched. Whiteleaf Cross is a prominent chalk landmark cut out of the beech woods on the scarp-face above. It has a triangular base and arms nearly 7 m wide with a span of over 26 m. Like Bledlow Cross, some 6 km to the south, its origins are obscure but as a charter of A.D. 903 refers to a boundary mark here, it is likely to have an ancient origin even if, like other chalk cuttings, it has been the subject of abuse and misinterpretation later.

Willen [5] A hamlet with an important Wren-style church, two farms and a few houses, predominantly in red brick, on a little hill

overlooking large ponds made by the Milton Keynes New Town Development Corporation. The church of St Mary Magdalene is in a graveyard enclosed with old brick walls and iron gates and is approached by an avenue of lime trees which, with the church tower, is a prominent landmark in the flat heavy fields of the Ouzel valley. It was built in 1680 for Dr Richard Busby, headmaster of Westminster School, and designed for him by his friend Robert Hooke, on the site of a medieval chapel. It is in red and black brick and limestone dressings with a square west tower and tall short nave. A little apsidal chancel was added in 1861 by T. H. Leeds. The main doorway is in a stone-faced recess in the tower, as at Wren's church of St Mary-le-Bow, and the upper storey of the tower has Corinthian pilasters at the angles and originally supported a little lead cupola. Pineapples now crown the tower and the little curving wing-walls linking two small rooms, originally vestry and library, which flank the tower. Inside are the plastered barrel ceil-

ing, wood panelling, chequered marble floor, pews, rails and stall fronts of the original design and a delicate white marble font on a black baluster which has an ogee-shaped cover carved by Bates who also worked for Wren. Hooke was a versatile inventor but this is his only remaining entire building. It was carefully restored in 1970. The Cotton Valley sewage works, with their handsome steel frame and glass buildings by the Development Corporation architects (1976), are to the south-east of the village east of the great ponds. The sewage works were originally planned, though in more modest form, to form the foreground of views south from the church. The ponds were designed to relieve flooding of the New Town but are being developed for sailing and other water sports.

Winchendon, Lower (or Nether)

[11] A soft village between soft rolling hills and the water meadows of the Thame with a brownish-yellow stone church, a stone mansion and colourwashed plastered cottages and farmhouses linked by chestnut,

Nether Winchendon: tower floor

Nether Winchendon House, home of the Bernards and their descendants for some centuries. This was formerly the Manor House, given by Walter Giffard of Long Crendon to Notley Abbey. It was granted in 1547, after dissolution of the Abbey, to the 1st Earl of Bedford, who sold it to a London merchant whose granddaughter married a Tyringham, owner of Cuddington and Notley Abbey, so that the properties were united. It passed by later descent to Sir Francis Bernard, Governor of New Jersey and Massachusetts (d. 1780), and then to his younger son, Scrope Bernard, who made extensive and picturesque, though naïve, additions on a large scale from 1790 to 1815. He inherited a largely timber house, medieval and Tudor, the medieval part including a great Hall facing across the Thame which he encased in stone and brick. The north-west wing was Elizabethan, of brick. It was then approached, as it still was till recently, by an avenue of lime trees. Scrope Bernard restored the old work, added stone towers at the ends of the medieval range, refaced the Tudor front keeping the Tudor brick chimneys, and extended the entrance side of the south-east wing, recased the Elizabethan wing in stone and then built a 'gothic' screen round the courtyard, made square by the addition of the present Garden Tower. When all this was done he retired to Kimble where he enlarged the former rectory, hurt, it is said, by his wife's continued dislike of their Winchendon home. The house was restored by Russell Cox in 1958, together with many other village houses owned by the family. The gardens, replanted from 1958 onwards, and the interior, with its tapestries and family portraits, are open to the public in summer.

Winchendon, Upper [11] A church, a house and scattered farms on a high limestone ridge near Waddesden, with tree belts, good arable land and views to north

sycamore and ash trees and old stone walls. The church of St Nicholas at the junction of three lanes is the pivot of the village, a simple, part-plastered, stone building with embattled west tower, plain nave, south porch and chancel rebuilt 1891. Its largely unrestored interior is delightful and has high box pews, a timber west gallery decorated with Royal Arms and a three-decker Jacobean pulpit. The north wall of the nave is covered with Tables of Commandments, the Lord's Prayer and the Creed. There is 15th-century glass (north), 16th-century Flemish glass (south), and brasses of 1420 and 1487. Of the numerous timber-framed buildings with brick infilling, the most imposing is the manor farmhouse, on the slope west of the church, which has severe gables but delicate framing. A door is dated 1620 but much of the house is earlier. The mansion is and west. The church of St Mary Magdalene is small, long and low, of limestone rubble with tiled roofs, with an embattled west tower and a cone-topped stair tower. The interior is pleasingly simple. The nave is early 12th century and the north aisle late 12th century with an arcade of three unmoulded round arches cut through the north wall. The late 12th-century south door has scalloped capitals, the chancel arch is early 13th century pointed and the screen of one-light divisions is 15th century. The pulpit was cut from a single block of oak and has panels with 14th-century Decorated tracery. The benches are 16th century. There is a brass to Sir John Stodeley (d. 1502) with a half-size figure. Adjoining is the long, two-storey, brick-faced house called the Wilderness. This was the kitchen wing of a mansion owned by the Whartons. The 1st Marquis was buried here but his son, who rose to be 1st Duke of Wharton, was later indicted for treason and forfeited the estates (*see also* Wooburn). Other relics of the Whartons' time are a two-storey brick summerhouse to the north-east, the large walled enclosure around it and several avenues of trees in the neighbourhood. Most of the land in the parish was acquired later by the Rothschilds whose property at Waddesden adjoins. (*See also* Eythrope.)

Winchmore Hill [14] (near Coleshill) A suburban-looking village between Coleshill and Penn, to the north of Beaconsfield, in rolling but not dramatic chalky hills. It has a triangular green and mainly 20th-century houses. Hazel hedges line the approaching roads.

Wing [8] Has an important Anglo-Saxon church and once had its own market and fairs: is now a relatively quiet large village with grey church and red-brick houses on a low limestone hill above the Vale of Aylesbury. It had another

Nether Winchendon House (*top*) and **Upper Winchendon** church

moment of glory in the 1960s in its fight against the siting of London's Third Airport on its disused wartime airfield (*see* Cublington and Stewkley). Rouse, a local patriot, says it is 'not particularly attractive', but it is pleasant enough, particularly on the hilly slope towards Aylesbury and in the little streets away from the main road. The church of All Saints on the pleasant

west side, nicely set in a well-treed churchyard, is mainly in creamy limestone rubble with stone and clunch dressings and lead roofs and is one of the most important Anglo-Saxon churches left, for it preserves all or most of the original seven-sided apse, crypt under the apse and complete nave and aisles, nearly 30 m long overall. Main alterations made since the

175

Wingrave: graffiti on south arcade

Conquest are the rebuilding of the south aisle in the 14th century, the addition of the west tower in the 15th, the addition of porches and the widening of most of the windows. The apse is considerably higher than the nave and has, below it, the rough-vaulted crypt with a hexagonal central chamber and ambulatory following the outline of the chancel above. The interior is tall, spacious and welcoming and the raised chancel, through its wide unmoulded arch, is inviting. But the main interest of the interior, after the crypt, is in its monuments. The most important are to members of the famous Bucks. family of Dormer, formerly of Ascott (east of the village) and Dorton. That to Sir Robert Dormer (d. 1552) blocks a north window. It has a garlanded tomb chest reces-

sed in an architectural composition of mixed English and Renaissance details, with coupled Corinthian columns carrying a heavy, wide entablature whose soffit is decorated with strapwork. It is probably the best monument of its time in the country. Other large Dormer monuments face each other across the apse. These are to Sir William (d. 1575) and wife with kneeling figures, completed in 1590, and to Sir Robert, 1st Lord Dormer (d. 1617) and wife, which has big kneeling figures between columns and smaller figures of children on the base. There are brasses of 1460, 1470 and 1648, the last being to a porter of Ascott Hall, 'now left his Key, Lodg, Fyre, Friends and all to have A Roome in Heaven'. Remains of the rood screen and the screen in the south aisle are of the 16th century while the octagonal font is 15th century. The base of a 12th-century Aylesbury-type font is in the porch. North of the church is the 17th- and 18th-century, white-painted vicarage; to the south is a picturesquely gabled school of 1850. Little streets of modest houses lead south to the main road. Here is Dormer's Hospital, a range of stone rubble almshouses founded in 1519, altered in the 19th century. At the north end of the village is a mound about 6 m high of a Norman castle and to the east of the village is the Ascott Estate, former home of the Dormers.

Wingrave [8] A Rothschild village without a Rothschild mansion, but with red-brick Victorian cottages and a grey Victorian-looking church between Ascott, home of one Rothschild and Mentmore, palace of another, in rolling, low, clay hills on the north side of the Vale of Aylesbury. The church of SS. Peter and Paul is at the central road junction and is a largely Perpendicular in detail, but over-renewed, grey-stone building with 13th-century west tower and turret rebuilt in 1898. Inside, the tower

arch has mature stiff-leaved 13th-century capitals, while stone corbels and wooden figures support the roof. In a vaulted chamber on the north side of the sanctuary are faded 13th-century wall-paintings, in part showing a soul being carried to heaven in a cloth by two angels. The font is a simple Norman tub with one cabled band. The Victorian 'Manor House', now an Anglican nunnery, east of the church, was the headquarters of the Czech government in exile during the Second World War. The village school and some tens of houses were provided by Hannah de Rothschild of Mentmore from 1876 onwards. The minor road south of the village has a simple but dignified United Reformed church built in 1852 and a wide view across the Vale to the Chilterns.

Winslow [8] A distinct little country town on the Aylesbury–Buckingham road with an important Wren-style house. Its centre is a small market square with two nice pubs: the 18th-century George, which has a wrought-iron balcony brought from Claydon House, and the early 19th-century-fronted Bell Hotel, which has a handsome columned door and bay windows. From here High Street runs north into an area of predominantly Victorian red-brick houses, which seem to have followed the coming of the cross-country railway between Oxford and Bletchley, to a little station (now closed) north of the town. Horn Street runs west from the Market Place and has a Congregational church with assymetrical elephantine tower by J. Sulman (1884) while in Market Walk is an admirably simple Baptist church of 1695 with complete Georgian internal furnishings. The parish church of St Lawrence peers over the Market Place buildings from the north. Its stone building, mostly of the 14th century, with a west tower, aisled nave and chancel looks 15th century thanks to the

Winslow Hall

north and south aisle windows of that century. Inside are effigies of Thomas Fige (d.1578) and wife and seven children; a brass to Dorothy Barnard (d. 1634); wall-paintings of the late 15th century showing the murder of Becket; St Christopher and a Doom; a Jacobean pulpit, and a valuable small library of early books including works by Bishop Jewel. Sheep Street, the road to Aylesbury, runs east from the Market Place and here, past the early 18th-century Brook Hall, and, almost in fields, is the finest house in the town, Winslow Hall. This was built in 1700 for William Lowndes, Secretary of the Treasury (*see* Chesham) with guidance from Sir Christopher Wren, woodwork by royal joiner and carpenter, and gardens by royal gardeners Wise and London. The house is tall, red and grey brick, with stone dressings seven bays

wide, with two high main floors and a shallower third under a hipped roof and big pedimented centre. The central doorway has a segmental pediment while the garden front is a mirror-image of that to Sheep Street. Off the High Street to the north, the only building of interest is the former workhouse, now part of the hospital, which was designed by G. G. Scott in his early classical style in 1835.

Woburn Sands [5] A place of dark browny-red brick houses and Victorian-looking shops on the main road (A50), in sandy, conifer-covered, slopes not far from Woburn, Beds. (pronounced Woeburn not Wooburn). The railway station of 1846 is one of the picturesque, gothicized, timber-framed, two-storeyed buildings put up by the London and North Western Railway on its Bedford branch.

Wolverton [5] A railway town created by, and for, the works of the London and North Western Railway which opened its first station in 1838 and locomotive and carriage works, and a second station (replaced in 1881) in 1840. The locomotive works were moved to Crewe in the years 1865–77 but the carriage works were expanded and flourished until the 1950s when many of them became redundant and were sold off to other industries. They are, however, still the hub of a large industrial estate encouraged by the establishment of the Milton Keynes New Town in which Wolverton is the largest town after Bletchley. Both railway works and the terraces of Victorian workers' houses are monotonous but it is still a mine for railway historians, as can be seen in Sir Frank Markham's *History of Milton Keynes*, volume 2. The old parish church, in

Great Woolstone church

◁ **Wooburn Green**: the screen

what is called Old Wolverton, though little of it is old, is the crude neo-Norman church of the Holy Trinity, hidden in yew and oak about 2 km west of the railway. In stone with west tower, transepts, a big west portal, a neo-Norman pulpit, walls and ceiling decorated by Daniel Bell (1877) and a monument to Sir Thomas Longueville (d. 1685) reclining in Roman armour on a big sarcophagus, it was built by H. Hakewill in 1815 to replace an older church. Next door is the former rectory, now 'Longueville Court', with a Corinthian-columned porch and pediment from the older manor house. In meadows to the north, a big square iron trough of 1811 carried the Grand Junction Canal across the River Ouse. New Wolverton, i.e., the railway town, has in St George the Martyr a big church by Wyatt and Brandon (1844) in a 13th-century style, with a north-east tower and mean spire. Transepts were added by J.O. Scott in 1894.

Wooburn [14] A small village with a flinty church and little brick houses dominated by the brick chimney of a Victorian paper mill, in the little Wye valley between Wycombe and the Thames. The church of St Paul is of medieval origins, and though never entirely rebuilt, it looks, in its shiny knapped flint exterior and scraped interior, a wholly Victorian creation for it was heavily restored by William Butterfield, internally in 1857 and externally in 1869. Inside are whitewashed walls and stout Norman piers and some brasses of late 15th and early 16th centuries with one later brass to the only son of Philip, Lord Wharton, who died in 1642 aged nine months. It is, however, greatly enlivened by the elaborate rood screen, with rood and two seraphim, designed by Ninian Comper (1899).

Wooburn Green [14] A larger village up the valley, separated from Wooburn by a field and a cricket ground. On its south side is Wooburn House, on the site of a palace of the Bishops of Lincoln and of a later large house, of the Whartons. The latter was one of the show houses of the country but was pulled down in 1750 following the disgrace of the Duke 'too rash for thought, for action too refined'. North of this is a large, kite-shaped, lime-fringed green with small brick houses of all ages around it.

Woodham [7] A civil parish 3 km west of Waddesdon, has no church or village, just two old farms and some scattered cottages and a disused and fast over-growing brickworks.

Woolstone, Great [5] A scattered hamlet in low-lying clay country, part of the parish of Willen-cum-Woolstone, now being radically transformed by lakes and housing in the creation of the Milton Keynes New Town. The church of Holy Trinity, built in 1839 as a chapel of ease to Willen, in a simple 'Commissioners' style with a main

179

Glass in the Greville Chapel, **Wotton Underwood**

velopment as part of the Milton Keynes New Town. Holy Trinity church is a small and much altered 12th-century building with nave and chancel and a western timber bell-turret and prominent 15th-century south porch. The chancel arch is early 13th century and the nave has big Decorated 14th-century windows. There is (or was) a Norman font with intersecting arches and a zigzag moulding on the cup and fragments of old glass in windows. Church Farm on the west was, till recent neglect, a handsome red-brick 17th-century building with a hipped tiled roof and prominent diamond-spaced chimneys, and an 18th-century brick front disguising its old timber frame. It was the centre of a large farm now partly drowned by the new lake.

Worminghall [10] The 'shabby Worminghall' of the old local rhyme which links it to Ickford and Shabbington, two other villages in the wet, elmy and willowy, meadows of the Thame valley near the Oxon. border. The church of SS. Peter and Paul is hidden in elms and farm buildings in a meadow at the end of a curving lane, the Avenue, that starts in a suburban-looking housing estate near the village centre. It is a small grey stone building with 14th-century chancel, 12th-century nave, 15th-century west tower and tiled roofs. In the plain interior is a brass to Philip King (d. 1592) with kneeling figures. He was the nephew of the last Abbot of Osney, first Bishop of Oxford. Two of his family born at Worminghall were also Bishops: John King, Bishop of London, born 1559 and Henry, Bishop of Chichester, born 1591. At the main street end of the Avenue is a memorial to Henry King, the Bishop of Chichester, in the unusually handsome almshouses founded by his son, a later John King, in 1675. They are in an H-shaped block in brick with stone quoins and mullioned windows.

façade to the road framed by turrets and angle buttresses, is now redundant. There are a few old farmhouses and cottages scattered around but the local population was never large.

Woolstone, Little [5] An empty brick farmhouse, a deserted boarded stone church and a ruined mill down a lane towards the Ouzel, make this look a ghost village. Much is waiting for rede-

The Clifden Arms on the south-west edge of the village is an exceptionally picturesque black-and-white thatched 16th-century pub. Around and between these is infilling with varied modern housing which includes some in Cornish concrete and some tall thin boxes of the 1970s with sharp gables. It is nevertheless an attractive rather than 'shabby' village.

Wotton Underwood [10] Within the medieval forest of Bernewood which stretched along the Oxon. border, has no real village, only a grand, early 18th-century house and landscaped park of the Grenvilles, Dukes of Buckingham, with a Victorianized church and estate farms and cottages, approached by an almost private road. The church of All Saints is a grey stone building with lead roofs in trees on the east side of a little green outside the House. It was built in the early 14th century but was given its west tower and lead spire in the early 19th century and much altered by G.E. Street in 1867 who rebuilt the south aisle (originally a chantry chapel of the Grenvilles) with a heavy neo-Decorated screen, raised the nave roof and restored the rest. At the beginning of the 19th century considerable alterations had already been made to this chapel when Grenville family internments were arranged in tiers like filing cabinets at the south end and an 18th-century wrought-iron screen brought in to close it. In the floor is a marble slab with brass figures of Edward Grenville (d.1585) and wife and, in a Victorian ogeed recess on the west wall, is an effigy in Elizabethan dress, supposed to be a belated monument to Agnes de Grenville (d. 1393). There is a tablet to the sole heir (d. 1836) of the 3rd Duke of Chandos who married Richard, 1st Duke of Buckingham, and Chandos, described as 'religious without enthusiasm' and having a kneeling woman and urn, and other, more Victorian, wall tablets together with a good deal of armorial stained glass of 1800 reset by Powell in Street's rebuilding. Wotton House was built for Richard Grenville, on the site of the family Manor House, in 1704 by a little-known architect John Keene and decorated by Sir John Thornhill. A central house of 11 bays in three (two tall and mean attic) storeys of red-brick, ochre stone dressings and green copper roof, is flanked by two one-storeyed pavilions with hipped roofs and lanterns which now look as important as, and more decorative than, the house itself. The latter was largely remodelled, but to the same external pattern, by Soane after a disastrous fire in 1820 and the house was gutted again in 1929 and remodelled by A. S. G. Butler. Little of the early work beyond the wrought-iron balustrade to the main stairs seems left. The landscape gardens with lakes and long avenues were laid out by Bridgeman who added temples, rotunda, bridges and grotto and the layout was softened by L. Brown who worked here for a short time before going with the Grenvilles to their inheritance at Stowe. Much of Bridgeman's work survives but many of Brown's gently curving vistas are overgrown. The area in and outside the Park to the west is thickly wooded. Of the rest of the parish there is little to be said but on the approach road is Wotton Row, a handsome terrace of timber-framed and red brick service cottages. The Wotton Tramway was built as an extension of the Metropolitan Railway, from Quainton Station to Brill through the estate in 1872. It was never very successful and closed in 1935.

Woughton-on-the-Green [5] Pronounced 'woofton' or 'wuffton', has a long wide green running across the grain of the country, from the Willen Road and the medieval church at the higher east end, down to canal and meadows on the west. There are old brick cottages and farmhouses round the green set back between trees, and extensive New Town development west of the canal. The church of the Assumption is a grey stone building with slate, lead and tiled roofs, restored by J. O. Scott in 1891. It has an embattled Perpendicular west tower in a reddish ironstone but is otherwise mainly Decorated. The south porch has little two-light openings on each side. Inside are a defaced effigy of a 14th-century priest, in a recess in the chancel, and a tablet to Martha James (d. 1735) framed between pilasters, pediment and urn. The early 18th-century Manor House in chequered brick above a stone plinth is at the west end of the Green while the Old Rectory is in a moated site just beyond the canal.

Wraysbury [18] Formerly Wyrardisbury, is a Thames-side place of too many bungalows and gravel pits, at the south tip of the old county. It was transferred with Slough and Eton and Datchet to Berks. in 1974. The centre is a triangular cricket green from which the tower and broach spire of the parish church can be seen to the south-east rising through trees. There are still meadows beyond the church, with views across the river to Coopers Hill but elsewhere are long ribbons of willow-fringed bungalows squeezed between flooded gravel pits, with only one substantial estate of older houses on the north-west side. St Andrew's church has a body of medieval clunch but this was faced in ragstone with oolite dressings by D. Brandon in 1862. At the same time he rebuilt the tower and spire, so that the church is externally entirely Victorian. Inside is whitewashed medieval clunch and Victorian furnishing. The piers of the arcades are oblong relics of the early nave wall and carved with little shafts. There are an early 16th-century brass to a knight and lady with double canopy and one to John Stonor (d. 1512) in lawyer's dress, a delicate urn on sarcophagus under an arched niche to Harriet (Gyll) Paxton (d. 1794) by Kendrick and a female figure with shield and anchor and obelisk to William Gyll (d. 1806). In the well-wooded Old Ferry drive 1 km north is 'King John's Hunting Lodge', a late 15th-century, timber-framed house, somewhat neglected after an early 20th-century restoration. It has a central two-storeyed porch and large parts of its medieval hall. A kilometre south in meadows facing Runnymede, are some old stone walls and a 13th-century window which are all that remain of the Benedictine Ankerwyke nunnery founded in the late 12th century.

Wycombe, High [14] Now that Slough has been transferred to Berks. and the Milton Keynes New Town has not yet congealed some disparate towns in the north of the county, High Wycombe, which has a population of 60,000, is the largest town in the county. It is a mixture of 19th- and early 20th-century industrial town, large mid 20th-century dormitory and the kernel of a small 18th-century market town hidden in mid 20th-century redevelopment. It stretches for 7 km from Loudwater on the London side, up the narrow chalk valley of the little River Wye, to West Wycombe on the Oxford side. The crossing of this valley by steep roads from Marlow and Amersham made it the market centre of the area; water power, beech woods, native skill and proximity to London markets made it a prosperous factory town. Nearness to London also increased its desirability as a dormitory and led to the rash of small houses and bungalows which flooded up tributary valleys and the main valley sides. The historic open spaces of the Rye, Wycombe Abbey and West Wycombe Park remind us what it once looked like. Its history is of little national importance though the valley floor has been occupied from Neolithic times. Its

rapid growth dates only from the time when market activities were overlaid by the upsurge in the furniture industry, for which, in spite of newer engineering and electronic factories, it is best known today. This started as a market for products of the local beech woods. Turning by 'bodgers' of chair legs and rails was done in the woods and assembly with wood planks, cane or rush was done in the town. But turning was slowly concentrated in the town and there are now no bodgers left in the woods. To visualize their way of life, which was once widespread in the Chilterns, a visit must be made to the Wycombe Chair Museum. Concentration of industry and market in the valley bottom and the distracting historic pattern of streets made congestion intolerable but nothing was done till after the Second World War. In fact matters were made worse in the 18th century by the Shelburnes, then owners of Wycombe Abbey, who pushed the park north, closing the old road on the south bank of the river and diverting it to the present London Road so that all traffic had to pass through the market place of the High Street. Shelburnes improved the town in other ways; they gave the eye-catching top to the church tower as well as the Guildhall and Market Hall. Chair-makers, however, concentrated along St Mary's Street on the old route which became an overcrowded slum with open sewers and common wells. The Carringtons, owners of Wycombe Abbey before the Shelburnes, made the next civic improvement by giving Queen Victoria Street, the approach to the Abbey Park, to the town on condition that it was used for civic purposes, and this is now the centre of local government services, with technical college, general hospital and law courts near by. There still remained the problem of relieving the High Street and this was done after the Second World War by driving a relief road round the south side of

the town centre connecting London Road to Oxford Road, wiping out the picturesque but slummy St Mary Street area on the way. Carriageways on its west side are raised over a new shopping area which provides a pedestrian link between the old shopping area and bus station and parking garages. The greater bypass south of the town, now part of M40 motorway, was opened not long after, but congestion on the steep approaches to the town seems as bad, at times, as ever. The parish church of All Saints is on a slight rise above the market place. It is still surrounded by traffic but is central to the town which has a large Woolworth on one side, Marks and Spencer on another and the Cornmarket just below. It is large and long and one of the few 'town' churches in the county. It was originally a cruciform Norman church with a central crossing tower but was much enlarged later in the 13th century. The central tower was pulled down in 1509 and the west tower was then built, and a slight extension to east was added later, but the church is predominantly Early English in style. The west tower is 30 m high, faced with squared stone. The upper part, with the quatrefoiled parapets and pinnacles which give it its distinctive but friendly outline, was given by Lord Shelburne and designed by Henry Keene in 1755. The rest of the church is flint-faced and looks hard and Victorian, due to the extensive restoration by J. O. Scott (1889). The interior with high and wide six-bayed nave and open crossing is impressive but again Victorian in feel, thanks to a 'purification' by G. E. Street in 1875. The chief monument is in the north chapel and is almost the full height of the church. This is to Henry Petty, Earl of Shelburne (d. 1751), and has reclining figures to the Lord and his Lady in Roman dress on a sarcophagus which has a medallion portrait of his father, Sir William Petty, the famous econom-

High Wycombe: the Guildhall

designed by Henry Keene in 1757. It is a two-storey brick building with open arcading to the ground floor, a projecting pedimented central bay on double columns, and, overall, a gay cupola with little Tuscan columns. The Market Hall, another Shelburne gift to the town, is on the north, a squat two-storey building with low, leaded, dome built by Robert Adam in 1761, though not one of his best works. The string course is inscribed 'To London 29 miles' and 'To Oxford 25 miles' which puts High Wycombe in its place. The High Street is wide and gives a general impression, in spite of poor infilling of the 1950s, of Georgian urbanity. The best buildings are the old Midland Bank (now Nat West), no. 39, no. 33 and no. 30, all early 18th century and on the south side. On the north side the Red Lion was of importance, but only its main elevation has been kept, and here the ground floor has been arcaded to give access to the over-large Woolworth which stretches back to Castle Street, while the porch and the Lion have been moved to the east end to make an entrance to offices above. In Queen Victoria Street, which runs south from central traffic lights, are the Town Hall in Edwardian neo-Georgian red brick of 1904, and a series of later and duller buildings ending with the Police Station of 1937. East along Abbey Way are somewhat more attractive dark brick Law Courts by the County Architect (1974). South of here, at the foot of Marlow Hill, is Wycombe Abbey, never a monastic place but the site of a modest old manor house owned by Archdales and Carringtons, and then rebuilt for the Lords Shelburne by James Wyatt in 1795. It is in grey stone with flint galleted joins, castellated and turreted, heavy and dull when it should have been picturesque. It was converted to the well-known girls' school in 1896. The Assembly Hall has the family pew of the Shelburnes pushed out of the church by

ist. The monument was erected by executors in 1784. In the south aisle are monuments to Lady Shelburne (d. 1771), 1st wife of William Petty-Fitzmaurice, 1st Marquis of Lansdowne, Prime Minister 1782–3, which has a standing figure with two children and an urn done by A. Carlini, to a Mrs Shrimpton (d. 1785), which has a 'Victory' and urn by Richard Westmacott sen., and a more seemly monument to J. Wheeler, a shoe-maker of London (d. 1621), which has an alabaster tablet framed with the tools of his trade. Much 17th- and 18th-century

woodwork was removed by Street, including the Shelburne pew now at Wycombe Abbey, but the 18th-century Mayor's desk survives in the south transept, while the medieval screen to the south chapel dated 1468 was much altered and restored. The font was designed by Street. Wrought-iron gates framing the view south into Church Square and the back of the Market Hall were made in 1762. Church Square flows round the Market Hall into the Cornmarket, the grand western end of the wide High Street. Here, closing the view west, is the Guildhall, given by Shelburne and

West Wycombe

Street. Early boarding houses and a chapel are by Caröe and the school has been extended to include Dawes Hill, the house to which Carringtons retreated after the sale of the manor. On the top of Marlow Hill are two modern schools of the 1950s and 1970s, the former by D. Clarke Hall with steel frames and curtain walling, the latter by the County Architect in dark brick, and beyond them a bleak-looking, steel-framed, Sports Centre overlooking the motorway. Back in the valley bottom, London Road comes in from the east along the pretty, meandering common known as the Rye and is adjoined by some pleasant Georgian buildings, while out to the east and a little south of London Road is Bassetsbury, the second historic manor of the town, which has a late 17th-century brick house, with details imported at its restoration in 1930, and an adjoining late Georgian mill. Easton Street, which joins London Street

to the town centre, was, till the Shelburnes moved the London road, a dead end into meadows. It has the scant 12th-century remains of the Infirmary Hall of the Hospital of St John, with, behind this, the former Grammar School buildings of 1883 and, further on, some mid-19th-century almshouses and a few pleasant 18th-century houses. On the north side of the valley the road to Amersham starts through two inter-war terraces of pompous neo-Georgian shops and offices. Castle Street leads west back to Church Street, and still has a few mutilated old houses, but then the railway cutting separates Castle Hill from the town. Here, in an attractive garden and a pretty flint house, is the valuable Wycombe Chair Museum with many items of local interest and, in its back garden, earthworks of a long vanished castle and a reconstructed bodger's hut. Up Amersham Hill are the newer buildings of the Royal

Grammar School of 1914 in a Queen Anne Style, with later additions by the County Architect, and, further north at Terriers, overlooking hectares of modern housing, is the church of St Francis, one of the best works of Sir Giles Gilbert Scott, consecrated in 1930. It is in a buff stone with a tall central tower, tall nave and two little entrance pavilions at the west end. There is no west or east window and light is effectively concentrated on the crossing by the lantern above and tall windows in the transepts. Terriers House, further north, is a late 17th-century brick house similar to Bradenham Manor but spoilt by plastering. West of the centre there is disappointingly little of interest outside the distant view of West Wycombe church on its hill 2 km away, but in Dashwood Avenue is the intriguing silhouette of St Mary and St George, a large church done cheaply in yellowish brick with a green central dome, by Wellesley

and Wills (1938). The golden ball of West Wycombe church beckons to better things beyond.

Wycombe, West [14] A National Trust preserved village in the infant Wye valley west of High Wycombe, between a handsome 18th-century house in an exceptional 18th-century park, and a pointed yew-fringed hill capped with a Georgian church with far-seen golden ball. The village was bought by the Royal Society of Arts from the Dashwood family in 1929 and transferred to the National Trust in 1934. The hill in 1933 and the house and gardens in 1943 were given to the Trust by the Dashwood family. The House of Wycombe Park is the centre of an estate acquired by the Dashwoods (London merchants) in 1698 and the present house, the church on the hill and park are largely the creation of Sir Francis Dashwood (1708–81), 2nd Baronet, and later Lord Le Despencer. He succeeded to his father's estate and a fortune when only 16 and was a man of considerable energy, taste, wealth and profligacy. He was a founder member and lasting supporter of the Society of Dilettanti (1724 on) and later founded the less reputable Knights of St Francis of Wycombe, better known as the 'Monks of Medmenham', which flourished at Medmenham Abbey and here until two members, John Wilkes, M.P. for Aylesbury, and Lord Sandwich, fell out. He was the 'worst-ever' Chancellor of the Exchequer in 1762–3 and was made Baron Le Despencer in 1763 'to decorate his fall' but he was to West Wycombe what Temples, Grenvilles and Thomas Pitt together were to Stowe. The House is approached from the flint lodge west of the village up a drive, past the Broad Walk to the lake, to the west portico and the west end of the house. This

West Wycombe Park:
Music Temple (*top*)
South front (*bottom*)

is basically a rectangular three-storey, Queen Anne, brick building, which was remodelled and extended in stuccoed brick by Sir Francis from 1735 to 1771, the north side being given a competent Palladian elevation with central pediment and the others extensive porticos. The tall Ionic west portico approached by the drive is not, however, the main entrance to the house but a garden ornament (and a screen for the older building) designed by Nicholas Revett (author, with Stuart, of *The Antiquities of Athens*). It was based on a Temple of Bacchus at Teos and indeed dedicated as a temple to Bacchus by Sir Francis. Visitors pass out again and into the long south portico, the double-storeyed colonnade with Tuscan pillars below and Corinthian above added by Donowell in 1754, to enter the hall of the house, through its centre. The Hall has screens of columns and walls painted in cool tones of brown, purple and cream to imitate marble and porphyry. From here a delicately inlaid staircase rises to a pillared gallery above. Ahead is the North Saloon, central to that side, which has a splendid view of the church and mausoleum on Church Hill to the left and to the Music Temple in the lake to the right. The yellow walls of the Saloon display the pictures collected by the 2nd Baronet. The Music Room was added by Donowell to the east, has a painted ceiling by Borgnis senior based on Raphael's *Banquet of the Gods* and a carved chimney piece by Henry Cheere, and leads out to the east portico with its heavy Tuscan columns added by Revett. The whole house was designed with the landscape in mind and largely for its external effect, as the best rooms face north and those on other fronts are darkened by heavy porticos. The Park itself is not as grand as that at Stowe but is more intimate and was, at one time, as loaded with garden temples as Stowe. The keystone of the present landscape is the Music Temple by Revett

West Wycombe:
the mausoleum

(1780), islanded in the lake, for this is the centrepiece of views from the house and of views up the valley towards Church Hill. Much of the other garden architecture was 'stage scenery' and has decayed or been swept away in later simplification but there remain, as well as the west Portico (the Temple of Bacchus), the Temple of Apollo, a monumental arch in flint enclosing a room used as a cockpit (and screening the Adam stables), the Round Temple, with a fan-shaped Tuscan portico screening a water-tank and dovecote, the Temple of the Four Winds by Revett (1759—earliest of five British copies of this Athenian temple), and a number of smaller temples which acted as lodges or shelters around the Park. The lake itself is maintained by a dam across the little River Wye, which was originally crowned with an immense arch of rocks capped by a statue of a river god, but this has been reduced to a modest cascade flanked only by nymphs, now in fibreglass copy. The river is dammed again at the 'sawmill', a group of flint and brick buildings across the river, and finally constricted again at the Pepperpot Bridge, decorated with little flint pavilions on Marlow Lane. Just north of this is a flint cottage disguised as small gothic church. Its narrow tower had a tall spire but this was removed contemptuously by Repton who was called to advise in 1800 and recommended much simplification and thinning. Much credit for the present, slightly overmature, beauty of the park should go to Thomas Cook, a pupil of Capability Brown, who softened the hard lines of the early design and harmoniously complemented Revett's garden architecture, but more still should go to Sir Francis who was the driving force of this creation. The parish church of St Lawrence is on the conical hill top across the valley from the park, in the ditch and bank of an Iron Age fort some 60 m above the village at its foot.

With its golden ball, heightened tower and Georgian nave provided by Sir Francis Dashwood, it looks entirely of his creation. John Wilkes in 1765 spoke of the 'church he has just built on the top of a hill for the convenience and devotion of the town at the bottom', but the church is medieval in origin and served other little settlements as well as West Wycombe. Dashwood added a stage and the golden ball to the old tower, rebuilt the nave using arched windows, marble paving, giant Corinthian columns, carved frieze and garlands and coffered and painted ceiling. He kept the medieval walls of the chancel but gave it a stuccoed arch, rococo scrolls and a low ceiling painted with a 'Last Supper' by the younger Borgnis (1765). The paganism of Dashwood's circle inspired its fittings, so that stalls and lectern are comfortable rosewood arm-chairs and the font has four doves round its bowl menaced by a snake creeping up the slender clawed tripod. The golden ball, which can be approached by an external ladder, is fitted with seats and table and was misused, like much else by Dashwood's circle, for John Wilkes described it as 'the best Globe Tavern I was ever in'. The east end of the earthworks, now partly concealed in yew and juniper, is cut by Dashwood's Mausoleum, which is set, like the golden ball, on the axis of the High Wycombe road. It is a large, open hexagon of flint with Portland stone dressings. The three eastern sides are in the shape of triumphal arches while the three western have niches to take funerary urns. The mausoleum was designed by the young John Bastard of Blandford and financed by a bequest from his friend with 'tasteless splendour', George Bubb Dodington (d. 1762). In the centre is an urn on a pedestal commemorating Francis Dashwood's wife who died in 1769, while on the west wall are monuments to the two wives of the 1st Baronet, taken here from the church. Half-way down

the hill towards the village street is the elaborate flint-walled entrance to caves made by Dashwood in 1750–52 to produce foundations for his straight new road to High Wycombe. A tunnel penetrates the hill for half a kilometre and has enlargements which are given fanciful names such as Banqueting Hall, Monks Cell and Inner Temple, as the caves are supposed to have been used for immoral or pagan meetings by Dashwood's friends after the break-up of the 'Monks of Medmenham'. The village itself is hidden by trees from both house and church and consists of 'picture-postcard' groups of houses of from 15th to 20th-century with hardly a jarring note, outside that of traffic on the Oxford road, which is now thankfully bypassed by the motorway to the south. The centrepiece on the north side of the High Street is Church Loft which bridges the lane to the church. It is a late 15th-century building with a meeting hall on the upper floor which oversails with bracketed and moulded beams and a clock into the street. Near by is the early 18th-century colour-washed and red-brick Manor House and opposite the friendly, early 18th-century, George and Dragon hotel with giant rusticated pilasters dividing its full four-storey height. Back on the north side, set on a high bank with trees, is the old vicarage, now called the Dower House, built for Dashwood in 1763. It is a delicate little Palladian, two-storeyed, flint house with an Ionic portico on its east. In its former grounds is the aggressive red-brick St Paul's church of 1845, a sad comment on the taste of Francis Dashwood's successors. Lastly in Church Lane there survives a late 18th-century building with red-brick ground floor and painted weatherboarding to two upper floors, which is one of the last of the old furniture workshops in the Wycombe area, to which industry the area owed so much of its prosperity.

Index

At **Medmenham** ▷

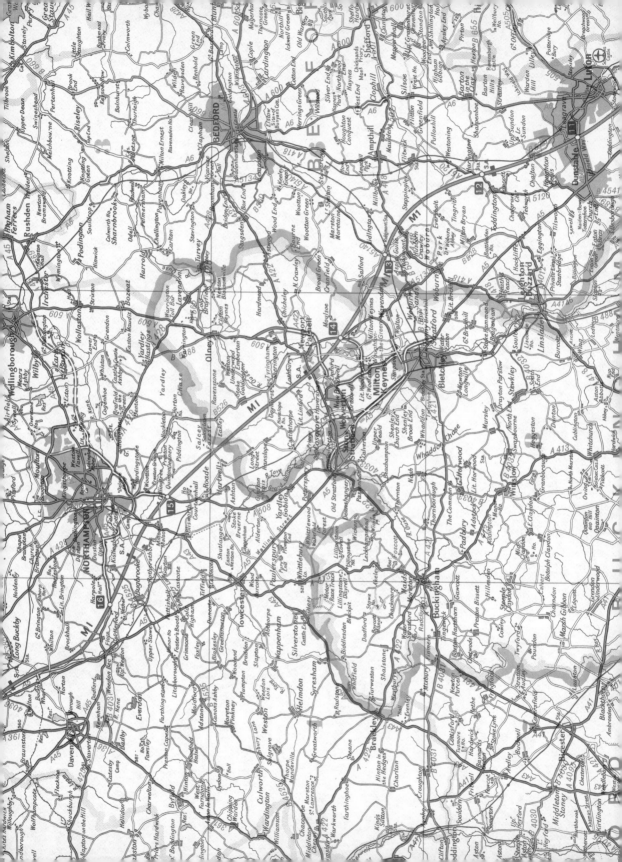